*"Man is not what he thinks he is;
he is what he hides."*

—André Malraux

The
SECRET LIFE
of
HIDDEN PLACES

Concealed Rooms,
Clandestine Passageways,
and the Curious Minds
That Made Them

STEFAN BACHMANN &
APRIL GENEVIEVE TUCHOLKE

WORKMAN PUBLISHING

NEW YORK

Library of Congress Cataloging-in-Publication Data is available.

ISBN 978-1-5235-1698-8

Design by Lisa Hollander
Cover photo credits:
Front cover (keyhole): Eye Ubiquitous/Universal Images Group. Back cover (left to right): Le Luxographe; © RIEGER Bertrand; Diego Grandi.

Workman books are available at special discounts when purchased in bulk for premiums and sales promotions as well as for fundraising or educational use. Special editions or book excerpts can also be created to specification.
For details, please contact special.markets@hbgusa.com.

Workman Publishing Co., Inc.,
a subsidiary of Hachette Book Group, Inc.
1290 Avenue of the Americas
New York, NY 10104

workman.com

WORKMAN is a registered trademark of Workman Publishing Co., Inc.,
a subsidiary of Hachette Book Group, Inc.

Printed in China on responsibly sourced paper.
First printing January 2024

10 9 8 7 6 5 4 3 2 1

Contents

Introduction

In 1996, in the Peruvian highlands near Lake Titicaca, a hiker discovered a door cut into a red stone cliff. The door had no hinges, handles, or seams. Locals called it "The Gate of the Gods" and claimed it could only be opened with a golden disk, slotted like a key into an aperture in the stone. The door was said to lead to the Incan afterlife, to a celestial realm of gods and spirits and endless feasts.

All across southern Europe and northern Africa are more of these unopenable doors—in the tombs of the Etruscans, the sumptuous death palaces of the Egyptians, and beneath the grassy Bronze Age grave mounds of Sardinia. Some of the doors are tiny, Alice in Wonderland–esque, no larger than a hand. Others are towering and ornate. Still others are painted, daubed onto the ancient stone in flaking lapis and crimson.

From Peru to Egypt, the religious explanation for these false doors is more or less the same: They were purported to allow the dead to return to the land of the living and enjoy the offerings brought to them. The psychological explanation is less altruistic and much more moving. The doors were built as a comfort to those left behind. They invited the mourner to dream of a place beyond the pain and hardships of life and the finality of death. They seemed to say, "We are locked and unopenable; you cannot see what lies behind us. But you can imagine it." And in countries and cultures across the globe, humanity did.

Few of us have met a locked door we weren't curious to look behind or a secret we didn't desperately want revealed. When Alice follows the white rabbit down its hole, she encounters at the bottom a hallway full of locked doors and one very small door that "led into a small passage, not much larger than a rat-hole: she knelt down and

looked along the passage into the loveliest garden you ever saw. How she longed to get out of that dark hall, and wander about among those beds of bright flowers and those cool fountains, but she could not even get her head through the doorway."

When you read the opening lines of this book, you most likely felt it too, that hot twinge of curiosity. You wanted to know more about the door carved into the cliff in Peru—why it was built, who built it, and, above all, what is behind it? Perhaps you began to imagine the answers, conjuring images of an underground city, a hidden temple, a secret tomb filled with treasure. This insatiable curiosity and willingness to imagine are hallmarks of the human mind. If something is hidden, it must be found out. If it cannot be found out, we will dig, investigate, and flat out invent until we have answers.

Why do we care so much about hidden things? According to Tom Stafford, a senior lecturer in psychology and cognitive science at the University of Sheffield, the roots of human curiosity can be linked to a trait called neoteny, a term from evolutionary theory that means the "retention of juvenile characteristics." Physically, it means we have large brains in relation to our body size, like babies. Mentally, it means we display certain childlike personality traits all the way into adulthood. Traits like curiosity, playfulness, and wonder remain inside us. They are what compel us to travel, read books, wander into a dark cave. No matter where we are, a persistent little voice calls to us, telling us that inside the old, the grim, the forgotten and abandoned—even inside the familiar, well-kept, and sumptuous—there is more than meets the eye, a hidden depth, a secret truth, a chance to discover something wonderful.

The mention of secrets, specifically secret rooms, hidden staircases, and sealed chambers, has the whiff of the lurid to it, of pulp mystery novels, Scooby-Doo, Indiana Jones, and gothic novels.

◄ *One of many unopenable doors across the globe, this one at the Srei Temple, Angkor Wat, Cambodia.*

▲ *A hidden door in the library of Admont Abbey, Austria.*

But secrets are more than a fun diversion. The things we hide are the things we are and the things we fear the most. When an emotion or fear is too important to share, too large and frightening to process, all that is left for us is to package it inside palaces, churches, tombs, and monuments, sealed chambers and tunnels, to lock it away behind doors, bury it under floorboards, or nestle it in jewels and gold, like the Egyptians and their fear of death (page 281) or Marie-Antoinette and her desperate search for meaning (page 183).

So many doors are still waiting to be opened. In distant parts of the world, in deepest jungles, or far below the feet of thousands of tourists, there really is more: the lost body of a saint, a heap of old love letters, a priceless painting, the story of a tragic life, a mystery answered, a glorious item rediscovered. In the Great Pyramid of Giza, new technology has revealed two unexplored voids. In the Russian imperial court, an enchanting room once stood, made all of amber, a room whose whereabouts is now utterly lost, as if it gathered up its skirts and stole away. And in Nottinghamshire, a quiet English manor sits upon a tangle of subterranean halls, trapdoors, libraries, and gaslit tunnels, built by a mysterious duke for reasons that are just beginning to come to light.

In *The Secret Life of Hidden Places*, we set about visiting these hidden places, opening their doors and delving into their obscure and forgotten histories. We have sought to find the human element in the architecture, not just the secrets themselves, but the tales of those who built them. We will lead you into a chamber of skulls high in the Swiss Alps, a Japanese temple full of traps, a Parisian apartment locked and untouched since World War II, a Prohibition-era speakeasy in Washington, DC, an underground alchemy lab, a trove of ancient erotica, the strange, enchanted garden of a nineteenth-century millionaire, and much more.

Albert Einstein once said, "The important thing is not to stop questioning," and humanity probably never will. We have so many questions and, like a child who must open every door she encounters, who will cry and weep if she is faced with one she cannot, we are compelled to seek answers. So we journey, we search, we dig, we slip behind the revolving bookshelf in a smuggler's house in Buenos Aires, investigate the buried ballroom of that lonely Victorian duke, and descend the mossy stairs of a well in Portugal, its walls carved with the symbols of a secret society. We rush along dusty tunnels beneath Mexico and travel the paths of ancient labyrinths on a remote Russian island. We ask ourselves, "Where will this lead me?" and the answer is always, "Who knows?" But there is always the chance, the hope, that it will be somewhere true.

1

The Sunken Manor

NOTTINGHAMSHIRE · ENGLAND

They call him the Prince of Silence and you are in his woods. You are not supposed to be here. You've heard so many tales: that the odd duke had a terrible accident as a child; that none of his servants are allowed to look at him, that if they do they are dismissed on the spot; that he only goes out at night and the rest of the time stays locked in five small, pink-painted chambers. He has no wife or children. He is all alone and apparently quite unhinged. And yet you could not resist coming here. Every day your friends troop in through the duke's gates to work on the construction of some massive undertaking. They have sworn not to speak of it. So you will find out for yourself. Whatever is happening here, you are going to see it with your own eyes.

◀ *The Duke of Portland's mysterious buried ballroom.*

You make your way among the black trees, the foliage whispering overhead, the night birds watching silently. And then you spot something: a figure, slipping through the woods. A ghost? No. A woman in an apron and cap, holding a lantern. She darts through the underbrush, brambles crackling underfoot. And there, forty paces behind her, ambles a tall, somewhat stooped man. You wonder if the woman knows she is being followed. But then she turns and waits for him, her eyes carefully averted, and it all clicks. He is here, the Prince of Silence himself. He is wandering, inspecting his realm, just like the

stories said. He wears a tall stovepipe hat and three layers of coats. He carries an umbrella, though it is not raining.

You stand, frozen in the dark. Then the servant moves on, and the duke hunches into his collar and follows. When you dare to breathe again, the lantern light and the figures are gone.

You stumble on in the dark. You do not see the building site until you are upon it, reeling at its edge. It is below you, a labyrinth of enormous rooms dug out of the earth. Beyond, the hall itself, Welbeck Abbey, rises pale and ghostly from the lawn, large enough to rival Buckingham Palace. But not even the King boasts rooms such as these.

You make your way carefully along the edge, looking down into the vast, unfinished spaces. Soon they will be covered, hidden away. And then what? What will the odd duke do down there? You are so engrossed in the scene that you do not hear the footsteps behind you, the soft sound of an umbrella tip punching the soil. When you do, it is too late. You turn, and there he is, staring at you from below his hat, his eyes very black. . . .

◄ *The visible, above-ground portion of Welbeck Abbey.*

For many of us, the great houses of the English countryside are what first springs to mind at the mention of hidden rooms and secret passageways, pointed gables looming out of a perpetual fog, ivied walls enfolding a hundred cobwebbed secrets, a door behind a tapestry, perhaps a walled-in corpse. The English manor has become an archetype, shorthand for secrecy and a slightly bohemian sort of wealth. But a little known fact is that there exist manors in the real world far stranger than those in any comic book or novel, crumbling estates hiding tales that Hollywood could only dream of.

One particularly intriguing example is Welbeck Abbey in Nottinghamshire. It does not merely have a hidden passageway or a staircase. Welbeck Abbey boasts an entire underground realm. Miles of gaslit tunnels radiate out from beneath the house like the overlong legs of a spider. A subterranean ballroom lurks under a rolling lawn, a vast library beneath a forest. Hydraulic elevators lie silent below blankets of vines, trapdoors forgotten under layers of dust, and all of it built for and used by one reclusive man: the mysterious "burrowing duke."

Who was he? Why build all these underground chambers? Most importantly, what secrets was he hiding in them? Let us take a peek into the mind of a particularly fascinating Victorian nobleman.

Welbeck Abbey began as a true abbey in 1153. It was next transformed into a country house and mostly rebuilt, though parts of the medieval abbey remain in the arches of the cellar and hidden behind the wainscoting of certain rooms. *Jones' Views of the Seats, Mansions, Castles, Etc. of Noblemen and Gentlemen, in England*, a three-volume guide to country houses published from 1829 to 1831, described the original house as "not remarkable for any particular beauty of architecture."

It would not stay unremarkable for much longer. In 1854, the 5th Duke of Portland inherited it and fled there with all his fears and psychoses in tow, slowly transforming it into a strange and beautiful mystery.

William John Cavendish-Bentinck-Scott was born in 1800, the forgotten fourth child of nine. It was his older brother who was the golden son, warmhearted and friendly, celebrated at school, and destined for a brilliant career in politics. Young William, on the other hand, was shy and sensitive. But when his older brother died suddenly in 1824, it was William who was forced to step into his shoes. Without warning, William became the heir in waiting to the family's properties and vast income.

> What pleased him most was to be invisible, to live in a beautiful world where he would not be judged or watched, where he was safe, and all was quiet.

At first, it seemed he might rise to the occasion. He fulfilled his duties as a military officer and took his seat as a member of parliament. Yet the work seemed to drain him. He complained often of ill health. The things he truly enjoyed were often solitary pursuits: opera—which he could watch from a private, darkened box—riding, and shooting. He also had a fascination for technology. He loathed social calls. When he traveled to Rome, he was overwhelmed with the attention from the other vacationing lords and ladies and refused them all. Instead he took a carriage into the hills outside of Rome, to the Villa Adriana, and walked through the cool, silent tunnels beneath it (see The Duke's Inspiration, page 16).

At thirty-four, William proposed to the celebrated opera singer Adelaide Kemble, only to discover that she had already secretly married another, an English landowner much more handsome than William.

The rejection appears to have wounded the sensitive duke deeply. He never courted anyone else after that and never married. Instead, he resigned from his military position, left London, and retreated to his estate in Nottinghamshire—Welbeck Abbey. Away from the public scrutiny he faced in the capital, William could finally do as he pleased. And what pleased him most was to be invisible, to live in a beautiful world where he would not be judged or watched, where he was safe, and all was quiet.

He began building this world almost at once, starting with additions to the manor and slowly expanding downward and out-ward across the estate, until he had constructed a vast architectural deception, a network of secret shortcuts and tunnels, underground galleries, and richly decorated chambers filled with art and books—an enormous stage where there was no audience, only stagehands and himself, the actor.

The so-called "Tunnel No. 1" was about 1,600 feet long and wide enough for two carriages to drive side by side, allowing the duke to drive in the direction of the nearby village of Worksop without being seen.

Many tales exist of his eccentricities during this time, including that his bed-room contained a trapdoor through which he could descend into his underground realm without the servants noticing. If a housemaid did happen to meet him in the corridors, she had to turn away and press her face to the wall. The story that begins this chapter is based on truth: If the duke went for a walk in the park, it was only at night and always accompa-nied by a servant carrying a lantern a hundred feet in front of him. Rain or shine, he wielded an umbrella and would flick it open and hide behind it when anyone turned his way. He was also never seen without two large overcoats, a stovepipe hat, and a double ruff.

Some of his employees did manage to get a glimpse of him. Elizabeth Butler, a laundry maid at Welbeck, wrote, "He was very tall and slim, with clear pale cheeks and dark eyes, which always struck me as mesmeric." But in general, he remained elusive. For the next eighteen years, he oversaw the expansion of his estate. The results were both strange and wonderful.

In 1878 Leonard Jacks was allowed to visit Welbeck Abbey, shortly before the duke's death. He reported his adventure in vivid prose in his book *The Great Houses of Nottinghamshire, and the County Families*. Of the house he wrote, "It is a vast pile, white and castellated, with innumerable windows, overlooking Sherwood

Forest, where the immemorial oaks grow, and the deer have a peaceful existence." He spoke of work yards, of 100,000 pounds a year paid to an army of 1,500 employees, of exquisite architecture and lovely gardens. The duke was obsessed with technological innovation. Braziers warmed the plants in his orangery so the fruit would ripen during the gloomy English summers. In the house proper, a miniature indoor railway had been built, tracks running to an elevator that would bring food up from the kitchens. Jacks wrote, "These rails—which are something like the rails of a tramway, terminate at a kind of iron cupboard, which is heated by steam, and in this the viands can be placed, and kept hot until they are required for consumption in the adjoining room."

But this was only the portion aboveground. Jacks was also admitted to the splendid world beneath the estate. This is where William's nickname, "the burrowing duke," came into full effect.

> One underground passage was connected with the old riding school, which is entered by a trap door [sic], opened by means of a crank. Only the few who have seen this great room can form any conception of its proportions, or of its magnificence. It is used as a museum of art, containing long rows of choice paintings. There must have been several hundred pictures in this room—portraits and landscapes by famous artists long since passed away.

Jacks goes on to write about walking between avenues of pictures and of books, "for there are several thousand volumes there, piled up in stacks upon the floor. The floor of this magnificent art gallery is of polished oak, and the inner portion of the roof, which is in the style of Westminster Hall, is painted to represent a glorious sky. The tall doors are wholly, and the walls partly, covered with looking-glass [mirrors], which gives effect to what would make one of the finest banqueting halls in the kingdom."

The duke's gallery was filled with Rembrandts and other old masters. There was a ballroom, said to be so skillfully made that you would have no idea you were underground, a billiards room large enough for six tables, and a marvelous underground library, called the Titchfield Library. It consisted of five interconnected rooms—including a reading room and a room devoted entirely to newspapers—all of them heated by steam for maximum coziness. "Down below the earth's surface," Jacks wrote, "there is not a sound to be heard in any one of the rooms, and a soft and subdued light is admitted through the large octagonal plate-glass arrangements in the ceiling."

All of these chambers were connected to the main house by underground passages. The so-called "Tunnel No. 1" was about 1,600 feet long and wide enough for two carriages to drive side by side, allowing the duke to drive in the direction of the nearby village of Worksop without being seen.

The 3,000-foot-long plant corridor runs between the main house and riding school and is wide enough for several people to walk side by side. It was filled with lush plants in the duke's day, a sort of subterranean greenhouse. Running parallel to the plant corridor is a narrower, rougher-hewn tunnel, which the duke had built for the servants, to ensure his own solitude.

There were many smaller tunnels: a grotto corridor, a fruit arcade, corridors with rails on which warm food could be brought on trolleys to the main house. The horse corridor was decorated with antler racks and led to the underground ballroom. According to Jacks, the passages and rooms were "lighted both by natural light and by gas. The light is admitted from above through circles of plate glass, which are placed in round frames. Appearing at intervals of about every ten yards amongst the grass of the park, these circular arrangements would puzzle any person who was not in the secret."

◄ *The plant corridor was the duke's underground garden, lit from above by skylights.*

Few people were in on the secret, besides the builders and servants. The duke rarely allowed anyone to see his constructions. Which begs the question: Why did the Duke of Portland build all this? Who was meant to dance in the ballroom and play pool in the vast billiards room beneath the park?

One suggestion is that he did it for posterity, that finding his own life to be lacking, he resolved to create a beautiful place for the progeny of his siblings to enjoy. But more likely he did it for himself. Perhaps he did indeed dance alone in the ballroom and play billiards by himself.

There can be little doubt that William was an introvert, possibly even an agoraphobe. His favorite carriage, which he had specially shipped to London when he was forced to travel, had a half dozen glass lenses sewn into its curtains, allowing him to look out at the world without the world looking back. Even his bed was specially built, with folding panels that would close him up inside something akin to a coffin.

Aside from trying to escape his crushing responsibilities, the duke may have also had health reasons for wanting to go into hiding. He suffered from acute psoriasis, an itchy, painful reddening of the skin, and was known to sleep between damp sheets to soothe himself. He may also have had neuralgia, a sensitivity to noise and light, which would explain why he skulked about at night and enjoyed moving via tunnel.

His poor health does not entirely explain why he chose to build a network of underground chambers and passageways, however, when he might just as well have used the rooms already built aboveground. Derek Adlam, a curator at Welbeck Abbey, thinks this had more to do with the duke's obsession with technology.

In his book *Tunnel Vision: The Enigmatic 5th Duke of Portland*, Adlam writes, "Unquestionably the Duke enjoyed the process of building and all its associated administrative organization. He must have enjoyed the copious, obsessively detailed correspondence maintained with his agents and managers, even though personal contact was limited only to a few trusted individuals."

Despite being known as a recluse, the duke closely managed, designed, and oversaw everything that went on within his estate. There are plenty of tales of William fraternizing with his employees, helping the servants' children gather chestnuts, even marching through the work camps "looking like a tramp," his trousers bound up with string to keep them out of the mud. And yet when aristocratic hunting parties visited the estate, he would not see them.

"It's odd," says Adlam, "that he is on the best of terms with his social inferiors but at arm's length from his social equals."

It suggests an interesting inferiority complex, this wealthy, powerful duke who only ever felt comfortable with those vastly below his station. But even among the working class, he was not truly at home. In four letters to Fanny Kemble, the older sister of the opera singer who had rejected him, he refers to the subsoil as "shelter" and the "only safe place."

"As the soldier digs himself in as a protection against the bombardment of shot and shell, so the duke dug himself in against the bombardment of ordinary everyday life."

A. S. Turberville, author of a two-volume history of Welbeck Abbey in 1938 and 1939, had this to say on the duke's psychology: "As the soldier digs himself in as a protection against the bombardment of shot and shell, so the duke dug himself in against the bombardment of ordinary everyday life."

▲ *The 5th Duke of Portland, also known as the "Burrowing Duke" and the "Prince of Silence."*

The duke's strange inclinations, then, most likely stemmed from a mixture of health troubles, paralyzing anxiety, and a desperate need for something to love. He had no close friends, no children or partner. He tried building for himself the place he was unable to find in other people: a beautiful sanctuary where he would not be judged or rejected.

Much about the burrowing duke is unknown. What we do know is that William was not all solitude and gloom. Letters speak of how he doted on his few acquaintances, sometimes sending them strange gifts, such as busts of themselves and, occasionally, a racehorse. He built his servants fine houses on his grounds and a skating rink that could be flooded and turned into an ice rink in the winter. He even bought his staff a fleet of black umbrellas, so that they too could make their way around his park with a dry head. (One cannot help but be reminded, here, of the opera stage again, of all the servants being extras, the umbrellas props in a choreography that only the duke could see.) He was not a monster, not some gothic creature skulking about underground. He was a very shy, complicated man, who preferred the dark and the silence to the staring eyes and noise of the surface.

Toward the end of his life, the duke's days were filled with intense loneliness. He lived in five rose-colored rooms in the west wing of his house and saw no one, only descending from time to time to wander his subterranean kingdom, read, and gaze at his collection of beautiful art. The only person allowed near him was his valet. On the rare occasion that he was spotted on the grounds, he would hide behind his umbrella, and when he arrived at his London townhouse for the occasional visit, he would hurry across the hall and into his study, where he would remain for the rest of his stay.

So complete was his hiding that when a woman came forward after his death claiming that he, in fact, had been her father-in-law and had led a secret life in London (including working in an upholsterer's shop and staging his own death in 1864), plenty of people believed her. To prove her case, Mrs. Druce made an application for the exhumation of her father-in-law's coffin, maintaining that it would be empty, the duke having been buried elsewhere. (The coffin was finally opened in 1907 and found to contain her father-in-law, who was decidedly not the Duke of Portland; Mrs. Druce was admitted to a mental asylum in 1903.)

Today nature has reclaimed many of the duke's tunnels. Trees and vines grow up their walls. Ceilings have collapsed. The passageways are a shadow of their former grandeur and have taken on a forgotten, primeval quality, like caves from a far more distant age. From the sky, their routes can still be clearly seen, long swaths of rubble running under hills and dales. Once they were the realm of the burrowing duke, darting about in his tall hat and ruffed collar. Now they are dark and unused, the realm of mice and birds and damp.

A distant branch of the family still inhabits one wing of the house. The rest was for many years occupied by a state-run military school. The underground ballroom was transformed into a gym, the music rooms into laboratories, the anterooms and dining room into classrooms. Opened in 1953, the Welbeck Defence Sixth Form College accepted boys (and later girls) with a scientific bent and was meant to supply the British military with soldiers adept at navigating rapidly changing technological landscape. It was a real-life version of the gifted children academy trope and one can imagine the delights and mysteries the students discovered in their free time, being taught military secrets by day and then sneaking from their beds at night and stumbling upon much stranger secrets in the tunnels below.

When the 6th Duke of Portland arrived at Welbeck for the first time during Christmas of 1879, shortly after the burrowing duke's death, he found the aboveground house almost in ruins. In order to access it, his servants had to place a trail of boards over a swamp of rubble and stagnant water. Once inside, the new duke observed, "The reception room had no floor, and a large tree peeked out from the basement." The burrowing duke had been so absorbed building his world below the earth that he entirely forgot what was happening on the surface. To him, there was nothing so dull, nothing so dangerous and hurtful, as that bright, loud place. Truth, happiness, and safety lay underneath. ◈

WILLIAM BECKFORD
AND THE FALLING ABBEY

William Beckford was a brilliant, dashing young aristocrat, the author of the gothic novel *Vathek* (written in French over the course of a frenzied few months at the age of twenty-one), the heir to a vast fortune, and soon at the heart of a scandal that rocked the English upper classes. In 1784, Beckford was caught whipping his lover, a young earl also named William, for sending letters to another man. When the earl's father discovered the affair, Beckford fled the country for Switzerland. He stayed on the continent for eleven years. When he at last returned to England in 1795, he was a social outcast, but richer than ever. What was he to do with all that money? Why, design one of the largest and oddest houses in England, of course, and conjure it up out of the tangled forests of Wiltshire.

Unfortunately no longer standing, Fonthill Abbey was a colossal feat, a Gothic Revival mansion masquerading as a house of God, a country estate that could easily be mistaken for an ancient abbey, with rooms called such things as the oratory, the sanctuary (used as an art gallery), and a "Staircase to the Nunnery." It was meant to give the impression of stepping back in time, into a realm of medieval romances and picturesque landscapes. One visitor described it as "a place raised by majick, [rather] than the labors of the human hand." It literally collapsed under the weight of its own hubris, a construction of the imagination that could not hold up to the realities of physics.

There are many parallels between Beckford and the 5th Duke of Portland. Both were second sons who lost their elder brothers early, and both became the heads of their families' fortunes. Both were art collectors and social outcasts who hurled themselves into eccentric building projects, creating monuments to their loneliness and isolation. But while the Duke of Portland focused his attention downward, Beckford built toward the sky.

He designed his fantastical abbey with an enormous central tower, 270 feet from base to top, and a surplus of soaring halls and galleries. Unfortunately, he also wanted everything to be built very

▶ *The remains of Fonthill Abbey after the collapse of its central tower.*

quickly. The builders cut corners at every opportunity, and when there were no more corners to cut, they began cutting other things as well. In 1807 the central tower collapsed and had to be rebuilt. The builders had failed to lay a foundation for it. According to another story, Beckford was so adamant that he spend Christmas dinner at the abbey that he told his workers to complete the kitchens post-haste. They collapsed as soon as the meal had been served.

The abbey was a crumbling dream, and Beckford seemed to realize this. In 1823 he sold it and shortly afterwards the central tower collapsed for the final time. The entire building was demolished two years later, its vast collection of treasures auctioned off. But Beckford's obsession with exceptionally tall structures did not end with the abbey. He built another tower in Lansdown, outside of the city of Bath, retiring there in the twilight of his life. That tower stands to this day.

THE DUKE'S INSPIRATION
The Tunnels Beneath Villa Adriana

No grand tour of Europe is complete without a stop in Rome, and when the young Duke of Portland arrived there he found himself very much taken with the city's secrets. Not only does it have its winding catacombs, subterranean churches, and any number of shadowy nooks and chambers where an anxious young duke might find solace, but far out beyond its edge, in the beautiful green hills of Tivoli, lies Villa Adriana, built by Roman Emperor Hadrian between 138 and 117 BCE. Beneath it a mysterious tangle of passageways crisscrosses the park and connects the many buildings of the estate. Rumor has it the Duke of Portland heard of this feature and made his way there to investigate.

Educated guesses have been made as to the use of the tunnels. One is that they were meant for servants so they could go about their duties without disturbing the carefully cultivated idyll above. Another more intriguing theory stems from academics William MacDonald and John Pinto, who suggest that they were religious in nature, used for secret rites related to the cult of Persephone. Called the Eleusinian Mysteries, this ancient religious movement involved the use of psychedelic drugs, visions, and a phase called the "Descent" meant to represent the journey into the underworld. The tunnels beneath the Villa Adriana could not have been a more ideal environment.

Perhaps the duke found some peace in the cool underground, away from the clamoring dinner parties and social calls of his class. After only a few weeks in the Italian capital, he set off for home, his mind no doubt buzzing with possibilities for a sanctuary of his own back in England.

THE MAD MOLE OF LIVERPOOL

Under a rather conventional hill in a downtown area of Liverpool lies a world of tunnels, cathedral-like halls, strange carvings, and passageways. Their purpose has been a matter of speculation for more than a hundred years, as has their builder, yet another wealthy eccentric named Joseph Williamson. Williamson made his money in property, and then used much of it to pay laborers to expand his subterranean realm. In later life, he was known as the Mad Mole. Over the years, he designed, financed, and had built several miles of tunnels beneath the Edge Hill neighborhood of Liverpool, England. The tunnels were dug as deep as fifty feet. Some were soaring and ornate, such as the Banqueting Hall, named so for reasons yet unknown. (Were banquets ever held there? Who dined in that damp, dark place?) Others were small, ending in bricked-up doorways and arches. By his death, an entire labyrinth of underground halls had been excavated.

A Liverpool antiquarian named James Stonehouse visited the tunnels in 1845. He wrote of "vaulted passages" and "yawning chasms," gigantic rats, including a snow-white one, as well as reports of a haunting, the locals speaking of agonized screams emanating from the depths. He even spotted a pair of three-story houses, equipped with sandstone spiral staircases, carved out of the solid rock beneath Smithdown Lane.

There are various theories as to why Williamson built these tunnels. One suggests that he followed an extremist religious sect that claimed the world would soon face Armageddon, and that Williamson built the tunnels as a place where he and his fellow believers could escape the catastrophe before reemerging to build a new city.

A more likely explanation is that Williamson was illegally excavating sandstone from beneath Edge Hill and had the archways built as a sort of decoy; if he was discovered by the authorities, he could claim he was simply building cellars, thus avoiding any income taxes on the rock he mined. Clever, clever.

2

The Book Thief
of
Mont Sainte-Odile

It starts small, on a warm summer day at the mountaintop monastery of Mont Sainte-Odile. Sweaty tourists linger outside in the sun, trying to catch a breeze as they gaze down at the Rhine Valley below. Saint Odile herself watches from atop a stone cupola, book in arm.

With your lanky six-foot-two-inch frame, you tower over the other visitors, something that normally doesn't bother you, but today . . . today you wish you were a little less conspicuous.

◀ *The Mont Sainte-Odile Abbey is now famous both for its secret passageway and the book thief who rediscovered it.*

You've studied Latin and, unlike the ignorant tourists who visit Mont Sainte-Odile, you can actually read the ancient texts in the abbey's first-floor library. You feel a mixture of pity and scorn for them as they circle the room, gazing at the books with polite boredom.

Finally, you find yourself alone. You begin to investigate the simple locks on the bookcases.

You leave with six books in your backpack. The monastery won't miss them. These priceless texts should belong to someone who can truly appreciate them. Truly love them.

You are a hero.

After the theft, you linger in the courtyard, watching tourists yawn in the sizzling heat. You do not feel drowsy. You feel invigorated. Ecstatic. You swat at a fly and notice that your hand is shaking . . . but it is not from fear. It is from excitement. For you are a library's best, and worst, patron: someone who loves books with such a passion that you will risk anything to obtain them.

The abbey bells begin to ring out over the valley and all feels right with the world. You climb onto your bicycle and pedal down the mountain.

The books, oh the books! You lay them out on a table when you return to your small flat, and sniff their earthy, vanillic, ancient book smell. You caress their leather covers and gently stroke their glorious spines. You gaze reverently upon the pages filled with beautiful Latin script. At last! There's no one to see, no one to judge. It's just you and the books and the endless, blissful hours that lie ahead.

But this first theft has merely whet your appetite. You need more.

You wait two months before you return. This time you steal nine rare tomes, religious texts, and illuminated manuscripts decorated with gold leaf, lapis lazuli, and silverpoint.

When you return for a third time, you discover that the library door is locked and the windows newly sealed.

Your first two thefts have not gone unnoticed.

Undeterred, you return the next day with a drill and attempt to open the lock. It fails. What are you going to do?

Several nights later, you are up late, poring over your beloved stolen items and swearing passionate oaths to steal just ten more books . . . or perhaps twenty. Thirty at most. But how will you get in now that the library is locked? It occurs to you that many ancient buildings contain secret passageways—you've toured countless castles that boast corridors behind bookcases or trapdoors that lead to hidden rooms.

Could you possibly be so lucky?

The next day, you visit the National University Library in Strasbourg and find exactly what you are looking for in an article about local history and Romanesque architecture: a hand-drawn floor plan of the abbey.

You thank God for this gift and take it as a sign. You walk outside into the bright sun and smile.

▼ A blueprint of Mont Saint-Odile Abbey, the secret room marked with a red dot.

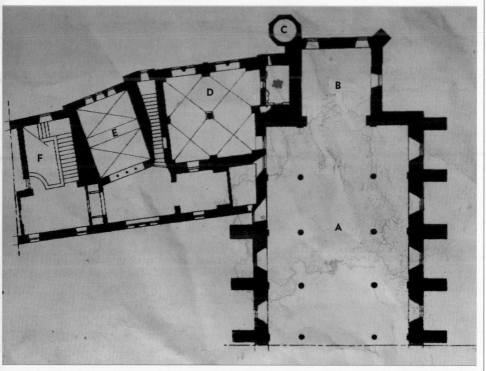

According to legend, Mont Sainte-Odile Abbey was founded in the eighth century by the Duke of Alsace under dramatic circumstances. When the duke decided to marry his daughter Odile off to a young prince, she fled into the Black Forest. The duke set off in pursuit, and a miracle occurred. The cliffs opened, revealing a narrow passageway through which Odile escaped. Upon witnessing this, the duke conceded defeat. Odile was spared marrying the prince and her father built her a monastery on the spot where the passage had appeared, allowing her to live out her life in worship and meditation as the queen of her own castle.

Lightning and fire did their best to destroy the abbey over the centuries, but the Benedictine nuns persisted, and today the abbey boasts a guesthouse and restaurant, visited by crowds of both non-believers and devoted pilgrims. Long before Stanislas Gosse's book thievery drew attention to Mont Sainte-Odile, it was famous for an illuminated manuscript titled *Hortus Deliciarum*, or *The Garden of Delights*, which was likely the first encyclopedia written by a woman.

Perched on a peak of the Vosges Mountains, the abbey's striking red stone walls and jagged roofs rise proudly above the sea of pines. The twelfth-century Golden Chapel of Tears and the Chapel of Angels are decorated with stunning mosaics in blue and gold, and the flower-filled courtyard is a peaceful place to sit and contemplate the moral relativism of book thievery. A short walk from the monastery lies what is known as the Pagan Wall, a seven-mile-long mystery that some claim was built by Druids.

In the mid-nineteenth century one of the monastery's vaulted rooms was turned into a library. Various institutions donated books throughout the years and by the time Stanislas Gosse arrived on the scene, it contained more than 3,000 titles, including several tomes of priceless incunabula*: 500-year-old Bibles and works by Cicero, Homer, Aristotle, and Virgil.

---

*A term used to describe books printed before the rather arbitrarily chosen date of 1501.

As for the abbey's secret passageway, it is concealed behind one of the library's bookshelves, a tiny door leading into a small, bare chamber with a trapdoor in the ceiling. No one knows when this room was constructed. Today it contains only rubble, a ruined stone bench, and several carvings of grim-faced cherubs. It's possible it was built to allow the abbot to eavesdrop on intriguing or unwholesome conversations, or it might have served as a vault for storing valuable items. Some argue it was used as a prison for naughty monks. Whatever the case, by the early 2000s, when the book heists took place, none of the tenants or caretakers knew of the passageway's existence and it was a stroke of luck that Gosse found it.

Gosse was a local teacher who played the organ at church. He lived alone and was said to be cold, even misanthropic, with no desire for the company of people. All of his love was reserved for books. "I'm afraid my burning passion overrode my conscience," Gosse told reporters. "It may appear selfish, but I felt the books had been abandoned. They were covered with dust and pigeon droppings and I felt no one consulted them anymore. There was also the thrill of adventure—I was very scared of being found out."

Discovering the secret room in the floor plan was only the beginning of Gosse's journey. Reaching it was quite another matter. The path to the hidden space was difficult and involved either dropping through a trapdoor in the bell tower via a rope ladder or climbing a narrow staircase and scaling an exterior wall facing the cliff's edge. Sources disagree on which treacherous path Gosse took into his secret chamber—perhaps this bibliophile cat burglar used both.

> "It was really a perfect mystery. The convent had the locks changed once, then a second and a third time, and the windows sealed."

Once inside the hidden room, Gosse slid open two wooden panels behind a shelf and slipped into the library. He moved through the room by candlelight, browsing titles at his leisure.

When a third spate of books disappeared, the head priest and librarian Alain Donius changed the locks again. But the books continued to vanish. Police were baffled. Monks and nuns hissed their suspicions up and down the abbey corridors, like characters in an Agatha Christie mystery.

Father Donius told reporters, "There was no sign of a break-in, yet our library was gradually being emptied. I thought to myself, 'One day I'll come in and there'll be nothing left.'"

Rare book dealers throughout Europe were told to keep an eye out for the stolen titles, but none surfaced.

"It was one of those frustrating but also rather thrilling cases," the public prosecutor, Madeleine Simoncello, told the press. "Quite extraordinary items were vanishing, sometimes singly, sometimes by the dozen. It was really a perfect mystery. The convent had the locks changed once, then a second and a third time, and the windows sealed. The thefts stopped for a while, then started again after Easter. That's when we started thinking seriously about the possibility of another entrance."

The police tore up floorboards, lifted ceiling tiles, tapped walls, and scrutinized every inch of the library in search of a mechanism that would open a secret door or reveal a hidden tunnel. Finally, in May 2002, a lucky gendarme stumbled upon the wooden panels that opened to the secret room. The police installed hidden cameras and waited.

On Pentecost Sunday, at nine o'clock in the evening, Gosse was arrested as he climbed down from the bell tower. The wild, heady days of his life as a smitten book thief were over.

Rare book thievery is not a new crime. In 1998, a 1623 edition of Shakespeare's first folio was stolen from the Durham University Library in England. Worth upwards of $3 million, it was missing for ten years, until an "eccentric antiques dealer" brought it into the Folger Shakespeare Library in Washington, DC, claiming it was from Cuba. Fifty-one-year-old Raymond Scott was quickly arrested. Though he'd been staying in five-star hotels and riding around in a limousine, he was, in fact, unemployed and living with his mother a few miles from the university. He was brought to trial, found guilty, and sentenced to eight years in prison.

William Jacques, nicknamed "Tomb Raider" by the press, stole hundreds of rare books in the 1990s from the London Library, British Library, and Cambridge University Library, including two copies of Sir Isaac Newton's 1687 publication, *Philosophiae Naturalis Principia Mathematica*, each worth approximately $135,000. He sold the titles at various auctions before eventually being caught and sentenced to four years in prison.

The police found approximately 1,100 stolen books in Gosse's flat, all of them carefully shelved, dusted, and unharmed.

What makes Stanislas Gosse unique is that he never attempted to sell his stolen loot. Perhaps he knew that he would be caught if the titles resurfaced at rare book auctions, or perhaps he simply couldn't bear to part with them.

"I have a consuming passion for ancient books," the twitterpated book thief pleaded.

He was not alone in his love. A character in Jane Austen's *Pride and Prejudice* declares, "I shall be miserable if I have not an excellent library." No doubt the feeling was based on Austen's own. The Dutch philosopher Erasmus stated, "When I have a little money, I buy books; and if I have any left, I buy food and clothes."

▲ *Stanislas Gosse*

Perhaps Virginia Woolf put it best: "Books are everywhere; and always the same sense of adventure fills us. Second-hand books are wild books, homeless books; they have come together in vast flocks of variegated feather and have a charm which the domesticated volumes of the library lack."

Gosse was charged with "burglary by ruse and escalade." ("Escalade," for you logophiles, is a historical term meaning "the scaling of fortified walls by ladders.")

The police found approximately 1,100 stolen books in Gosse's flat, all of them carefully shelved, dusted, and unharmed.

"I know it can seem selfish," Gosse said at his trial, "but I was under the impression that those books had been abandoned." Raised Catholic, he had visited the abbey often since he was a small child. He'd watched as the books, unused and unloved, slowly decayed on the library's shelves, year after year, until he finally decided to do something about it.

Rather than being outraged, locals were quietly delighted by Gosse's theft—here was someone so devoted to rare books that he would risk prison for a chance to possess them. The "gentleman thief," as he was called, was let off easy, with a suspended prison sentence, a $20,000 fine, and community service at the abbey, helping to catalog the very books that he'd stolen. ◈

ANN RADCLIFFE
IS TO BLAME ONCE AGAIN ...
or is it Horace Walpole?

A secret passageway hidden behind a library bookcase—this concept is so ubiquitous that a person can find it everywhere in modern popular entertainment, from The Addams Family to Batman Begins—Bruce Wayne must strike three dissonant chords on his grand piano to open the passageway to his lair. In real life, any number of stately British homes have a similar feature. Oxburgh Hall, for example, boasts a secret door disguised as a shelf, the false spines featuring satirical joke titles such as The Art of Increasing the Pouch and Paunch and the rather scandalous Charles's Introduction to the Italian Tongue, with "The Italian tongue" being an old-fashioned euphemism for cunnilingus.

Where did the idea spring from? While secret passageways date back to the Egyptian pyramids and were used, along with booby traps, to guard the burial chambers against tomb robbers, there's speculation that they first appeared in popular culture via gothic literature.

Ann Radcliffe published five gothic novels in the 1790s and is considered a pioneer of the genre. She was wildly successful (the highest-paid writer of the time) and influenced countless future writers, including Sir Walter Scott, Victor Hugo, Edgar Allan Poe, Alexandre Dumas, and Fyodor Dostoevsky.

In her book *The Mysteries of Udolpho*, the protagonist Emily finds a secret door in her bedchamber, through which the villain Morano creeps in and attempts to kidnap her. Did this spark the entire secret passageway trope? Is Radcliffe to blame for creating a long-lasting cliché from this harmless plot device?

Perhaps not. Horace Walpole's gothic classic, *The Castle of Otranto*, published in 1764, also featured "a subterraneous passage which led from the vaults of the castle to the church of St. Nicholas." This predates Radcliffe's tunnel by some thirty years. *The Castle of Otranto* is also overrun with ghosts, prophecies, trapdoors, monasteries, monks, and characters locked in towers. Perhaps Walpole is the writer who should be praised (cursed?) for establishing this enduring element of the genre.

WHAT LIES BEHIND BOOKCASES

Helpful tip: If you are in the business of black-market art buying or have some heinous secret that must never see the light of day, don't hide it behind a bookcase. Every Hercule Poirot wannabe will take one look at those shelves and pounce.

This was the case in 2017, in a suburb of Buenos Aires, when authorities raided the house of a collector suspected of smuggling Chinese antiques into South America. Wisely checking behind the bookcase, investigators stumbled upon a secret passageway leading to a hidden chamber. What they found inside was not at all what they expected, however. Instead of ancient Chinese art, it was filled with dozens of pieces of Nazi memorabilia, among them a box of swastika-emblazoned harmonicas, an hourglass, bayonet, magnifying glass, and photograph of that self-same magnifying glass in the hands of Adolf Hitler. The disturbing trove may well have found its way to Argentina in the hands of high-ranking Nazi officials, many of whom managed to escape to the South American country after World War II.

BOOK TOILETS
and Other Book-Shaped Mysteries

The really cool people in the eighteenth century didn't just keep a stack of reading material next to their privy. Their privy was *made* of reading material. Inside the Hofkamer, a grand townhouse tucked at the back of a private courtyard in Antwerp, Belgium, there exists a bathroom camouflaged as a sweet little corner library, complete with a toilet disguised as a pile of large books. Faux bookshelves line the walls, constructed from leather and wood. A large window lets in the sun.

As it turns out, book toilets were something of a running joke in the eighteenth century—right alongside book-shaped musical instruments, book-shaped playing card sets, and book-shaped smoking kits. How did it come to this? Hollowed-out books had long been used to smuggle vials of poison, knives, and other contraband. They were viewed as inconspicuous, innocent, even virtuous items. It was only a matter of time before their wholesome reputation was exaggerated for giggles. For example, the United States Pottery Company, which was in operation from 1847 to 1858, made drinking flasks in the shape of books, their spines stamped with such titles as *Hoo doo Bible, Departed Spirits,* or *Ladies' Comfort.* As far back as the sixteenth century, book-shaped alcohol flasks, often painted with saints and crosses, were produced in Spain and Mexico. Apparently, things become infinitely more respectable when wrapped in a book.

Today, there is an entire subgenre of these curiosities, now known as "Blooks" (book + look = things that look like books). It encompasses everything from 1950s' book radios to a particularly meta book-shaped box titled *The Care and Feeding of Books,* inside which is a book repair kit. There is even a prank book called *World's Greatest Jokes* by R. U. Laffin, which, when opened, explodes.

If your head is spinning? Let's just get back to the book toilets. In 2020 the rare book firm Daniel Crouch Rare Books listed a large, heavy "volume" for sale titled *Histoire des Pays Bas,* which translates to *History of the Netherlands* (Netherlands = nether regions). The volume, unclasped, opens to reveal a wooden stool and a hole meant for a chamber pot. This portable "book" was produced in France around 1750. The current price? Nine thousand dollars.

◄ Seventeenth-century book toilet in the grand townhouse of Hofkamer, Antwerp, Belgium.

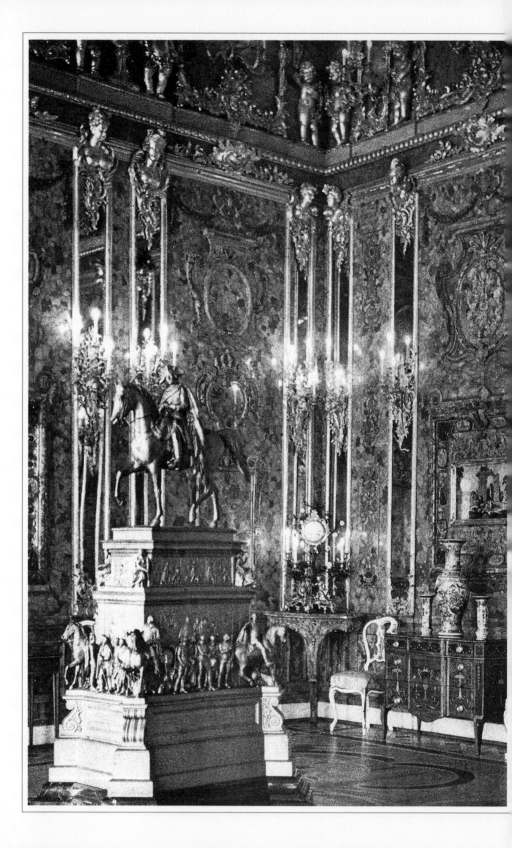

3

A Room Like Warm Honey

TSARSKOYE SELO • RUSSIA

You wander the palace unseen. Birds nest
beneath the painted clouds of the ruined
galleries. Soldiers mill across the parquet or
sleep on the divans where, thirty years before,
the Romanov children argued and played and
daydreamed. Dirty boots scuff threadbare satin.
Gilt doors have been nailed with placards—
"Kp 1," "Stab"—portrait halls and drawing rooms
repurposed as sleeping quarters for the troops.
You recognize their uniforms: gray wool, a black
eagle clutching a wreath, a hooked double cross.
The Nazis have reached Russia. They've taken
the Catherine Palace and are waiting, bored and
restless, for orders from Berlin.

◄ *The original Amber Room in the Catherine Palace in 1917. After it was dismantled and shipped to Germany, the original chamber vanished without a trace during World War II.*

After a while, you lose your way. The rumble of the soldiers' voices echoes and fades. And then, out of the dark, you enter a room. It stands in stark contrast to the splendor of the other rooms you've passed through. The floor is covered in sand. The walls have been hastily hidden behind masses of rag pulp and cloth. But the disguise is being picked at.

Two soldiers, guns slung, are pulling at the wall coverings. And suddenly, in the dimness, you see a faint glimmer, not gold, but deeper, richer. You glimpse carved garlands of acanthus leaves, rosettes, mirrors, mosaics made of agate, onyx, and lapis, and panel upon panel of softly shimmering, lustrous brown gems, their colors whirling, like a drop of milk in tea, like perfectly glazed pastry. The room seems to radiate its own light, from lemon to honey to coffee, a thousand tones of warmth. The men cry out. Their superiors arrive and shoo you away.

You return sometime later hoping for another glimpse. You walk the empty halls, searching for the extraordinary room, but when you finally find the place where it should be there is nothing there, only a hollow, empty shell. The soldiers have left and the room has left with them. You shuffle across the sand and gaze at the bare walls and you wonder if perhaps you imagined it, that bewitching glimmer, that glow like warm honey, like the final embers of life in the desolate, gutted palace.

Friedrich Wilhelm I, King of Prussia, a man whose greatest hobby consisted of kidnapping giants from London and Vienna and forcing them into service as his personal bodyguards, was not what you'd call an artistic sort of fellow. He was miserly, rough mannered, obsessed with military protocol, and did not like to read. He loved his wife but despised what he considered her idle affection for painting and music. Fearing his offspring might grow up more like her than him, he assigned them all strict lessons in political economy and the art of warfare and, at one point, gifted his six-year-old son a regiment of 131 small children to drill and train.*

It was under this unpromising star, however, that one of the most enduring and fascinating pieces of art of the last 400 years first appeared on the world's stage: a jewel box of a room so bursting with beauty and detail that it boggles the mind. Théophile Gautier described it in his book *Voyage en Russie* as something from a fairy tale or *The Thousand and One Nights*. "The eye," he wrote, "is amazed and blinded by the wealth and warmth of tints, representing all colors of the spectrum of yellow—from smoky topaz to a light lemon."

The more one digs into the Amber Room and its past, the more tangled and odd the narrative becomes.

The Amber Room is not secret the way other rooms in this book are. It was visited by thousands during its heyday, admired and envied, moved between multiple royal courts, used as a czarina's personal wellness room, and as a political chess piece to broker alliances between nations. Everyone who saw it had something to say about it. A German chambermaid glimpsed it and sent an awestruck letter back to her lover in Weimar, writing breathlessly of an indescribably beautiful room whose "price could never be calculated." Contemporaries named it the eighth wonder of the world. But today the Amber Room is a secret in the truest sense of the word, hidden

---

*This son, the eventual Frederick the Great, went on to become an accomplished flautist, a passionate proponent of the arts, *and* a military genius. That he might be capable of possessing all three of these qualities at once did not seem to have occurred to his father.

not behind a panel or under floorboards, but within history itself, a room lost in layers of time, obscured by the flames and political paperwork of a great war. It had a long, eventful existence, traveled farther than most rooms do, and was last seen in Königsberg, now Kaliningrad, Russia, in 1944, just before the city was carpet-bombed into oblivion. Then it vanished, leaving a thousand traces in its wake.

What became of Friedrich Wilhelm's fabled fairy-tale room?

Dr. Alfred Rohde, the director of the Königsberg museum where it was last housed, swore to his superior that the room's amber panels had been rescued from the bombs, yet weeks before told a family friend that they had been destroyed.

Six hundred miles away, in Gotha, tales sprang up of children skipping pieces of delicately carved amber across ponds.

In Bremen in 1997, a mysterious "Mr. X" attempted to sell one of the room's four colored marble mosaics, causing a sensation and swift government intervention.

In a Bavarian wood, a treasure hunter who had dedicated years of his life to searching for the room was found ritualistically disemboweled, fueling rumors of Soviet assassinations and government sanctioned cover-ups.

The more one digs into the Amber Room and its past, the more tangled and odd the narrative becomes. Was the room destroyed? Did Dr. Rohde manage to hide it from the Soviet secret police and is it somewhere out there still, in a basement or mineshaft, waiting to be found? The room's story is long, winding, and still unfinished, but to understand even a sliver of its legend we will have to go back to the very beginning.

The Amber Room first began to take shape in the workshop of Andreas Schlüter, court architect to Frederick I, the father of the aforementioned artistically challenged Prussian king. Baltic amber, fossilized prehistoric tree sap that can be polished to an array of lovely hues, had begun to be stockpiled in Danzig during the 1600s, and in 1701 it was decided that something should be done to showcase these gems. Work began on a Bernstein-Kabinett, or amber cabinet, taking thirteen years and multiple master craftsmen to complete.

The room was first installed, rather inauspiciously, in a corner of the third floor of the Berliner Stadtschloss. It had only been there a handful of years before it caught the eye of the visiting Peter the Great, czar of Russia. The czar, along with bringing the Prussian king another giant for his collection, was there for business and personal gain. Well aware of

▲ Catherine the Great of Russia, who used the Amber Room as her personal meditation chamber.

Friedrich Wilhelm's wish to secure his aid against Sweden, he took full advantage of the situation and made a point of loudly admiring all the things he wanted for himself, including the dazzling new Amber Room. Friedrich Wilhelm took the hint and, preferring troops over a frivolous piece of art any day, gifted the czar the room along with a yacht. The alliance was made and the room was packed up. It would not see Germany again for three centuries.

In early 1717, the room arrived by sled in St. Petersburg, where it was installed in the old Winter Palace. Then, in 1755, when the Russian court moved out of the city, the room went with it, to the Catherine Palace in Tsarskoye Selo, or Czar's Village. (Even kings had to keep up with the Joneses, or in this case the Bourbons, and the king of France had recently moved his court out of Paris to the bucolic meadows of Versailles.)

In the Catherine Palace, there was a slight problem: The designated space for the Amber Room was six times the size of the original humble cabinet. Not wanting to spread the grandeur too thin, the czar ordered that it be expanded. Here is where it transformed into a true masterpiece. Two Italian architects took on the task of extending the amber panels, decking the room out with Venetian mirrors, gilded figures, Florentine mosaic panels, and mother-of-pearl inlays, and turning the little cabinet into the most majestic of the state rooms. Nine hundred and ninety pounds of amber became 13,000 pounds. Even the floor was a work of art, inlaid with fifteen sorts of wood.

Once finished, it became Catherine the Great's favorite room in the palace, one she used both for gatherings with her inner circle and for her personal meditations. It was a bright space, especially by candlelight, the amber conjuring a warmth that no other room in the palace could replicate. During an endlessly gloomy Russian winter, the room might have been the equivalent of a SAD lamp or wearing orange-tinted spectacles. Perhaps adding to its appeal, amber was considered healthful at the time, a wonder cure for a host of ailments. In Russian folklore it was thought to be a powerful deflector of the evil eye and was worn in necklaces and bracelets and hung from children's cradles. Paneling an entire room in it, then, might have been the equivalent of creating a bunker, insulating its inhabitants from all the horrors of the world.

For many years it did just that. The room passed unscathed through the rise and fall of multiple monarchs, as well as the bloody Bolshevik revolution. Then, in 1941, Hitler's Operation Barbarossa knocked at the doors of the USSR. With enemy troops swiftly approaching St. Petersburg and the Czar's Village, the palace caretakers were thrown into a panic. Anatoly Mikhailovich Kuchumov, a young museum curator, deemed the room far too large and heavy to be moved. Over the centuries the amber had grown brittle, and it was decided it could no longer be taken down for fear of ruining it. So Kuchumov had it glued with cloth and padding, and the floor covered in sand in a futile attempt to disguise it from the Germans, who, 300 years later and no longer in need of aid against Sweden, were fully intending to snatch back Friedrich Wilhelm's gift.

⊶☛ Curiously, on September 2, 1944, several weeks after the room's supposed total destruction, Rohde wrote to his superior in Berlin claiming that "The Amber Room has survived, apart from six dado panels."

In September 1941, German troops arrived at the now deserted palace. The Amber Room's disguise did little to fool them. A pair of soldiers found the panels under the covering and within thirty-six hours the room had been packed up and sent by train toward the Baltic Sea. (How the Nazis managed to dismantle the room and spirit it away more or less undamaged while Kuchumov and his staff could not, is a question that appears to have haunted the Russian curator for the rest of his life. He never stopped hunting for the room.)

In the autumn of that year, the room took its final known journey, arriving in Königsberg on October 17, 1941. Over the next few months Dr. Alfred Rohde, the city's premier museum curator, had the room reassembled on the upper floor of the Palace of the Teutonic Knights, also known as Königsberg Castle, a fortress at the center of Königsberg's historic quarter. Rohde was an expert on amber art and had campaigned for the Amber Room to be saved

◀ *The Rococo Catherine Palace, summer residence to the czars and home to the Amber Room for almost two centuries.*

and sent to him. When he found that two doors were missing, he had them sent for, the errant doors passing through a treacherous landscape of battles and war-torn countryside to reach him.

On November 13, 1941, the *Königsberger Allgemeine Zeitung* carried the headline "Amber Walls in the Palace" and the display was opened to the public. The room was a sensation and a brazen propaganda tool, meant to bring a sense of hope to the beleaguered citizens of Königsberg. The display was attached with the message that if you could steal the Amber Room from under the Soviets' noses, their troops would soon be defeated too. But behind the scenes, the war was not going well. Superiors in Berlin were concerned with losing ground—and loot—to the Allies. Not long afterward, the room was once again dismantled, packed into crates.

Here, the road splits into dozens of barely visible trails. At the end of August 1944, Königsberg was bombed extensively by the Soviets in retribution for the bombings in Moscow. A family friend of Rohde's, Liesl Amm, remembers going into the town by bicycle the next morning to ensure the survival of her friends and family. She met Dr. Rohde in the ruins of the castle courtyard. He took her to the basement where it was claimed the Amber Room panels had been stored for safekeeping. In an interview with Anthony Wilson in his documentary *In Search of the Amber Room*, Liesl spoke of a honeylike mass covering the stones. "It's all gone," she remembers Rohde telling her.

Then, curiously, on September 2, 1944, several weeks after the room's supposed total destruction, Rohde wrote to his superior in Berlin claiming that "The Amber Room has survived, apart from six dado panels." Rohde's son, a young soldier, remembers seeing his father for the last time and being told that the Amber Room had been "moved to a safe place."

So did Liesl misremember the scene in the ruins of the castle? Or did Dr. Rohde lie to her? Or was the room only partially destroyed and Rohde led Liesl to believe it had been destroyed in its entirety? There are myriad reasons why Rohde might want to obscure the truth about the fate of the room. If it was destroyed, nobody wanted to be blamed, certainly not Dr. Rohde, whose pride and joy was his museum and its exhibitions. And if it had survived, Rohde, a patriotic German, would not have wished to give up this information to the Soviets or to anyone but his closest confidants and family. Some claim he managed to get it out of the city and took the secret of its location to his grave. Others say that the room was so heavily damaged by smoke in one of the initial attacks on the city that Rohde hid it away out of shame for failing to protect it. According to this theory, the unrecognizably scarred and ugly panels were eventually burned as rubbish.

Yet another theory claims that the room, having survived the bombing and invasion of Königsberg by the Soviets, was then accidentally torched by Russian soldiers in celebration of their victory. This would not have been something the Soviets would have readily admitted to, and theories persist that they falsified statements and documents and strategically kept the hope of the room's existence alive both to avoid responsibility for its embarrassing loss and also to aid in claims for restitution against Germany in the decades following the war. The Soviets also looted artwork from Germany during World War II, some say as many as 1.6 million pieces, and as long as the Germans were responsible for the loss of the priceless Amber Room, talks of restitution might remain one-sided.

▼ *Königsberg Castle before and after it was bombed by the Soviets during World War II. The castle acted as a museum and housed the Amber Room during its time in Nazi Germany.*

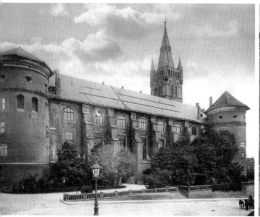

Then there is the matter of Kuchumov, the curator who poured sand across the Amber Room's floor and papered over its walls. After the war, he founded a special commission of Soviet researchers, code-named poetically "The Choral Society," to search for the room and keep the hope of its survival alive. Yet right after the war, Kuchumov went to Königsberg and investigated the case firsthand, where many think he found ample proof of the room's destruction. Was he simply a pawn in the political post-war game or did he truly believe the room still existed?

Finally, all trails went cold. And no sooner had they than conspiracy theories began to proliferate. What better way, it was whispered, to stop speculation on the whereabouts of what was called the eighth wonder of the world than to say that it has been annihilated? There are hypotheses of billionaires with parts of the Amber Room paneling their yachts, of Lenin having replaced the crates containing the room with decoys and rushing away with the real room at the eleventh hour. A trawl through the depths of internet sleuthing message boards reveals questionably sourced stories from people claiming to be neighbors, friends, or descendants of the soldiers who had wired the bombs used to destroy the Amber Room.

> The legend of the Amber Room persists precisely because there are just enough conflicting reports and tantalizingly obscured trails to set imaginations alight.

Some theories veer wildly into the realm of the supernatural, speaking of an "Amber Room Curse" and a trail of corpses left in the missing room's wake. Dr. Rohde and his wife died of typhus in postwar Kaliningrad while the KGB was investigating the fate of the room and the doctor who signed their death certificate supposedly was never heard from again. General Gusev, a Russian intelligence officer, was killed in a car crash after being interviewed by a journalist about the Amber Room. Amber Room hunter Georg Stein died gruesomely in 1987 in a Bavarian forest, purportedly laid open with a scalpel, though others say he died of a gunshot wound to the head. However, it is there in that small discrepancy that stories were born. Some claimed he was killed by Soviets trying to keep him from revealing information about the Amber Room. The more levelheaded said he had committed suicide out of disappointment over discovering the room was gone forever. Who was right?

The legend of the Amber Room persists precisely because there are just enough conflicting reports and tantalizingly obscured trails to set imaginations alight. Over the past decade alone there have been countless headlines trumpeting the news that treasure hunters have found the priceless room or pieces of it. The mysterious Mr. X in Bremen who attempted to sell one of the mosaics turned out to be Hans Achterman, the son of a Wehrmacht truck driver who claimed to have helped pack the room during one of its many escapes. (The mosaic hung above the man's couch in his apartment for years before being relegated to the basement. The son told reporters he did not like the look of it.)

While the truth is often stranger (and duller) than fiction, there are compelling reasons to believe the room might have escaped the conflagration at Königsberg. The Nazis were known to spread valuable items far and wide across the globe in an attempt to confuse pursuers. Loot was removed as far as Iceland, as was the case with the *Minden*, scuttled with $110 million worth of gold from the Dresden Bank in its belly. In 2020, the *Karlsruhe* was found sunk off the coast of Poland containing military vehicles and crates that could possibly hold remnants of the amber panels.

It's entirely possible the room is still out there. But perhaps its trajectory will be comparable, in the end, to the search for Anastasia, Grand Duchess of Russia and youngest daughter of Czar Nicholas II. Long rumored to have survived her family's bloody assassination in 1918, the search for her lasted close to a hundred years and featured a steady string of impersonators, false claims, and wild theories. The truth was that Anastasia died in Yekaterinburg together with her family, but as long as there was some doubt as to where her body lay, legend persisted that she had escaped.

Likewise with the Amber Room—where there is no body and no answers, all answers are possible and there are much more pleasant answers than to acknowledge that something beautiful has been lost forever. No answers allow the collective imagination to run wild. It's why cold cases are more exciting than closed ones, why lost treasures have the power to fascinate, while found ones might barely garner a glance in a crowded museum exhibition. It's why humans will always persist in their slightly delusional search for . . . not the truth exactly, but something better, something more hopeful than the bones of a princess, or a pile of carved gemstones melted to an oozing mass in a cellar.

A reproduction of the Amber Room exists today. Artisans have built a version of it in the Catherine Palace using the same techniques as the amber craftsmen in the 1700s. (It is a wonder of its own, made possible through a financial alliance between Germany and Russia.) And in Königsberg, now Kaliningrad, close to the place where Dr. Rohde's museum once stood, a red brick castle houses an amber museum, its displays full of delicate wonders: amber portraits, amber clocks, a ship with amber sails, and an amber trinket with a prehistoric lizard suspended inside.

But the real Amber Room, the one whose panels soaked in the perfumes of Catherine the Great and echoed the voices of the greatest minds and leaders of Europe, that room remains lost. Perhaps it is gone forever, lying at the bottom of an ocean, slowly succumbing to seawater and decay. And maybe it's just as well it has a little peace now. The room has seen wars and bloodshed aplenty. Even Friedrich Wilhelm of Prussia might have been proud of it in the end. ◈

THE LOST LIBRARY OF IVAN THE TERRIBLE

Ivan the Terrible, czar of Russia from 1547 to 1584, is best known for massacring the people of Novgorod, killing his own son, and the myth that he gouged out the eyes of the architect of Moscow's colorful onion-domed St. Basil's Cathedral to ensure the man would never design anything so lovely again. Less well known is that he may have been something of a bib-liophile. According to documents uncovered in Estonian archives, he owned more than 800 rare texts, ranging from Egyptian scrolls to Chinese, Greek, and Latin manu-scripts. Unfortunately, the bloody monarch, whose collection was called the Libereya, was extraordi-narily paranoid and had the library hidden away in the warren of pas-sageways beneath the Kremlin, Russia's capitol building.

▲ *Ivan the Terrible looking, indeed, terrible.*

Originally built in 1156, the Kremlin is one of the world's oldest fortresses still in use. The passage-ways beneath it have to this day not been completely mapped.

Since the late nineteenth cen-tury, archaeologists and treasure hunters have been trying to locate the lost library without success. Legend speaks of a curse, that Ivan cast a spell on his library so that anyone who came close to unearth-ing it would go blind. Some historians are skeptical that the library exists at all. Others think it almost certainly did but has been sold off piecemeal over the centuries or burned to ashes during the fires that routinely devastated Moscow. And, of course, still others believe that the fabled Libereya not only existed but that it is still hidden in some unmapped chamber beneath the Kremlin, waiting to be found.

4

A City on an Anthill

PUEBLA · MEXICO

You blink up at the sun-parched apartment
building, then down at the slip of paper in
your hand. Can this be the right address?
In front of you is a slightly shabby tenement
painted a dusty blue. Wrought iron balconies
jut over the gauntlet of bustling street vendors
below. The aromas of grilling elotes and tacos
árabes drift in the air. A great oak tree spreads
its branches overhead, cooling the flagstones
and the vendors. But you are left to sweat and
squirm in your stiff uniform, cursing the one
who called you here.

◄ *Centuries-old tunnels are rumored to criss-cross the underbelly of almost every major city in Mexico.
Some of these rumors are now being discovered to be true. But who built these tunnels and why?*

An anonymous tipster has informed you—the police—of an ongoing disturbance inside the building. Visitors enter at all hours of the day and night, arriving with full baskets and leaving with empty ones. This person insists that a group of nuns is living illegally somewhere inside the building. But where? In the walls? Under the floorboards? They are certainly never seen by anyone in the street. Nuns, and their convents, are outlawed in Mexico. As of the reforms of 1859, the church's vast properties have been seized, their meddling finally suppressed.

Is this all an elaborate prank?

You and your fellow officers enter the building, pressing up the staircase to the second floor. Down a hallway, you reach the apartment you were told to search. In the back wall, hidden behind a tapestry, you find a low, square door. You duck through it first, crouching to fit under the lintel.

You don't know what you were expecting—dust, darkness, a cramped hideaway, the nuns huddled together, peering at you like

startled rabbits. Instead, you find yourself standing in a whitewashed study, finely furnished. Beyond, through an arched doorway, is a courtyard, trees, tiled fountains, airy colonnades. You walk through room after lovely room and see recent evidence of inhabitation, dishes sitting in soapy water, a dipped pen on a desk.

In the library, you encounter a statue of a golden-robed monk, his finger to his lips, beseeching everyone to be silent. And they have been silent, the nuns, silent as crucifixes behind that secret door, in their own, hidden world.

In the crypt, you finally find them. They do not resist arrest. They go with you freely and soon you understand why. They are only a distraction.

As the other officers fan out through the convent, they discover that the building has been amended over the years. They find hidden rooms, hidden staircases, even spy holes allowing the nuns to peek down onto unsuspecting people. Beneath a tile in the church, one officer discovers a tunnel leading away. Many of the nuns have escaped down it, jewel-studded reliquaries and treasures hidden inside their robes. They will exchange their black habits and wimples for dresses and bonnets. They will slip back into the fabric of society or into the homes of their wealthy families.

The police chief orders workers to come and collapse the tunnel beneath the floor of the church. You watch them arrive with hammers and shovels and you shake your head. Pointless. Pointless even to try. Everyone in this city knows what lies just under their feet: miles of tunnels, stretching far and deep, and back through history. This city is built on secrets. It aches and groans with them. The workers carry out their job. The tunnel is blocked. Only one little gap has been stopped up.

◀ *A photograph of the Mother Superior's office in the Convento Santa Monica, showing the hidden door that connected the convent to its false front.*

In Italo Calvino's Nebula-nominated 1972 novel *Invisible Cities*, a fictionalized Marco Polo describes a series of fantastical metropolises to an aging Kublai Khan—from cities built of spiderwebs to cities built of pipes to one city hidden underground, a mirror version of the city above it. For every church on the surface, there is one directly below it. Every street features a parallel tunnel beneath it, every house, a dark reflection.

While the city he describes is invented, almost every city of a certain age in our own world has an underworld, or many underworlds, stacked one atop the other, layer upon layer of defensive structures, tunnels, catacombs, and cellars that have slowly accumulated over the centuries. Paris's catacombs are the most famous, but the list is long, including the tiny country of Luxembourg, which features more than ten miles of tunnels cut into the rock beneath its capital, built in the seventeenth century to house the entire population at the time—up to 16,000 people—in the event of war. (Families had their own little cave-compartments, their names written above the archways. During the Holocaust, the tunnels were used to shelter Jewish families from the invading Nazi forces.) Even Portland, Oregon, not exactly high on the list of mysterious places, has its tales of Shanghai Tunnels, nineteenth-century constructions said to run from the basements of the city's hotels and taverns to the docks of the Willamette River. They were used to ferry supplies from the river to the taverns and, some say, to kidnap unwary drinkers to be conscripted to ships bound for Asia. Even less well known are the mysteries beneath the city of Puebla in Central Mexico, with its miles of low brick tunnels, almost all of them connecting a convent or religious institution.

For as long as anyone can remember, rumors have persisted of tunnels worming their way beneath the colonial city of Puebla. In 1929, a local publication described something called "The Devil's Cave," a dark passageway behind the vocational school, sloping down into the earth. Children were warned away from it. It was believed that this tunnel led to another, and another, that you could wander in and never find your way out. Whispers spoke of thieves living in the tunnels, dangerous outlaws, and wicked spirits.

In 1935, three pots of gold and silver doubloons were stolen from the basement of the Hospital Church of San Roque in the city's historic center. While investigating the theft, authorities discovered a well in the building and, halfway down it, a tunnel.

In a laundress's home, another mysterious entrance was found. And in the north of the city, close to the old fort, a nobleman's house featured a staircase leading down. A constant cool breeze wafted up from the darkness below. The nobleman had an iron gate placed over it, just in case.

Then, in 2015, the truth came to light. During the excavation of a seventeenth-century bridge known as the Puente de Bubas, or

▼ One of the many tunnels recently discovered beneath the bustling city of Puebla in central Mexico.

Syphilis Bridge thanks to the syphilis hospital that once stood at one end, workers uncovered an underground gallery almost a mile long. Inside, they found artifacts reaching back centuries: children's toys like marbles and wooden horses as well as the accoutrements of more adult pastimes—weapons, beer bottles, and coins. The excavation of the Puebla tunnels began.

The initial theory was that the tunnels had been built by the Mexican military in the weeks before the famed Battle of Puebla. On May 5, 1862, the vastly outnumbered Mexican troops managed to smash the French army, one of the most powerful in the world, on a muddy hill outside the city. Journalists across the globe asked how this could have happened and, while there were many factors, a little discussed one was Puebla's network of tunnels. While the French forces crept nearer, the Mexican army feverishly expanded an existing tangle of underground passageways until it reached Fort Guadalupe on the hill, even raising the ceilings so that they could ride their horses along them. During the subsequent fighting, the tunnels were used to carry messages, transport ammunition, and allow troops to burst out from underground and ambush the French.

However, while the Mexican army enlarged the network, someone had already built most of it hundreds of years before. But who?

The medieval French poet Alain de Lille famously stated that all roads lead to Rome. In Mexico, the more accurate wisdom would be, "All roads lead to a church." All of the miles of tunnels beneath Puebla end in the crypts of a church, convent, or monastery.

Between 1519 and 1533, the Spanish conquistadors swept across what is now Mexico. Following the conquest, temples and pyramids were pulled down, stone gods had their faces shattered and eyes scratched out. In their place, great baroque cathedrals were raised. Catholicism reigned supreme. And throughout this time, tunnels were dug beneath the streets, connecting churches to seats of government. According to locals, they exist in Puebla, Guadalajara, and Mexico City, even though that city was built on the marshy soil of a drained lake and plagued by earthquakes. In Monterrey, a tunnel has long been claimed to lead from the old city hall to the ornate, canary yellow bishop's church of Obispado perched high on a hill overlooking the glittering metropolis and its brightly painted slums.

These tunnels were not just built in Mexico. A number of towns and cities across Europe feature tales, and often physical proof, of tunnels connecting churches to government buildings and castles. The English town of Merseyside is said to have a tunnel running from its main church, St. Chad's, to the courthouse. In Tomar, Portugal, tunnels and hidden chambers were recently discovered that are suspected to lead from the church to the one-time castle of the Knights Templar a mile away. Likewise, the picturesque island town of Mont-Saint-Michel, rising like a wizard's trick from the flooded planes of Normandy, features a veritable snake's nest of tunnels beneath its crowning church, passageways that wriggle downward through crypts, an underground chapel, and into the cellars of the public buildings lower down the hillside.

> **According to salacious local lore, the tunnels were used by monks and nuns as a secret meeting place where they could make love away from God's watchful eye.**

Why might this be? The answer is much less kooky-conspiratorial than it sounds. Until the 1700s, the separation of church and state did not exist. Religion and government worked hand in hand to maintain the power structures of every country in Europe. Before long, this became the case in Mexico as well. Bishops were often elected as viceroys, the political head of municipal districts. Since there were no banks in the early days of Spanish rule, businessmen went to the church for loans. If a prominent aristocratic family had too many children, it was often expected that a younger member would join the clergy as a way to benefit the family, the equivalent of marrying off a daughter to a well-connected gentleman. Though they butted heads over certain practices, it was no secret that the

government and the church were closely intertwined. What *was* secret was that the primary buildings of these two institutions were linked through physical means, as well as spiritual ones.

What were the Puebla tunnels used for, before the revolutions, thieves, and myths? Records are murky and mostly nonexistent. According to salacious local lore, the tunnels were used by monks and nuns as a secret meeting place where they could make love away from God's watchful eye. (This author was told several stories of infant skeletons being found in the tunnels, purported to be the unwanted offspring of these unholy unions.)

A more plausible theory is that the tunnels were simply practical ways of moving about away from the heat and danger of the streets above. They also functioned as escape routes in times of political turmoil. Churches and government buildings tended to be the most sturdily built in any given city and the most easily defensible. Should one institution be in danger, they might be able to flee to their brethren, colleagues, and relatives at the other. An added benefit was that churches were, for many centuries, exempt from violence altogether, allowing them to be as safe a refuge as any fortress in time of war.[*]

Then there was the matter of the gold; during the church's zenith in Mexico, convents and monasteries were treasure troves of art and beautiful things, as well as hubs of craftsmanship and skilled labor. Nuns and monks could be goldsmiths, writers, craftsmen, and painters. The tunnels would have been a practical way for these religious communities to stay in touch with one another and transport their wealth.

[*]As far back as Greek and Roman times, religious buildings were respected as places of sanctuary for fugitives. To spill the blood of someone in the presence of the gods was to bring misfortune on yourself. This tradition persisted all the way into medieval times and beyond, which is why it was such a scandal when Thomas Becket, the Archbishop of Canterbury, was killed inside his own church by followers of King Henry II in 1170.

◄ *Mont-Saint-Michel in Normandy was once a prison, abbey, and fortress. Researchers are still uncovering new secrets, hidden chambers, and passageways.*

By the end of the 1700s, the influences of the Age of Enlightenment and French Revolution in Europe had taken effect in Mexico as well. The delicate symbiosis between church and state crumbled, and Mexico began fighting not only for its independence from Europe, but also for freedom from one of Europe's tools of colonization, the Catholic church. In 1859, the first of a series of laws were passed, restricting clerical privilege, weakening church courts, and commanding religious orders to hand over their monasteries, convents, and lands to the state. Overnight, nearly all the country's convents and monasteries became public property. The great connectors between church and state fell away and were forgotten. The physical tunnels did too, becoming the realm of rateros, bandits, and devils.

> The authorities found secret passageways galore, as well as staircases and another well, also connected to the network of tunnels, and recently stopped up by the nuns themselves.

But the nuns of the Convent of Santa Monica in Puebla were determined to survive. For almost seven decades, they managed to remain in their sprawling convent, making use of the centuries-old infrastructure beneath the city to move about and adapting their buildings into places of concealment.* Using the help of sympathetic city officials, they even orchestrated their convent's registration as a streetlamp factory in city documents. They then bricked up external entrances, learned to live in almost complete silence, and survived more or less peacefully behind the false front of the apartment building—right up until it was searched on May 20, 1934, and their operation was blown open.

La Opinion published an article about the discovery of the convent the next day:

---

*In 1917, due to shifting political tides, Mexican nuns were briefly allowed to return to their convents. In 1926, this was once more made illegal. Whether the nuns of Santa Monica ever left their convent in the first place is doubtful.

*It was practically besieged by federal forces. . . .
They found a whole system of underground roads
connecting with the church that is under the surface of
the earth. The underground paths are partly covered in
dust, but are otherwise of a perfect construction and offer
archaeologists the opportunity to carry out a real study,
as they date back to very remote times. . . . Some of these
roads lead to the lower apartments of the convent.*

The tunnels were only the beginning of the hidden convent's secrets. The newspaper went on to write:

*The convent, which encompasses numbers 101 and 103
of Avenida 18 Poniente, is something of a marvel. . . .
Beneath the surface of the earth there is a temple built
especially to serve as a chapel, invisible to those not in-the-
know. An electric button is pressed on the leaf of a double
door, and an entrance opens in the floor leading to the
subterranean temple. . . . Up to four people stand upon a
square mat and when the bell is pressed, the mat descends
to the bottom of the subterranean sanctuary and, giving
the necessary time for people to remove themselves from
it, rises again, positioning itself in such a way that it is
impossible to know there is anything beneath it.*

The authorities found secret passageways galore, as well as stair-cases and another well, also connected to the network of tunnels, and recently stopped up by the nuns themselves. (The fact that so many of these wells were plugged in the early twentieth century implies that thieves had indeed come across the old tunnel network and were increasingly making use of it.)

Despite the sensational discovery of the hidden convent and the tunnels beneath it, no detailed archaeological exploration was undertaken at the time. The discovery was a curiosity for locals, a political tool for those in power, and a boon for the whistleblower, who was given a percentage of the treasures found in the convent and swanned off to Mexico City, where he lived in opulence for the rest of his life.

As for the nuns, it is likely local authorities knew all along that they were there and turned a blind eye or even actively discouraged interference. Many of the women in the convent were from upper-class families with powerful positions in the economy and government. Still, the nuns were immediately evicted upon discovery. Their convent passed into state hands.

The convent is now a museum, bright and airy. Little remains to suggest it was once almost entirely cut off from the world. Its bricked-up doors are open to the street. In the library, the statue of the golden-robed monk still holds his fingers to his lips, urging all who enter to be silent. And who knows? Perhaps there is still the odd nun lurking in some hidden room or scurrying through Puebla's tunnels. What's certain is that only a fraction of Puebla's—and Mexico's—tunnels have been explored, only a thimbleful of their secrets uncovered. ◊

THE MAZE IN THE MOUNTAIN

Puebla has its tunnels, Paris has its catacombs, but few cities can boast being *entirely* subterranean, as is the case of the ancient underground city of Derinkuyu in the Nevşehir Province in central Turkey.

In 1962, a local man found a room hidden behind the wall of his house. This room led to staircases, passageways, and, eventually, to an entire city, abandoned and reaching down eighteen floors into the earth.

Archaeologists believe there may be as many as 200 under-ground cities in this region of central Turkey, though so far, only a handful of them have been explored. At a depth of approximately 280 feet, Derinkuyu is the deepest of those discovered. The sub-terranean network of tunnels and rooms was thought to have been cut into the soft yellow volcanic rock by early Byzantine Christians seeking refuge from raids. Sliced down the center, the city resem-bles a honeycomb or a particularly advanced anthill and includes all the institutions and rooms you might find in a regular, supra-terra-nean city: stables, churches, storage rooms, refectories, wineries, and living quarters said to have been capable of holding more than 20,000 people. When danger arose, citizens fled down shafts and through hidden entrances into their secret city before rolling thick, round stone doors across the openings and sealing out the violence above.

SECRETS OF THE TEMPLE OF THE PLUMED SERPENT

While the Catholic church was going wild digging tunnels through-out Mexico in the 1500s, they were not the first to do so. The country's earliest secret tunnels were dug more than a thousand years earlier and filled with the bodies of sacrificial victims. In 2003, archaeologists discovered a 330-foot-long tunnel beneath the Temple of the Plumed Serpent in the ancient city of Teotihuacán, on the outskirts of what is today Mexico City. Another such tunnel was found under the neighboring Pyramid of the Moon. That pyramid had already proven to be a grisly treasure trove, its crypts contain-ing everything from jade masks to a mosaic statue surrounded by eighteen obsidian knives, a man sitting upright on a chair, facing west, the cadavers of jaguars and other jungle cats, as well as twelve human bodies, ten of them missing their heads. The finds beneath the Temple of the Plumed Serpent were even more macabre: 137 corpses, their hands tied behind their backs.

While much of Aztec religion and customs is shrouded in mystery, both tunnels were thought to be the paths toward ritualistic burial sites. Similar to the practice of hitobashira in Japan (see page 73), victims would be ritualistically killed or walled in alive in order to ensure the gods' blessings upon the massive architectural undertaking ahead. The tunnel beneath the Temple of the Plumed Serpent was sealed with a boulder and remained untouched for almost 2,000 years.

More wonders found beneath the temple include 600 clay spheres decorated with pyrite, or fool's gold, purpose unknown, and tiny landscapes laid out on the floors of two of the underground chambers. The landscapes feature miniature mountains and streambeds that once contained liquid mercury, as well as four small greenstone figures, all looking up at the same point on the ceiling. What are they looking at? An adventure novel would say a secret door, a road to treasure. The truth is that no one yet knows. The exploration of the temples is ongoing.

EL CHAPO'S ESCAPE TUNNEL

Secret tunnels aren't always hundreds of years old and dripping with myth and history. Sometimes they are built within a matter of weeks in the modern age, using the near unlimited funds of a bloodthirsty drug lord. This was the case when Joaquín "El Chapo" Guzmán escaped from a maximum security prison near Toluca, Mexico, in July 2015. His first escape fourteen years earlier involved paying $2.5 million in bribes to various prison personnel and police, who allowed him to be wheeled out of the prison in a laundry cart. His second escape proved much more elaborate and also slightly more dignified.

At 8:52 in the evening, Guzmán entered the tiny shower area of his cell and ducked below a low wall, out of sight of the security cameras. He did not reemerge. When guards entered the cell, they found a small square of concrete had been cut out of the floor. Underneath, a ladder led down thirty feet into a tunnel. And not a spoon-dug tunnel—this tunnel was as solidly engineered as any mineshaft, ventilated, reinforced, and electrically lit. It ran for almost a mile, ending inside a partially constructed house in the middle of a cornfield. The house had been built solely to mask the digging of the tunnel beneath it. For Guzmán, his expensive trip to freedom was short lived. In January 2016, he was recaptured and is currently being held in a supermax security prison in Colorado, ADX Florence, nicknamed the "Alcatraz of the Rockies." Locked away behind countless motion detectors and 1,400 remote-controlled steel doors, his cell is built entirely of concrete, even the furniture. It is soundproof, and the windows are just four inches wide, with no way for him to know where in the structure he is located. Even if his henchmen started digging, it would be almost impossible to find him.

▲ *The motorcycle El Chapo drove down a secret, mile-long tunnel during his escape from a Mexican maximum security prison.*

Travis Dusenbury, a one-time prisoner, said, "I've been locked up in some isolated, rural places, but at least at those places I could always see a highway, see the sky. But at the ADX, you can't see nothing, not a highway out in the distance, not the sky. You know the minute you get there you won't see any of that, not for years and years."

5

The Oddly Built Temple

KANAZAWA · JAPAN

You watch the lady from around a half-closed screen, the cool paper brushing your cheek. Slowly, delicately, she makes her way across the courtyard toward her husband. Her wooden sandals tap against the stone, echoing among the castle roofs. In the maples and the ginkgo trees the birds are silent.

Her husband, the warlord Maeda Toshiie, stands his ground, but his officers are disquieted, shifting like grass in a cold wind. The lady is dressed for death, five-crested, pitch-black silk, snow-white tabi* glowing in the sunlight. Behind her, in the shadows of the porch, the men's wives wait, all of them clad in funereal black as well.

*Traditional Japanese split-toe socks, often worn with elevated wooden sandals.

◀ An Onna-Bugeisha, or female samurai, one of a small group of upper-class women who were trained to defend their castles and homes in the event of war.

When the lady reaches her husband, she takes a folded slip of paper from her sleeve and hands it to him. A gentle missive? A declaration of loyalty? The warlord reads it, but his eyes do not light up with warmth. He barks something curt and hurls the message on the ground. But the lady is already leaving again, tapping away across the courtyard.

Were a stranger to stumble across the scene, they might find it tragic: a mournful wife bidding her husband farewell in the most dramatic way possible. But you are the lady's faithful servant. You know the truth. Lady Maeda is no mournful wife. She is a warrior, a politician, and the mother of eleven children. Only a year earlier, she maneuvered her way across the battlefield at Shizugatake to broker peace with the enemy. Today, her actions have been meticulously planned, from the funeral clothes to the carefully composed message. Lady Maeda is making a statement.

In a few moments, Toshiie will set off for Nagoya, 124 miles away, in an attempt to break the siege at Suemori Castle. It is a battle he has no sure chance of winning and one he does not want to fight. If he fails, it is only a matter of time before the enemy comes here, to the golden city of Kanazawa, to plunder, kill, and conquer.

Lady Maeda knows it is not lovelorn words that will move her husband to bravery. She knows he needs a challenge, a spike at the back of his neck.

Once the warlord and his men have thundered away, you go out into the courtyard and lift the piece of fallen paper. On it, Lady Maeda has written, "If fortune fails you at Suemori Castle, do not intend on returning home alive. Everyone here, including myself, shall set this castle ablaze and bring our families here to perish."

Behind you, you hear the tapping of sandals. You tuck the paper away and dart out of view. Lady Maeda passes under the gates, her silks dragging over the stone and the fallen leaves. You know where she is going: to the Myōryū-ji, the oddly built temple.

"To pray for victory," the foolish stranger might think, "to beg for good fortune for her husband." But again he would be wrong. The temple, like its mistress, is not what it seems. Beneath its serene exterior, it is a maze of traps and staircases, locking doors, secret rooms, and escape tunnels. At its top is a row of little windows where Lady Maeda will watch the plains of Kaga and wait for signs of victory or defeat.

She is not going to the temple to pray. She is going to prepare for war.

◄ *Kenrokuen Garden, the Maeda clan's personal park just outside the castle walls, still stands today.*

Far from the neon signs of Tokyo and the graceful temples of Kyoto lies the city of Kanazawa, curled against the western coast of Japan like a small gray dragon. Not many tourists find their way here on the bullet trains. Though it offers winding alleyways, cherry-painted teahouses, and some of the finest public gardens in the country, even Japanese citizens don't exactly flock there. But the Kanazawa of several centuries ago was a completely different beast—rivaling seventeenth-century Amsterdam and Rome in size, it was the gem of an empire and the location of a particularly interesting sort of architectural mystery.

> They arranged streets around Kanazawa Castle to turn back on themselves, leading attackers on a merry chase away from the keep.

On the surface, the city was a place of porcelain makers and silk printers, famous for its elegance and sophistication. It was dotted with Shinto shrines, Buddhist temples, wondrous gardens, stone lanterns, and kami houses—homes for the gods and spirits perched among the lily pads, reflecting in the mirror-smooth waters.

But it was all a front.

Beneath the city's thick gilding of temples and manicured greenery, it was a bear trap built for war, a thousand defensible positions disguised as innocent structures, a street plan designed to thwart and befuddle, and a little temple where all these architectural techniques came to a point.

Why the subterfuge? What compelled the Maeda clan, and Japan in general, to hide their defenses and lay a veneer of decorum across everything from spousal interactions to war buildings?

By the time Lady Maeda and Toshiie traded their careful barbs, Japan had been in a slow-burning civil war for more than a century. Warlords routinely sacked each other's cities. Clans rose and fell. Kanazawa was a fruit any number of enemy nobles might like to pluck. It needed defenses. Unfortunately, building those defenses was all but illegal.

Japan in those days was essentially a military dictatorship. While the country still had its divinely appointed emperor on the Chrysanthemum Throne, he was kept quiet and out of the way in his palace in Kyoto. (His main task consisted of "controlling time," aka organizing Japan's complex calendar system, which, though ceremonially important, was somewhat akin to giving a child a toy to occupy him.) It was the shogun, the emperor's head general, who led the country. He was the one with true power and thus lived in perpetual fear of losing that power. If it came down to it, he wanted to be able to knock aside an unruly warlord with as little trouble as possible.

The best way to do so was by implementing building restrictions in the warlords' cities to keep them from becoming too defensible: no new structures more than three stories and no new fortifications of any sort.

▼ The sprawling Kanazawa Castle, home of the Maeda clan.

Of course, the rulers of Kanazawa immediately found ingenious methods to circumvent these restrictions. Their goal? Find a way to preserve their wealthy city against attack while still appearing to be a docile vassal of the shogunate. Their method? Construct a host of defenses that looked like innocent, everyday structures. They arranged streets around Kanazawa Castle to turn back on themselves, leading attackers on a merry chase away from the keep. They disguised military outposts as houses and scrambled the insides of preexisting structures to fit new purposes. It was the equivalent of Hollywood making a Hays Code movie and the scriptwriters finding clever ways to express taboo themes without mentioning them outright. The result casts a layer of artfulness and mystery over things that would otherwise be only half so interesting.

> ⚷ The temple boasts no less than twenty-three tiny rooms and twenty-nine staircases, as well as locking doors, secret hiding places, and a tunnel said to connect the temple to the castle, allowing messengers, soldiers, and escaping nobles to travel unseen.

One of the most intriguing architectural examples from this time is a little known temple outside Kanazawa Castle. Called Myōryū-ji, or literally "the oddly built temple," it was meant to look like any other Buddhist place of worship: a beamed porch, steeply pitched roof, and large room inside for prayer and burning incense. But hidden behind the sliding paper screens, below the floorboards, and up in the rafters was an entirely different world. The temple boasts no less than twenty-three tiny rooms and twenty-nine staircases, as well as locking doors, secret hiding places, and a tunnel said to connect the temple to the castle, allowing messengers, soldiers, and escaping nobles to travel unseen. It was a temple first and foremost, but it was also a safe house, a watchtower, and a microcosm of the defense strategies of the city. (The Myōryū-ji is one of the only structures of its kind that survives to this day and is well worth a visit. Though tours are only in Japanese and must be reserved via telephone, you'll be able to see with your own eyes many of the tricks it has up its sleeve.)

The temple was built around a core strong enough to withstand typhoons. Though it looks like a law-abiding two-story structure from the outside, it holds a total of seven levels—three main ones and several mid-levels, where defending troops could crawl about and hide. It is also full of traps. Next to the main altar, right where an assailant might pause to catch his breath before storming upstairs, is a trapdoor. One wrong step would hurl him into a basement room where troops could make short work of him. And if he did make it to the stairs, it was unlikely he would get very far. Perhaps the temple's most dastardly architectural trick is the use of paper insets in the staircases, allowing soldiers concealed in hidden compartments below to stab at the feet of assailants.

And if all those precautions fail? One small room in the temple was built for seppuku, the ceremonial self-disembowelment that nobles were expected to perform to avoid capture. Were a lord or a high-ranking individual to become trapped in the temple with no chance of victory, this room had a flame in it, kept always burning, and a self-locking door. Much like Lady Maeda vowed to do in her message, a noble could retreat here, use the flame to set the wooden temple alight, and commit the ritualized suicide undisturbed while the troops fought outside.

While it is unknown whether Lady Maeda ever set foot in the temple, she would have been acutely aware of the city's defenses and secrets. She certainly would have known of a possible refuge she could use should the enemy reach Kanazawa. Wars were particularly difficult for women. Left to defend the city in the absence of their husbands, they were faced with rape, enslavement, and massacre should their armies fail. A fifteenth-century wood carving of the fall of Fukane Castle shows a thousand heads on spikes, many of them women. In this light, Lady Maeda's message to her husband is less of a threat and more of a tragic warning.

In times of war, it was practically expected that a person would take his or her own life before allowing the enemy to do it. One story tells of Lady Sakasai, who, when her castle was stormed, escaped the bloodshed in a particularly striking fashion. Wearing her finest kimono, she cut down a heavy bell used to signal troops and heaved it over her head and shoulders. Then, stumbling through the courtyard and over the bodies of fallen samurai, she threw herself into the moat and drowned beneath its weight. Another story tells of how the Catholic convert Hosokawa Gracia—an aristocratic woman who studied both Portuguese and Latin at a time when such practices were extremely rare in Japan—refused to commit suicide due to her faith and ended up being stabbed by her own servant to avoid disgrace.

Humanity often casts a veil over its functioning urges, a fig leaf of rules and traditions disguising base necessities. Japanese folklore might call ritual disembowelment an act of dignity or honor, but really it was to spare a samurai the horrible, prolonged pain of dying at the hands of the enemy. Almost every tradition, no matter how seemingly emotional or spiritual, can be traced back to something much simpler: an attempt at not-dying or, at the very least, dying on one's own terms.

In the Heian period (794 to 1185 CE)—a "golden" stretch of time when around 5,000 nobles ruled in splendor over five million poverty-stricken peasants—beauty was the highest virtue among the aristocracy. To be charming and elegant and to exhibit good taste (and good handwriting; lives were lost and fortunes won over good handwriting) were valued above all else.

Why would beauty matter so much when most of the population was living in squalor? Like the nebulous "good taste" of today, the Heian traditions were a way to consolidate power, to distinguish sharply between the haves and have-nots. It was, once more, a smoke screen for something else, for survival, at least for the rich.

Eventually, the excesses of the Heian court were reined in. Under the shogun dictatorship, Japan became more militaristic and severe. But a strong undercurrent of the Heian philosophies remained, melding with the famous minimalism of later centuries. In short, everything should have a purpose, perhaps even multiple purposes, and should also be beautiful.

Kanazawa Castle, for example, had white-tinged tiles made of lead. They were not only pleasing to the eye but also fire-resistant and could be melted down for bullets if the need arose.

Another example was the practice among the Japanese aristocracy of blackening their teeth. Though it caused an open mouth to look like a toothless void, it was collectively decided that it was a sign of maturity and elegance. White teeth were ugly. "They look just like peeled caterpillars," one observer wrote venomously of a woman who refused to partake in the custom. But blackened teeth also served a practical purpose: The substance used to darken the teeth acted as a sealant, preventing enamel decay in a time when a lack of dentistry could cause serious pain and even death.

And then there was the oddly built temple, innocent-looking, pious—strength and ambition disguised as quiet submission. Despite the effort that went into making Kanazawa defensible, the oddly built temple was never put to the test. Toshiie won the siege at Suemori Castle and, by the end of the seventeenth century, Japan had entered into an unprecedented stretch of peace. Many of the wooden structures burned down and though the Myōryū-ji survived, it was used only for its original purpose: prayer, meditation, and the burning of incense, its trapdoors and hidden rooms gathering dust, its escape tunnel forgotten.

And how did things end for Lady Maeda? Even after her husband's victory at Suemori Castle, her life was far from uneventful. After many adventures including a lengthy stint as a political hostage in Edo, Lady Maeda died a respected hero, seventy years old and surrounded by her children and loyal cohorts. Toshiie, it is said, loved her to the end of her days. ◈

NIGHTINGALE FLOORS AND HAUNTED WELLS
Secrets of the Samurai Castles

During the Edo period, a rash of shogun castles were built across the green fields and atop the defensible rises of Japan. Today, only a handful of them still stand, most having fallen victim to fire and war. Those that remain are testaments to a specifically Japanese style of fortress, unlike any other in the world and rife with architectural curiosities.

Take the elaborate, many-roofed Nijō Castle in Kyoto, where so-called nightingale floors "sing" hauntingly as you walk across them. Built so that the nails beneath the floorboards rub against their clamps and create a gentle chirping noise, these floors were engineered to make eavesdropping—and silent assassinations—all but impossible.

Then there's the black-lacquered Matsumoto Castle in Nagano, picturesque with its blood red and bone pale trim. Walking through the surrounding park, it's easy to forget that such an elegant building is not an enormous garden gazebo but rather has been built entirely with violence in mind. Matsumoto Castle has 115 gun and arrow slots hidden behind its exterior panels, along with sloped channels and openings for pouring boiling oil and catapulting out stones. There is also a hidden, windowless half-level called "the dark floor" that was used to confuse attackers and make them think they had reached the top of the building when in reality there was still one level above them. Were the castle to have been stormed, samurai would have waited for the attackers to reach this floor before striking them down, thwarting them before they reached the warlord on the topmost level.

▲ A nineteenth-century scroll painting of Himeji Castle illustrating the intricate maze of streets, walls, and buildings protecting the keep.

Greatest of all the fortresses is Himeji Castle, elaborately tiered, blazing white, and the subject of many a postcard and cherry blossom–strewn gift shop bauble. Known as the White Heron Castle, it has survived any number of disasters, from fire to a direct bomb strike to that time it was nearly auctioned off for about $2,000 to a local resident who was going to demolish it. (It was rescued from this fate at the eleventh hour by an army colonel who appreciated the castle's historical significance.)

Himeji Castle bristles with secrets. Like Kanazawa and its network of hidden temple-fortresses, Himeji Castle's defenses started well beyond the keep. Streets around the castle were arranged for maximum confusion, leading enemies in an endless loop without ever getting any closer to the walls. And if they did manage to breach the gates, they were confronted with a fresh hell of walled roads, bottlenecks, and baileys. The distance from the Hishi Gate to the main keep is only 430 feet as the crow flies, but attackers would have no choice but to follow a much more circuitous route: 1,066 feet of walled and winding roads, the defending forces pummeling them with matchlock fire, arrows, and rocks every step of the way. Even today, despite copious signs and markings, the routes inside the castle walls confuse tourists.

In the main keep, there are six floors plus a basement. Its upper floors boast mushakakushi, or warrior hiding rooms; the walls are dotted with what look like small, square cupboard doors, some near the floor, some halfway up the wall. These opened into spaces where warriors hid and from which they could crawl out at a moment's notice.

Himeji Castle is also the setting of several ghostly folktales, including one called "The Manor of the Dishes." In it, a maid is falsely accused of stealing one of her master's Delft plates after rejecting his advances. As punishment, she is thrown down the castle well. To this day, her unquiet ghost can be heard counting to nine from the bottom of the well, over and over, desperate to find the missing tenth plate and prove her innocence. According to some tellings, her spirit can be dispelled, or at least placated, by shouting "Ten" at the top of one's lungs. (If the story of a bitter ghost living in a well sounds familiar, you just might have seen it before. It was one of the inspirations behind the oft-remade Japanese horror classic *The Ring*.)

HUMAN PILLARS AND
THE PRACTICE OF HITOBASHIRA

One hundred twenty-four miles south of Kanazawa, in the city of Sakai, stands perhaps the oldest surviving Japanese castle. Maruoka Castle—often called "Mist Castle" because of its penchant for being hidden by mist whenever the enemy would approach—is small, rather unassuming, and has a gruesome and tragic tale behind it. Or rather, beneath it. According to legend, builders tried and tried to get the foundation to stand. When it kept toppling over, they decided the best solution would be a human sacrifice to appease the nature spirits. A one-eyed woman named O-shizu agreed to the task. She was desperately poor, with two sons and no prospects. Her one request in return for being the pillar on which the castle would be built was that one of her sons be made a samurai. The lord of the region agreed and O-shizu was placed at the center of the castle's foundation. The stones were stacked around her until they crushed her, after which the castle was built without incident.

Unfortunately, the lord moved to a different province before he could fulfill his promise to O-shizu's son. Because of this, Maruoka Castle was thought to be haunted by her spirit. When the moat would flood, it was said O-shizu's tears were the cause, and visitors often reported a dark shape lurking in corners of the keep.

While the haunting is debatable, the practice of burying humans in the foundations of structures in an attempt to appease the gods has been recorded many times throughout history and across cultures. In Japan, the practice is called hitobashira and was seen as a noble and patriotic act, a sacrifice of one for the benefit of many.

Another example of hitobashira is Matsue Castle, also thought to have been built upon a human pillar. Though the sacrifice's name has been lost to time, she was said to have been a beautiful young woman who loved to dance. After her death, a law was passed forbidding girls from dancing in the street. If they did, it was said Matsue Castle would shudder from top to bottom, the maiden's unhappy spirit trapped in the dark beneath the crushing stones, shaking with envy to hear the dancers' joyfully tapping feet.

6

Doll's Eye View

AMSTERDAM • NETHERLANDS

You have walked the Rijksmuseum until your feet ache, admired the Vermeers signposted by the flocks of tourists in front of them, inspected the baroque cabinetry with its hundreds of tiny drawers, sighed over the vases and glaring masks stolen centuries ago from Dutch colonies. There have been so many rooms, such a density of marvels, that what you find next feels like a breath of fresh air: a dimly lit room containing a sumptuous dollhouse behind glass. It is taller than you, filled with tiny treasures—a mercury mirror the size of a plum pit, a board game with pieces as small as spider's eggs.

◄ Jacob Appel's painting of the dollhouse (c. 1710) shows a mysterious funeral scene in the lower corner that no longer exists.

You stand in front of it, staring at the splendid miniature world. Around you, the room is quiet. The house seems to be calling to you, every one of its objects whispering a little story. You glance over the information tablet. An eighteenth-century woman—Petronella Oortman—assembled this house. It was her life's work. You circle the room, wondering who she was and why she did it. And then, on the wall next to the dollhouse, you see a painting.

It depicts the dollhouse you just saw . . . and yet not quite. The painting was completed by Jacob Appel in 1710, at the time when Petronella still owned the dollhouse. It shows a spinning wheel that is no longer there, a ruffled curtain that has long been replaced. And on the first floor, one of the rooms is completely changed. Five child dolls stand solemnly around a cradle draped in black. A woman doll stands watching them. Behind her, a panel the same color as the wallpaper—a secret door—is slightly ajar, opening into a square of blackness. You don't remember a panel in the doll-house. And there were no dolls in it either, no tragic wake. Who is the dead child? What is hidden behind the wall?

You hurry back to the dollhouse, squint through the glass. You want nothing more than to reach into the display, to worm your fingers into the secret door and discover what hides behind it. But, of course, that is not allowed. You can only look, and imagine, and long to know more.

There is something innately fascinating about the miniature, moveable worlds of dollhouses. They allow us to shift our perspective of ourselves, rendering us suddenly masters of a tiny universe. They allow us, for a moment, to feel as if we are in control of all the wild complexities of life. Sometimes they allow us to explore and process things too painful to face in the real world, such as a tragic death or a lonely life.

The precursor to the dollhouse was the curiosity cabinet. By the sixteenth century, kings were displaying their most unique possessions in cabinets especially designated for this purpose. Holy Roman Emperor Rudolf II was well known for owning a particularly vast and esoteric range of strange objects, including astrolabes, celestial globes, and a miniature clockwork ship, its sails painted like a tiny Sistine Chapel, its crew moving across the deck to the dainty tune of a music box. (The ship was used to impress the king's dinner party guests; the climax occurred when it fired its tiny cannon into the soup.)

Everything in the house is perfect. But was it simply to show off? Or was something deeper seeking expression?

By the seventeenth century, curiosity cabinets were no longer only for kings. Danish physician Ole Worm gathered entire flocks of taxidermy beasts and fossils, and Athanasius Kircher's curiosity cabinet contained the first megaphone as well as designs for a "catastrophic lamp," the parent of the magic lantern and grandparent of our modern-day cinemas. By the eighteenth century, anyone with a bit of money was assembling a cupboard full of peculiar treasures and keepsakes—"mermaids" from Asia, poison mushrooms, saints' bones (or cat bones—no one was really going to argue), kings' teeth, phoenix feathers, dirt from the Garden of Eden, rope from the hangings of murderers. A curiosity cabinet was a way to show how interesting, well traveled, and educated its owner was, a highlight reel, if you will, an antiquated form of an Instagram feed.

But curiosity cabinets were almost solely the domain of a gentleman. What of the gentleman's wife? Her equivalent was the dollhouse.

Through our modern lens this seems particularly unfair. Men had the contents of the entire world to show off how wonderful they were, while women had to make do with the domestic sphere. But the dollhouses of a small circle of wealthy Dutch women were equal in cost and wondrousness to many a kingly curiosity cabinet, tiny artistic masterpieces built with the utmost skill and furnished with tiny, exotic luxuries.

Called baby houses, or pronk poppenhuisen, the grandest of these dollhouses belonged to a seventeenth-century woman named Petronella Oortman. Crafted by a French cabinetmaker, the dollhouse was built of mahogany and tortoiseshell. It stands more than eight feet high and six feet wide. Even during Petronella's life it was famous throughout Holland. The Duke of Savoy was unable to get a meeting to view the house, though he desperately wanted to, and the widow of the Duke of Orange was twice denied entrance to the Oortmans' home before she was able to finagle a viewing by showing up at the door unannounced. In total, the dollhouse was said to be worth 20,000 to 30,000 guilders ($1.2 to $1.8 million in today's dollars). By comparison, a human-sized house on one of the most elegant canals in Amsterdam cost about 28,000 guilders at the time.

The level of detail is astounding. Commissioned to mark the occasion of her second marriage, the dollhouse signified the beginning of a new chapter in Petronella's life, an ideal world. Everything from the miniature napkins to the pillowcases were stitched with their initials: "B" for Brandt and "O" for Oortman. The porcelain pieces were shipped from Asia, the baskets hand-woven with a needle. A tiny board game in one of the rooms features miniaturized silver kopecks, such as those in circulation in Russia at that time. These coins, which weigh only 0.68 gram each, were cut from silver wire and then stamped. Real 300-year-old salt fish is kept preserved in the pantry. The house even envelopes the male world, bringing it down to size by including a tiny, black-painted curiosity cabinet filled with its own array of minuscule seashells.

The dollhouse contains only rooms Petronella would have liked and used herself. There is no study, no barn or work room, no smoking room where the gentlemen gathered after dinner and where women were not allowed. On the first floor is the kitchen boasting only the best, mostly fashionable blue-and-white china. It is a fantasy of a kitchen, a so-called "good kitchen" or false-front kitchen that existed in many Dutch houses of the day, a place where you could show guests your fine china and drink tea, while sparing your hair and petticoats from the fumes and grease of the actual kitchen. On the top floor are the maidservants' bedrooms, each with a different colored curtain and tiny twin chamber pots. There are even tiny foot warmers in some of the rooms, as women traditionally sat farthest from the fireplace. Everything in the house is perfect. But was it simply to show off? Or was something deeper seeking expression?

Petronella had suffered much grief before she commissioned the building of her dollhouse. Born to a gun maker in Amsterdam in 1656, she married silk merchant Carel Witte at age twenty-one. For eight years they tried to have children, but Petronella's first daughter died in 1684, having lived less than twelve months. Her husband passed away the following year. All of this was recorded and expressed through her dollhouse.

How do we know this? A painting survives, made while Oortman was alive, giving us an intriguing glimpse back in time. It shows the

Dollhouses have long been used to make sense of one's situation on a small scale, to compress the complexities of life into something that can be taken in at a glance and manipulated in ways the real world resists.

▲ *Close-up of the mourning room and its hidden door. The black cabinet contains a collection of minuscule seashells.*

dollhouse in its original condition, before its rooms were redecorated and changed by subsequent generations. Each of them is painted as its own little world, with its own perspective and vanishing point, not fitting together in any sort of logical way. The painting also shows what are likely to have been Petronella's original dolls, now lost, which included many children, and a lying-in room upstairs where a mother sits with her baby.

Most intriguing, it shows a room on the first floor in which a dead infant is surrounded by five living children. Upstairs, two men play backgammon, perhaps craving distraction from their pain, perhaps locked in another world, unaware of the mourning taking place below. Meanwhile, on the first floor, a woman stands slightly apart from a cradle and children, and watches. Most likely this was the way the house was arranged when Appel painted it, a mausoleum, and a space for Petronella to enact her grief.

Dollhouses have long been used to make sense of one's situation on a small scale, to compress the complexities of life into something that can be taken in at a glance and manipulated in ways the real world resists. Famed children's author Beatrix Potter was given a glass-fronted dollhouse by her editor in which she kept two pet mice, eventually immortalizing them in *The Tale of Two Bad Mice*. (In the story, a pair of mice break into a dollhouse and are driven to wrath when they discover the beautifully painted food is made of plaster. In the end they ransack the dollhouse, smash the food, and throw all of the dolls' clothing out the window. The whole thing is rather anarchic and thought to represent Beatrix Potter's fears regarding the stuffiness of Edwardian domestic life.)

Then there was Frances Glessner Lee's murder dollhouses, called *The Nutshell Studies of Unexplained Death*. Lee, known as the godmother of forensic science, was a millionaire heiress who built tiny depictions of real-life murder scenes to aid police investigators in solving crimes. In a more recent example, artist Cynthia von Buhler built miniature scenes and dioramas to sort through her feelings about her grandfather's mysterious death. One day in autumn, he had been walking along a street in Manhattan when he was shot dead without warning. The shock was so great that his wife, von Buhler's grandmother, went into labor.

"Nobody still living in my family knows why my grandfather was shot," says von Buhler. "Nothing was known about the killer, his motive, or a trial. My grandmother took these secrets to her grave." And so von Buhler recreated many of the events, building everything from a tiny speakeasy like the one her grandfather owned, to the room where his body was laid out. By creating the scenes, she was able to bring clarity and tangibility to a subject that up until that point had been kept in a deliberate haze. In miniature, the vastness of a sudden, unexplained death was suddenly fathomable. Her family secrets were no longer beyond her reach.

And what sorts of secrets did Petronella hide in her dollhouse?

While the house might look like a simple collection of spaces for cooking, laundry, entertaining, and child-rearing, there is more to it than meets the eye. On the first floor, blending into the golden wallpaper of the morning room, is a secret panel. Behind it, a hidden room holds perhaps the most extraordinary objects in the dollhouse: eighty-four tiny books, dating back to the 1680s and containing everything from illustrations of small black hats, to snipped-out pieces of maps from life-sized works, to handwritten words, all perfectly legible, though the pages are barely the size of a child's fingernail.

Most of the books are filled with narrow strips of text taken from Der Hoveniers's 1693 work, *Almanach van Amsterdam*, but there is one exception: the miniature *Gebede Boeck*, or prayer book, dated 1683, the year Petronella's first daughter lived her brief life. This tiny volume contains the full texts of the Lord's Prayer, the Ten Commandments, and Psalm 105. The inclusion of that particular psalm is telling. It is a long passage, beginning jubilantly but soon turning bleak. "He sent darkness, and made it dark; for had they not rebelled against his words? He turned their waters into blood, and slew their fish. Their land brought forth frogs in abundance, in the chambers of their kings. . . . He smote also all the firstborn in their land, the chief of all their strength."

Oortman's firstborn was struck down. Her first husband died. Her new marriage signified a fresh start, a careful reorganization after a period of earth-shattering grief. The psalm in the tiny prayer book ends on a hopeful note: "He fed them well with the bread of heaven. He opened the rock, and water gushed out; it flowed like a river in the desert, for he remembered his holy promise."

When Petronella died at the age of sixty, her dollhouse passed to her only living daughter, Hendrina. The house was specifically mentioned in her will, indicating it was one of her most treasured possessions. It passed through many hands over the ensuing centuries, was misattributed as being built for the czar of Russia, and has now finally found its place in the Rijksmuseum in Amsterdam, only a few canals away from where Petronella once lived.

Interestingly, there were three Petronellas in the Netherlands, all living at roughly the same time, and all of whom curated extraordinary dollhouses that have survived to this day. One of them was

Petronella de la Court, a distant relative of the other Petronellas. Born in Utrecht, where her dollhouse currently resides, she had ten children and, together with her husband, owned a very profitable brewery in Amsterdam. Her dollhouse is not quite as grand as Oortman's, edged out by the secret room full of books and the sheer sumptuousness of the details. However, it too illustrates the character of its owner. Where Oortman's dollhouse is filled mostly with leisure and household rooms, de la Court's features an office, where a doll representing herself is doing paperwork next to a stack of ledgers. (After her husband died, de la Court and her sons took over the family's brewery. She guided it until her death, when it was closed.) Her dollhouse also contains a "garden room," a rather claustrophobic approximation of the outdoors, with shrubs and garden beds, statuary, a white gazebo, and walls and ceilings painted with blue skies and darting birds.

The third Petronella was Petronella Dunois. Her dollhouse is the smallest of the three and perhaps the coziest, with bright floral wallpaper in the upstairs drawing room and many original dolls, including dogs and a number of children. But unlike the other Petronellas, Dunois's dollhouse did not reflect her true life. Born

▲ The early twentieth-century dollhouse, Titania's Palace, features eighteen rooms and was even wired for electricity.

into a wealthy family, Dunois was orphaned before the age of ten and lived with her older sister in loneliness for some time, imagining through the lovingly crafted details of her dollhouse exactly the life she wished for. She never achieved it. Though Petronella Dunois did eventually marry, she died without children in her early forties.

There is a hint of warmth to her story though. In the dollhouses of both Petronella Oortman and Petronella Dunois are beer kegs bearing the swan sigil of Petronella de la Court's brewery business, indicating that the three Petronellas knew one another and exchanged items as gifts, perhaps coming around to view each other's extraordinary creations, perhaps even becoming friends.

"I sometimes think that houses are interesting because they are so like dollhouses," the philosopher and art critic G. K. Chesterton once wrote. "I look forward to the day when I shall have time to play. . . . I shall retire into this box of marvels; and I shall be found still striving hopefully to get inside a toy-theater." It's a beautiful thought, that the things of imagination and childhood are more real and appealing than any of the approximations we manage to build as adults. For these Dutch women, paradise was not to be found in the world around them. It was one step down, one step smaller, quiet and hidden away, a step closer to the light.

A Brief History of Dollhouses

The first dollhouse recorded in history was commissioned in 1558 by Albrecht V, Duke of Bavaria. An idle pleasure-seeker who adored the arts and amassed great debts by luring crowds of painters and craftsmen to his court, he ordered a splendid miniature house built that included a stable, a wine cellar, and a tiny Kunstkammer, or art gallery. Some say it was commissioned as a gift to his daughter, though this is likely conjecture from later centuries when it was decided that dollhouses were strictly interesting to young girls. More likely the dollhouse was a recollection, a pleasant memory that the duke tried to capture for himself. He called it his baby house, as it was said to be modeled after his childhood home.

Duke Albrecht's dollhouse was lost to fire in 1674, but since then countless other miniature wonders have been built, some of them truly jaw-dropping.

Titania's Palace is a dollhouse that was built in Ireland between 1907 and 1922, commissioned by British army officer Sir Nevile Wilkinson. Despite being a veritable giant, Wilkinson had always held a keen interest in the little things in life. According to his own telling, he was walking in the garden with his daughter, Guendolen, when she spotted a fairy running away into the roots of a syca-more tree. She asked Sir Wilkinson why the fairy had gone into the cold, damp dark beneath the roots and he had answered that fair-ies were not fortunate creatures like humans; they had no homes, only caves to keep their treasures in. Guendolen, feeling sorry for the fairies, asked her father to build a home for Titania, the queen of all fairies. Sir Wilkinson complied, commissioning a palatial doll-house containing eighteen rooms and more than 3,000 tiny works of art, some of them fashioned out of real artifacts. According to his detailed handbook of the dollhouse, Titania's boudoir is kitted out with a folding screen made from seventeenth-century Persian playing cards, like something out of Mary Norton's classic children's book *The Borrowers*, where tiny people snatch household items to fur-nish their home. The chapel features "an Italian casket made of old amber inlaid with marvelously wrought ivory carvings, which was repurposed from the base of a 17th-century crucifix," and the stair-case is crowned by what looks like the statue of a horse but is actually the last surviving piece of a Ludwigsburg porcelain chess set. The doll palace has been uprooted many times, fairy inhabitants not-withstanding, and currently resides at Egeskov Castle in Denmark.

Another curiosity is the doll apartment complex built by John Carlson for his sister in 1912. Modeled after a New York City tenement, this doll high-rise features several apartments, a functioning elevator, and an elaborate fire escape system. It also functions as a handy cross-section of social strata, with the shabby furnishings of the lower floors giving way to chandeliers and velvets in the penthouse.

But perhaps the most wondrous of all dollhouses resides in Chicago. It is a miniature castle built by a Hollywood star over a period of thirty years and inspired by fairy lore. Each of its rooms was arranged to look as if a fairy had been present—reading, eating, dancing—and had simply popped out moments before the appearance of you, the visitor.

Colleen Moore looked exactly the way you might imagine a silent film star would: bow lips, a fashionable black bob, and an effervescent smile. Her first dollhouse was built out of cigar boxes by her father when she was two years old, but after a successful acting career and savvy investments with Merrill Lynch, she was soon able to make use of much finer materials—in fact, the finest materials money could buy. Nothing else would do.

Designed by Horace Jackson, an architect and Hollywood set designer, and Harold Grieve, an art director and interior designer, the Fairy Castle is nine feet tall and ultimately cost $500,000 ($10

▼ Silent film star Colleen Moore dwarfed by her massive fairy-tale dollhouse.

million today) to build and furnish. It features soaring turrets and creeping ivy, Gothic doorways, art nouveau–style stained glass, a swooping, gravity-defying staircase, even running water and electricity. Its rooms boast a miniature bear rug Frankensteined from an ermine pelt and a mouse's head, a pipe organ with mother-of-pearl keys the size of rice grains, and a set of mugs made from wood splinters gathered from the bombed-out rubble of Westminster Abbey during World War II.

The entire castle is filled with references to famous fairy tales. In the kitchen, a pie is filled with four-and-twenty tiny plaster blackbirds. The dining room is furnished with King Arthur's Round Table, and in the front hall stand the chairs of the Three Bears, so small that museum curators must wear masks so as not to accidentally inhale them.

But not all the castle's furnishings are sweet. On one shelf stands a miniature iron maiden, a torture device designed to enclose the wicked in a coffin lined with spikes. And in the chapel there is an alleged shard of the true cross, given to Moore by her friend Clare Booth Luce, the American ambassador to Italy in the 1950s, in remembrance of Luce's daughter, who died tragically at the age of nineteen in a car accident. The piece was originally housed inside a medallion, bequeathed to Luce by the pope himself. Moore, however, had an ornate miniature monstrance made to hold the shard instead, setting it on the chapel's altar. "I didn't care for the pope's taste in the medallion," Moore quipped during an interview in the 1980s. "But I kept the cross."

Like Petronella Oortman's dollhouse, the castle's most distinctive feature is its library. Decorated with a seafaring motif, verdigris green furniture, and murals (appropriately depicting scenes of the Lilliputians from *Gulliver's Travels*), its shelves are lined with more than a hundred tiny books. Agatha Christie, F. Scott Fitzgerald, Aldous Huxley, Willa Cather, Daphne du Maurier, and John Steinbeck all lent their names to books on those tiny shelves. Some wrote only a line or two or scrawled a quick signature inside. Others, like Edgar Rice Burroughs, went all in. The author of *Tarzan of the Apes*, he wrote *Tarzan, Jr.* expressly for Moore's dollhouse, a multichapter story about a princess journeying into a forbidden forest, and had the whole endeavor illustrated by his son John.

Though the entire endeavor might seem the vain hobby of a faded star, Colleen Moore managed to turn her passion into something quite noble and far reaching. "Now that it is completed, I would be selfish not to do some real good with it," Colleen Moore told the *New York Times* in 1935. And that she did. Between 1935 and 1939, as the Great Depression swept the United States, she took her Fairy Castle on tour, traveling across the United States in three specially built train cars. During this period she raised more than $650,000 (nearly $13 million today) for children's charities, bringing joy—and a touch of magic—to thousands. ◈

OUR LORD IN THE ATTIC

On a bustling canal in Amsterdam stands a tall, narrow brick house, almost identical to the houses around it. This one, however, holds an exquisite secret: Hidden away inside its attic is a cramped church, complete with a faux marble altar, mauve-painted balconies, a miniature pipe organ, brass gaslights, and enough pews to seat 150 worshippers.

The church was built in its strange perch because of the persecution of Dutch Catholics in the seventeenth century, when Protestant authorities were known to burst into services, arrest priests, and smash religious icons with mallets. In response, schuilkerken, or clandestine churches, began popping up across the Netherlands, hidden inside everything from barns to back gardens.

Our Lord in the Attic could only be reached through a hidden door in the downstairs living room, which led to a narrow staircase. Worshippers would then troop past bedrooms and parlors before arriving in the sumptuous nave under the roof. Loitering outside the townhouse was forbidden, as was the parking of sleds. Anything that brought attention to the fact that this was a place of worship was carefully avoided and the congregants would hold their soft sermons during the day, when the noise from the canal would drown out their songs.

There is even a secret within the secret: In the left-hand column of the altar is a small seam that looks as if the wood has begun to buckle. It opens to reveal a pulpit, which can be folded out on an extendable arm. A priest may then climb into it to deliver his sermon. (The hidden pulpit was a way of retaining the visual balance of the church, as symmetry and godliness were thought to go hand in hand.)

Today the church is a museum and still regularly holds services, which one can visit with no fear at all of Protestants arriving to smash things with mallets.

THE JIB DOOR

The door in Petronella's dollhouse, Marie-Antoinette's secret door (see Marie-Antoinette's Secret Escape, page 183), and the library bookcase doors of English country houses are all subspecies of a particular genus of secret door called the jib door, or invisible door. Jib doors are made to meld into the decor of a room, papered over in the same pattern of wallpaper or flush to the wall, without a frame, handle, or visible hinges. What many don't know is that the jib door did not necessarily begin as a secret. During the seventeenth century, jib doors were meant to preserve the symmetry of a room while still allowing access. In bedrooms, the hidden doors often led to dressing rooms or studies, the "back rooms" that were meant for more intimate pursuits, as well as to servants' passageways and staircases. In Dutch homes during this time, a door would sometimes be added, instead of subtracted, for symmetry, such as in the house of Our Lord in the Attic (page 88). In the main parlor of that house, there are two doors, side by side in the wall. One of them allows entrance into the room. The other cannot be opened and leads nowhere.

▲ *An example of a disguised "jib" door, this one in an abandoned château in France.*

The hidden jib door sprang from an inversion of the same concept and eventually became ubiquitous in great houses across the world, slowly developing a reputation of mystery. They could easily be overlooked and, over time, they were built to be as cleverly disguised as possible, with wall sconces mounted on them or a painting.

Where does the curious name come from? In eighteenth-century Scotland, to "jib" meant to squeeze the last drop of milk from a cow's udder or to rob someone of their last possessions. The door was probably given this name much later, once its reputation for clandestine pursuits was cemented, as it allowed people to slip in and out of rooms without being noticed.

One more detail: You can identify jib doors meant to be used by servants by the thick, fuzzy fabric called green baize that was used to cover the back, nonpublic, side of the door. This served to muffle the sounds of the servants from the masters of the house.

SECRETS INSIDE STATUES

During restoration work on an eighteenth-century Spanish statue of Jesus, preservationists found letters in an unlikely place: his buttocks. The letters were written in 1777 by Joaquín Mínguez, a priest at the Burgo de Osma cathedral, north of Madrid. The letters' contents are mostly mundane: Mínguez wrote of how he had successfully harvested wheat, rye, oats, and barley and that he had a great deal of wine in storage. However, he also mentions the bloodthirsty Spanish inquisition and Charles III's rule of Spain. The fact that the letters cover such a wide range of topics implies that the priest intended for them to be found, the statue acting as a time capsule for future generations.

A more grotesque discovery was made within a wooden statue of Jesus in Mexico, where researchers found eight human teeth lining the 300-year-old carving's mouth. A number of macabre explanations were suggested, from the wood-carver pulling out his own teeth in a frenzied attempt at realism, to the concealment of the remains of a murder victim. Most likely the teeth were simply donated by a devout member of the church—*after* the individual had died, of course. In those days, it was common for church members to donate hair for the wigs of holy statues or fabrics for the statue's clothes. To give one's teeth to Jesus must have been considered a very fine honor indeed.

Less grim, in Verona, Italy, a bronze sculpture of Juliet from Shakespeare's *Romeo and Juliet* stands in the ivied courtyard of what is purported to have been the young lover's home. During a recent restoration, researchers found the statue's hollow interior full of love notes dating back to the statue's unveiling in 1969. For years, visitors had been slipping letters through tiny cracks in the statue's exterior. The letters usually asked for successful relationships or romantic advice, though how Juliet scammed her way to becoming the patron saint of matters of the heart is a mystery of its own, considering that her romance ended with both her and Romeo dead due to poor communication.

Today, those seeking Juliet's ear must make do with hanging letters on the wall behind her statue or sending notes to her secretaries. A letter addressed to "Juliet, Verona, Italy," will find its way to the fictional character's real-life assistants at the so-called "Juliet Club," where volunteers will handwrite a reply.

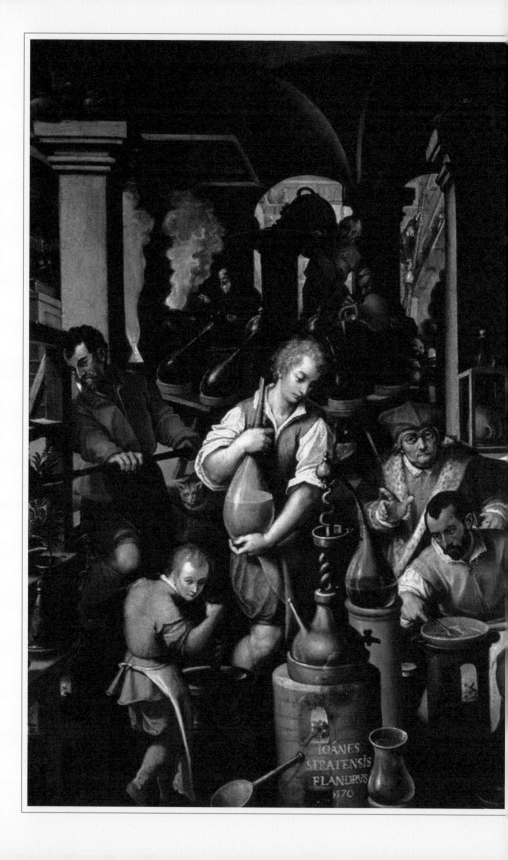

IOÁNES
STRATENSIS
FLANDRVS
1570

7

Alchemy, Frankenstein, and "Evil Scientist" Laboratories

VARIOUS

Ever since your mother began studying alchemy, she has been odd, distracted, and reclusive. Over the last decade her letters have grown increasingly strange, and for the past six months she has stopped signing them, "Your loving mother," but instead she has simply written, "The Mage."

You are aware that your mother is now obsessed with finding the elixir of life, the magical panacea that is said to bring immortality to all who drink it. When she invites you to visit her workshop, you take the next coach out of town.

◀ The Alchemist's Laboratory, *Jan van der Straet, 1570, Palazzo Vecchio*

You reach Paris in the cold, eerie hours of pre-dawn. You know your mother works at night and sleeps during the day, so you head straight to her laboratory in the heart of Pigalle. The area is seedy and ominously quiet. You breathe a sigh of relief when you reach the heavy wooden door marked with a series of odd symbols.

You wind through a twisting underground passage, dodging the rats and other vermin that scurry around the edges of your wool cloak. You turn a corner and spot the secret yellow mark. You press on the hidden latch and step inside a large room. You immediately cough. The air is thick, acrid. You smell woodsmoke, vinegar, sulfur, and other vile, unnameable things.

You briefly wonder if this is the scent of hell.

You do not see your mother. You are alone.

The tall, cylindrical brick furnace in the center of the room radiates warmth and you draw close, out of the shadows, away from the damp and chill. You peek inside and see an egg-shaped glass vessel percolating among the gray ashes.

You trip over half-empty burlap sacks as you ease toward the hearth near the far wall, where small flames lick a large cauldron. You lean over and gasp as a whiff of the concoction hits your nose. Inside the pot bubbles a thick, inky goo that smells sweetly earthy and horrid, like rotting flowers, freshly turned soil, and blood.

Your eyes focus on a workbench. You see copper tongs, pincers, ladles, and several things far less benign—a human skull and a diverse collection of small dead animals, dried insects, and other creatures preserved in large jars.

Various vials and crucibles cover the nearby shelves. You scan containers with labels describing exotic liquids and powders, such as Salt of Urine, Camel Dung, Spirit of Hartshorn, Saltpeter, Oil of Vitriol, Lime, and Balsam of the Soul.

Hanging beside the shelves are dozens of glass receptacles of various sizes. Some are gourd-shaped, some oval, like transparent ostrich eggs, and others have long, narrow spouts that are stoppered with corks. They come in a variety of colors—sea green, flame red, sapphire blue.

"They have names, you know."

Your mother appears behind you, quietly and suddenly, as if conjured out of thin air. Her blond hair swings loosely down her back. She is barefoot and looks even younger than you remember, though you haven't seen her in a decade.

"Mother." You run to her. You clutch her in your arms, but she doesn't return the embrace.

"These are my babies," she coos, stepping away from you and gesturing toward the vessels. "I blow the glass myself. The red ones are known as the Skull Cup, the Cup of Babylon, and the Mother of the Stone. The green are Spirit Holder and Moon Vessel. And last of all is my favorite, the blue Tomb of the Dead."

"I'm so close," she whispers, "so close to finding the elixir. It's taken me years of sweaty experimenting, but I've finally realized what is missing."

"And that is?" you ask in a soft voice as you slowly sidle backward, toward the door.

"The final ingredient," she whispers. "The blood of an innocent."

She grabs your arm and slashes your wrist. She is steely, stronger than you remember. Stronger than she looks. Impossibly strong.

She drags you to the hearth and forces your hand over the cauldron. You watch as your blood slips down into the bubbling sludge, a pint of it, a bucket of it.

The simmering alchemical potion begins to separate, to thin . . . and then, with a flash of light, it changes color from inky black to a brilliant, bright, starshine silver.

"It worked," she screams.

You can hear the sickening triumph in your mother's voice, the sting of it ringing through your ears even as you feel yourself growing weaker and weaker, even as you feel your knees hit the stone and you crumple onto your side.

"IT WORKED!" the Mage screams.

The image of a frenzied scientist in his secret lab—wild-eyed, white lab coat, unkempt hair—can be seen in everything from Mary Shelley's *Frankenstein* to *Back to the Future*. But where did it originate?

It's possible that the trope of the "evil scientist" traces back to medieval alchemy. When she started writing *Frankenstein* in 1816, Mary Shelley was likely inspired by stories of a German alchemist who conducted disreputable experiments in a place known as Frankenstein Castle, the ruins of which Shelley may have visited. She was a folklore enthusiast, and she was possibly introduced to the topic by her stepmother, who was the English translator of the Brothers Grimm fairy tales.

> The goal of every alchemist was to find the Philosopher's Stone, a mythical substance with the ability to turn base metals into gold or silver in a process known as transmutation.

And the fact that scientist-villains in films so often speak with German accents? Just an offshoot of this trope's Frankenstein Castle origins.

Indeed, alchemy—as well as astrology and mysticism—were highly fashionable in fifteenth-century Europe (though the roots of alchemy date back much further and can be found in ancient Chinese, Greek, Arabic, and Indian texts). Shakespeare wrote of love potions in *A Midsummer's Night Dream* and sleeping draughts to feign death in *Romeo and Juliet*. Royalty patronized alchemists, astrologists, and mages. Even popes practiced alchemy and employed their own astrologers and magicians.

Both women and men studied the art and most practiced in secret workshops hidden across Europe. Why? Women feared that they would be persecuted as a witch and both sexes believed that the thoughts and feelings of strangers could affect their fragile experiments and skew the results. Little is known about the locations of these workshops, but (thanks to Shelley) it is easy to picture them existing in cavernous, semi-abandoned castles located on lonely hilltops above small, German villages. In truth, alchemy was illegal in some countries and often considered heretical. Furthermore, alchemists wished to keep their activities hidden from the public eye, to protect any magical formulas they might discover. Their labs were more likely hidden in underground, windowless stone chambers, notable only for their inconspicuousness.

The "hermit alchemist" was so ubiquitous that in 1607, Andreas Libavius, a German doctor and alchemist, published *Alchymia Triumphans*, which urged alchemists to avoid isolation, and instead be social and have a family, so as to make alchemy a respectable science.

The goal of every alchemist was to find the Philosopher's Stone, a mythical substance with the ability to turn base metals into gold or silver in a process known as transmutation.* Some alchemists believed the Philosopher's Stone was the amalgamation of common substances that, when combined,

Left: Princeton's Ripley Scroll. Above: A toad represents 'prime matter'.

Above left: A child of Sun and Moon. Above right: A bird eats its wings.

▲ *Bizarre scenes from the Ripley Scroll.*

would create something magical. The pursuit of this unique substance led to the future studies of chemistry, pharmacology, and metallurgy.

*The Ripley Scroll is a twenty-foot-long manuscript that supposedly provides a recipe for the Philosopher's Stone. It depicts alchemical flasks, biblical scenes, dragons, lions, a phoenix, and the Philosopher's Stone itself, which is portrayed as three orbs of red, black, and white. Some people believe that a series of round medallions on a doorway of the Notre-Dame in Paris also depicts a recipe for its creation.

In the typical alchemical workshop you would find books, a celestial globe, a corner where the plants were stored, a still or retort where plant matter was distilled, an oven for percolating potions, and a glass-blowing furnace—alchemists often made their own glass vials and pear-shaped crucibles in order to avoid discovery.

Eventually alchemists moved away from the goal of transforming base metals into gold and toward the pursuit of new medicines and a panacea known as the "elixir of life." Johann Konrad Dippel was a devout believer in the possibility of this miraculous concoction. Born in Frankenstein Castle in 1673, he was an occultist, theologian, physician, alchemist, and recluse. People viewed him as a dark sorcerer who shunned society and brewed up diabolical potions in secret lairs.

According to rumor, Dippel also fiddled with electrical therapies on bodies stolen from the local graveyards and attempted soul transference through the use of a funnel. Yes, a funnel.

Built circa 1252, Frankenstein Castle sits on a hill overlooking the area known as Odenwald. The castle was likely a gloomy, medieval stone fortress, but little is known about the original structure. The surrounding woods were a wild place of thickly shadowed glens and foreboding fortress ruins. Many legends still exist about the location, including tales of dragons, witchcraft, buried gold, and eerie magnetic fields. It's all a bit too perfectly atmospheric. An alchemist conducting demonic experiments in the nearby castle would have fitted perfectly into the forest's gothic charm.

Dippel soon patented something he called "Dippel's oil," which also came to be known as "bone oil." Dippel claimed his potion was a universal medicine with many uses. It was made from the distillation of various animal parts, a murky, viscous substance that tasted even worse than it smelled. Dippel's oil was once used by troops in World War II to poison wells, so to speak. It wasn't lethal, but it made the water undrinkable, causing the enemy significant hardship without breaching the Geneva Convention.

Frankenstein Castle fell into ruins in the eighteenth century but was semi-restored in the mid-1800s (in a Gothic, historically inaccurate fashion) and is still a lightning rod for various occult rituals in the area. However, it is only one of many possible locations for secret alchemical lairs. Here are a few of history's most intriguing examples:

The Studiolo of Francesco I de' Medici, Grand Duke of Tuscany
FLORENCE · ITALY

The Palazzo Vecchio, with its soaring clock tower, was the seat of the Florentine Republic in the fourteenth century. Built between 1298 and 1314, it has served many roles and gone by many different names throughout the years. It stands in the Piazza della Signoria, where Michelangelo's statue of *David* once stood (a replica now stands in its place). Every Florentine tourist eventually ends up at this piazza, but the ones who leave behind the sun and the gelato to venture into the Palazzo Vecchio discover a building with many marvelous secrets.

In 1540, the court of the Medici was transferred to the Palazzo Vecchio and the interior redesigned to include a labyrinth of apartments, terraces, hidden corridors, and courtyards, with chambers displaying art from Michelangelo and Donatello.

The palazzo held several monumental frescoes and wondrous rooms, such as the Hall of Maps, where fifty-three hand-painted maps from the Renaissance era reside, and the Lion House, a place designed for Cosimo the Elder's menagerie of lions. But arguably the most interesting is the Studiolo. Hidden inside the palazzo, down its mazelike halls, lies the barrel-shaped room that served as Francesco I's hiding place, refuge, personal museum, and alchemical workshop.

Francesco inherited his dukedom from his father, Cosimo I, in 1574. He was a complex man, sometimes tyrannical, but also a scholar and a patron of the arts. The Studiolo could be reached only via a single door in the duke's bedchamber. He used the tiny room to display rare items he found on his world travels, as well as art from more than thirty artists, including a portrait of himself in a work by Jan van der Straet entitled *The Alchemist's Laboratory*. The painting shows a bustling laboratory complete with metallurgical work, bellows, furnaces, and flasks (the duke is in yellow).

Francesco was a known scientist and alchemist, and he also used the Studiolo as a place to experiment with chemistry and alchemy. Unfortunately, this caused the hidden room to be dismantled after Francesco's death, in the later years of the Counter-Reformation, when alchemical practices were seen as heretical.

Holy Roman Emperor Rudolf II's Alchemical Workshop

PRAGUE · CZECH REPUBLIC

Enter a museum in one of the oldest buildings in Prague's Jewish Quarter, locate the statue in the library, and turn it to reveal a secret door and a set of stairs that leads down to a medieval alchemical laboratory.

The museum, called Speculum Alchemiae, purports that Rudolf II, the Holy Roman Emperor from 1576 to 1612, had it built as a place to conduct experiments and develop magical elixirs for love and eternal youth. It was rediscovered in 2002 during a renovation, still filled with taxidermied animals, old barrels, feather quills, rolled parchments, and dusty bottles.

Rudolf II had a keen interest in astrology and alchemy and spent much of his wealth luring alchemists to his court in his obsessive quest to find the Philosopher's Stone. The workshop beneath Speculum Alchemiae is likely just one of many hidden underground laboratories that he had built throughout the city.

▶ *Francisco I's Studiolo, a hidden room in the Palazzo Vecchio, Florence. Its thirty-six paintings depict scenes of mythology and magic, and nineteen of them open to reveal cabinets in which he stored his collection of curiosities.*

Like Cosimo the Elder in Florence, Rudolf was a great lover of art and helped make Prague a leading center of art and science during his reign. He patronized philosophers and poets and kept a menagerie of exotic animals. (According to Simon Winder in *Danubia: A Personal History of Habsburg Europe*, a lion and tiger were allowed to freely wander Prague Castle. The castle's account books list compensation paid to victims of feline attacks.)

Rumors persist that Rudolf may have been the first owner of what is now referred to as the Voynich manuscript. Thought to have been written in the fifteenth century (which has been confirmed by radiocarbon dating), it contains an indecipherable code and features elaborate illustrations of dragons, small nude women connected to tubes that appear to contain liquid, astrological signs, and diagrams of plants that are assumed to be medicinal. Its author, purpose, and language remain mysterious to this day. The manuscript would have been part of Rudolf's stunning cabinet of curiosities, one of the finest and most extensive in Europe. The cabinet filled three large rooms in the castle and included astrolabes, telescopes, sixty clocks, and (according to the emperor) a basilisk and two nails from Noah's Ark. Some scholars claim that Prague inherited its gothic, mystical reputation directly from this alchemist emperor's peculiar obsessions.

Nicolas and Perenelle Flamel's Secret Workshop

PARIS · FRANCE

Nicolas Flamel! He found the Philosopher's Stone! He drank from the elixir of life and cheated death! He's so famous he was featured in the first Harry Potter book! Most people have heard his name, either from reading J. K. Rowling's series or Victor Hugo's *The*

Hunchback of Notre-Dame. (Hugo claimed that he had been contacted by the spirit of Flamel during a séance in 1854.)

Perhaps you have seen the portal-to-hell flick *As Above, So Below*, where the main character studies Flamel in an effort to find the Philosopher's Stone. Or maybe you've played *Assassin's Creed: Unity*, which has several Flamel-themed quests.

Are any of the stories about Flamel true? Did he have a clandestine workshop in Paris devoted to discovering the secret of eternal life?

Folklore about Nicolas Flamel (born in 1330) and his wife, Perenelle, is diverse and plentiful. According to legend, Flamel dreamed of a famous alchemical text, which he later found to be a real book, supposedly called *The Book of Abraham the Jew*.* Flamel and his wife spent years trying to decipher the text and unravel its mysteries, traveling from France to Spain and meeting with many scholars. They apparently cracked the code, discovered the stone, and managed to produce gold and silver from base metals.

The Flamels returned to France, now fabulously wealthy. They founded hospitals and churches and helped the poor (their philanthropy is verifiably true), all the while writing alchemical texts and laboriously cooking up magical potions in their secret workshop, endlessly searching for the elusive elixir of life.

Of course, some people argue Flamel never did anything remotely alchemical, mystical, or magical, that he and his wife were simply solid, church-going philanthropists, and his house contained absolutely zero secret workshops cluttered with mystical tomes, apothecary jars, cauldrons of bubbling potions, and ominous vials secreting noxious smells. And perhaps all these legends could

---

*This was a copy of a previous work titled *The Book of Abramelin*. It told the story of an Egyptian mage and later became an important text for Aleister Crowley (page 161).

be dismissed, except for two odd circumstances: Flamel designed his own tombstone, currently displayed in the Musée de Cluny in Paris, and it teems with strange, alchemical symbols. According to lore, some years after the death of both Nicolas and Perenelle, a grave robber opened their tombs and both bodies were found to be missing.

It's easy for people to infer from this latter fact that the Flamels did find the secret to immortality and are still alive today. Eighteenth-century aristocrat Comte de Saint-Germain also claimed to have discovered the elixir of life and boasted to several members of royalty that he was hundreds of years old. Many alchemical fanatics believe this was in fact the immortal Flamel.

Of course, Saint-Germain might have been fibbing, either to avoid assassination (he was possibly the son of a prince and heir to a Transylvanian throne) or simply to make himself appear more interesting to bored nobles.

Not to be outdone by Nicolas Flamel, the comte has also made fictional appearances—he pops up as a ruthless time traveler in Diana Gabaldon's *Dragonfly in Amber*, as the mystic in Alexander Pushkin's short story "The Queen of Spades," and as an occultist in Umberto Eco's *Foucault's Pendulum*.

The Alchemical Laboratory and Astronomical Observatory of Uraniborg

VEN · SWEDEN

In 1576 the Danish astronomer Tycho Brahe was granted the island of Ven in the Øresund, the strait that separates Denmark and Sweden, by Frederick II, King of Denmark and Norway, for the purpose of building a three-story brick observatory where upwards of thirty astronomers could comfortably study, live, and host visiting royalty. It was an elegant building featuring spires, balconies, and spiral staircases, placed in the center of a formal garden. Illustrations from Brahe's *Astronomiae instauratae mechanica* (1598) indicate that the square rooms in the center were mainly used for eating, sleeping, and to house visiting scholars and royalty. The gatehouse contained a small prison for unruly guests and a printing workshop. The observatory had three towers and was surrounded by galleries containing astronomical instruments. A large mural quadrant was located on one wall, which the scholars used to "measure the altitude of the stars as they passed the meridian."

Called Uraniborg, after Urani, the mythological Greek muse of astronomy, the observatory was funded by the king and state, but Brahe, in true alchemical tradition, kept a secret underground laboratory for his medical alchemy studies, and the gardens supplied many of the herbs that Brahe used in his experiments.

While Brahe contributed greatly to science, he was a controversial, demanding figure who was in no doubt of his own genius. He lost part of his nose in a duel when he was twenty years old (apparently with a fellow scholar over who was the greater mathematician) and he wore a prosthetic brass nose for the rest of his life. Brahe was forced to abandon Uraniborg in 1597 after he and Frederick II's son Christian IV quarreled. Uraniborg was destroyed in 1601 and the Rundetaarn (Round Tower) in Copenhagen became the leading astronomical observatory. Eventually Holy Roman Emperor Rudolf II took Brahe in and he moved to Prague and became the Imperial Mathematician. He died a year later, at the age of fifty-four.

The popular rumor at the time was that Brahe had accidentally poisoned himself while attempting to cure an illness with one of his own potions—his body was later exhumed and this was proven to be false. No poison was found, but it was noted that he had been exposed to an excessive amount of gold in the latter months of his life. Perhaps Brahe had stumbled upon the Philosopher's Stone in his studies? Or perhaps he'd begun drinking his ale flecked with

▲ *Tycho Brahe's Uraniborg observatory on the island of Hven, Denmark.*

gold leaf, in the common alchemical belief that this metal was a potent healer.

Regardless, Brahe died the true alchemist in the end—his pockets, and even his physical body, brimming with gold.

Popular culture has long had a love affair with alchemy, one that extends far past *Frankenstein* adaptations. Chemist-wizards and potion-sorcerers ripple through the pages of fiction and their evocative, flame-filled workshops have enchanted film lovers for nearly a century.

H. P. Lovecraft published a short story titled "The Alchemist" in 1916, which contains a dark wizard, a ruined castle, fallen towers, a trapdoor, and an alchemist who discovers a potion for immortality. Terry Pratchett features alchemy in his Discworld novels, as does George R. R. Martin in his A Song of Ice and Fire series.

Disney's *Fantasia* (based on a poem by Johann Wolfgang von Goethe called "The Sorcerer's Apprentice") depicts a wizard creating bewitching images with the eerie light emanating from a skull. The evil fairy Maleficent in Disney's *Sleeping Beauty* throws tantrums in her barren stone lair and surrounds herself with fluorescent green flames. The evil stepmother in *Snow White and the Seven Dwarfs* brews potions in an underground lab in her castle, complete with strange glass bottles and spell books entitled *Poison, Black Magic, Black Arts, Sorcery*, and *Astrology*.

The 1982 cult classic *The Dark Crystal* has nightmare-inducing scenes of villainous Skeksis in a laboratory filled with terrified animals in cages and ominous contraptions. The Skeksis drain the life essence of the Pod People and Gelfling in an attempt to prolong the evil emperor's life.

Even many video games boast alchemical elements, from *The Witcher* to *Elden Ring* (which some claim was inspired by ancient alchemical literature).

Where is the line drawn between chemistry and alchemy? Science and magic? Who cares? We are having too much fun with this to give a damn. ◆

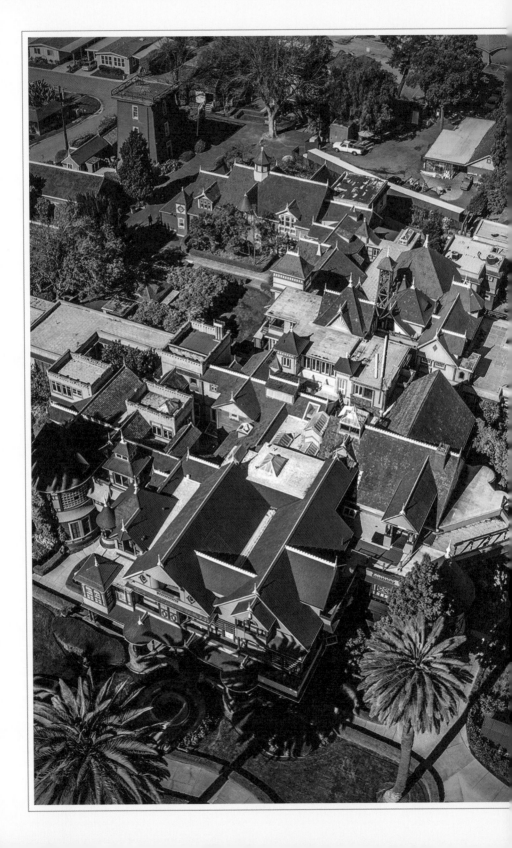

8

The Winchester Mystery House

SAN JOSE • CALIFORNIA • USA

On the other side of the bedroom door, you hear the stairwell clock chime twelve times.

It was the scent that woke you—the scent of a graveyard, of burial, of six feet under, of upturned earth and decaying flowers, bruised skin and white, cold limbs, of coffin dust and sharp embalming elixirs.

It is the scent of sin.

It is the scent of ghosts.

The evening before had started off warm and humid,

◀ An aerial view of the "haunted" labyrinthine mansion, the Winchester Mystery House, San Jose, California.
▶ Sarah Winchester

then crescendoed into a summer thunderstorm, one of the cacopho-
nous, heart-rattling kinds that shake a house down to its bones.

Bones.

Sometimes you lie awake in the middle of the night and imagine
the bones of all the dead, all the men, women, and children slain
by the weapons sold by your father-in-law's Winchester Repeating
Arms Company. So many bones. Bones enough to fill an ever-
expanding San Jose mansion.

You told the workmen to go home for the night. They couldn't
continue in the rain and thunder. Four years ago, a young, handsome

carpenter named Henry had nearly been struck by lightning as he stood on the roof, nailing down a plank in a raging storm. People already whispered that you, and this house, were cursed. What would they say if you let a young man die?

You push back the covers, climb out of bed, and slip across the cold bedroom floor, the hem of your nightdress sweeping gently across your bare toes.

The spirits always come when the house goes still, when the hammers and nails cease, when the men disappear and it's just you and the sins of your family sitting in the silence, waiting.

You open the bedroom door and enter the long, twisting hallway. On nights like these, you retreat to the kitchen to drink warm milk and wait out the hellish dark, until dawn finally arrives and the vengeful spirits return to their own grisly, supernatural realm.

You stumble up a flight of stairs to the servants' quarters, hoping to find someone who can light the kitchen stove and keep you company. But you can't remember, in the shadows, in the quiet, which door opens to the housekeeper's room and which one opens out into the empty air. One turn of the wrong knob and you will fall to your death.

You spin right, then left, then right again. You reach for a door handle, then pull back with a shudder.

You put your hand to the wall to steady yourself. It feels sticky, almost hot. You recoil and hold your palm up to a shaft of moonlight spilling through a nearby window. Your palm begins to drip. Red droplets splash across your white nightdress.

"The walls," you whisper, "the walls are bleeding again. . . ."

◀ The infamous door that leads to a dangerous thirteen-foot drop to the ground.

This is the common (mis)representation of what is now known as the Winchester Mystery House: a place of horrors, where one tiny, elderly woman in black battled ghosts, along with her own mental health, while endlessly expanding her California mansion until it was a labyrinthine monstrosity with zigzag stairways that lead nowhere (47 in all), as well as:

- 6 kitchens
- 13 bathrooms
- 47 fireplaces
- 52 skylights
- 10,000 panes of glass

According to legend, Sarah Winchester was haunted by the spirits of all the people killed by the Winchester repeating rifle, which was the source of her fortune. She famously kept workers continually building onto her Queen Anne Victorian home for thirty-eight years in a frenzied attempt to confuse these ghosts, so they could not harm her.

There are the tales of how she was obsessed with the number 13, and she built 13-paned windows, 13-step staircases, drains with exactly 13 holes, 13 bathrooms, and commissioned a stained-glass spiderweb window made by Tiffany, with 13 glass "water drops" on the web.

There are rumors that Sarah was involved in a secret society, perhaps the Rosicrucians or the Freemasons (see page 127), or both, and the strange features in her house are a series of encrypted puzzles that only the followers of these sects can understand. The list goes on.

How much of this is accurate? No one knows. Windowpanes are easy to count, even 10,000 of them, but the personal fears and motivations of an eccentric, wealthy woman who died a century ago? This is harder to pin down. What is known is that the influence of Sarah Winchester, and her mammoth house, looms large. Several ghost-hunting shows have searched for spirits on the property and a horror film starring Helen Mirren titled *Winchester* was released in 2018. The author Shirley Jackson grew up near the Winchester House and it has been cited as an inspiration for her famous *The Haunting of Hill House*. Disneyland's Haunted Mansion ride is said to be inspired by the Winchester house, in particular its grand ballroom.

In fact, you might be able to pin the entire "haunted mansion" concept on the Winchester Mystery House. But is this truly a story of a grief-stricken woman on the run from ghosts? Or was there some other purpose to Sarah Winchester's obsessive building?

Sarah Winchester (née Pardee) married into the Winchester family in 1862, just a few years before the first Winchester repeating rifle hit the market in 1866. The Winchester family was already wealthy. Their patriarch, Oliver Winchester, had founded a successful shirt production company. Sarah herself was born into comfortable circumstances—her father, Leonard, was a skilled carpenter and housebuilder, frequently employed to build elaborate Victorian-era homes for the elite in New Haven, Connecticut. The Pardees and the Winchesters were neighbors and Sarah married the "boy next door," William Wirt Winchester, in a simple ceremony one year into the Civil War. By that time, Oliver Winchester had purchased a failing arms company and, with the engineering acumen of his star employee Benjamin Tyler Henry, designed and patented the repeating rifle.

Rumor has it that this decision came after she sought advice from a psychic, who cautioned her that the deaths of her loved ones were karmic payback for all the death caused by her family's business.

The Winchester repeating rifle, sold as the Henry and marketed as the "gun that won the West," became a runaway bestseller, selling more than half a million each year. President Theodore Roosevelt used a Winchester, as did Annie Oakley and Buffalo Bill Cody.

The Henry could be reloaded in a matter of seconds, substantially decreasing the time between shots, which almost single-handedly changed the nature of armed conflict. The rifle was used heavily by the United States military, Euro-American settlers, and Indigenous American tribes. Buffalo hunters used the rifle to wipe out herds, as did the US Cavalry to massacre entire settlements of Indigenous American peoples. An enormous death toll followed in its wake.

William helped his father run the Winchester company and the couple had a daughter, Annie, born in 1866. She lived only forty days. Officially, Annie died from marasmus, a severe form of malnutrition. William himself was also sickly and was plagued by tuberculosis for much of his life.

Tragedy struck again in 1880 when Sarah's mother died, followed closely by her father-in-law. On Oliver's death, ownership of the company passed to William but he too died, a year later in 1881.

The full weight of the Winchester's bloody empire fell on Sarah's shoulders. She inherited $20 million (approximately $580 million in 2020), along with a 50 percent ownership stake in the Winchester Repeating Arms company. This gave Sarah an income of approximately a thousand dollars a day, equal to about $30,000 by modern standards.

Five years later, Sarah permanently left for the West, moving to the San Francisco Bay area. Rumor has it that this decision came after she sought advice from a psychic, who cautioned her that the deaths of her loved ones were karmic payback for all the death caused by her family's business. The psychic then informed Sarah that she must "go West" and continually build onto her home as a way to "appease the spirits."

Perhaps Sarah did see a psychic, as spiritualism was extremely popular at this time. The famous Fox sisters had been holding séances up and down the East Coast for four decades at this point.[*]

*The three Fox sisters first demonstrated their "psychic skills" on November 14, 1849, at the Corinthian Hall in Rochester, New York. It was the first public display of spiritualism and sparked a long run of similar such demonstrations by spiritualists and mediums. The sisters quickly became famous—the audiences for their séances numbered in the hundreds.

Regardless, if this spiritualist had the good sense to tell Sarah Winchester to leave her hometown, which was full of sorrow, and move out West because it might prove a pleasant distraction, then it was wise advice. Furthermore, her brother-in-law had recently accepted a position with Occidental College in Oakland, and Sarah decided to accompany her two sisters on their move to the Bay area. With her substantial fortune, she intended to build a large enough house for all of them to inhabit. In 1886, she purchased Llanada Villa, a two-story farmhouse, and its surrounding ranch, in San Jose, which at the time was an unremarkable rural community south of San Francisco.

However, Sarah's sisters quickly moved on. Within a year, one sister had left California for her husband's new university job in North Dakota, while the other had decided to move into San Francisco proper, leaving behind her daughter, Marion.

Her original goal stymied, Sarah seems to have caught the building bug. Hard. For the rest of her life, which would stretch on for nearly four decades, Sarah kept up a near constant stream of construction, using the best materials money could buy.

Notable features included:

- A wood-paneled Venetian-style dining room with low ceilings, leaded glass windows, and Italian marble. (It's said that the chandelier in this room spookily swings with no known cause.)
- A basement "Steam Alley" filled with radiators. The most frequently sighted spirit lives here. People claim to see the "Wheelbarrow Ghost" pushing its namesake down a long, dark corridor.
- The Daisy Bedroom, where Sarah was trapped for hours during the 1906 earthquake, until her servants finally freed her. The mark of a crowbar can still be seen on the bedroom door.
- A stained-glass window that cost $1,500 (approximately $46,000 today).

- A door that leads to a thirteen-foot drop down to the lawn below and another to an eight-foot drop into a kitchen sink.
- What's known as the Witches Cap—a turret or tower shaped like a cone. Psychics claim this room is filled with "spirit energy."
- A large bell tower, where every Friday the thirteenth its bell is rung 13 times at 1300 hours (1 p.m.) in "tribute to Sarah."
- A staircase that leads nowhere and ends in a ceiling.
- The grand ballroom's stained-glass windows, which feature two odd, obscure Shakespearian quotes: "These same thoughts people this little world" from *Richard II* and "Wide unclasp the tables of their thoughts" from *Troilus and Cressida*.
- A séance room, where Sarah is said to have communed with the dead in the middle of the night. Local folklore dictates that she rang the bell at midnight to summon the spirits and then again two hours later to release them. There is no concrete evidence that Sarah ever participated in or held séances in her house. (Also, one wonders why she would have wanted to summon ghosts when the prevailing thought was that she was haunted by them.)

▼ *The alleged "séance room" where Sarah supposedly cavorted with spirits in the dead of night.*

While Sarah Winchester did not employ craftsmen twenty-four hours a day, seven days a week to work on the house, as some maintained, its expansion was ongoing and endless, without any obvious reason or decipherable goal. Her house was never, in her view, "finished." Later, the gothic rumor sprang up that it was because she was afraid she would die if construction ever ceased, that the ghosts she was fleeing would overtake her at last. Perhaps the truth is a mix of many things and, above all, building the house and fussing over its details gave Sarah Winchester a sense of purpose.

"I am constantly having to make an upheaval for some reason," she wrote in a letter to her sister-in-law in 1898. "For instance, my upper hall which leads to the sleeping apartment was rendered so unexpectedly dark by a little addition that after a number of people had missed their footing on the stairs I decided that safety demanded something to be done so, over a year ago, I took out a wall and put in a skylight."

Not quite as compelling as "ghosts made me do it."

In 1895, an article about Sarah and her house appeared in the *San Jose Daily News*, which provides insight into just how strange the house began to appear to others.

> *The first view of the house fills one with surprises. You mechanically rub your eyes to assure yourself that the number of the turrets is not an illusion, they are so fantastic and dream-like. But nearer approach reveals others and others and still others. . . . From every point of view new towers appear, and one has to make a circuit of the building to see all of these, for every addition to the many that is made has one or more separate roofs, and every roof is elaborated into a tower or resolved into a dome. . . . Although no part of the structure is over two stories high, the house is large enough to shelter an army. . . . As fast as new rooms are finished—and they are all made with the*

latest and most modern of accessories—they are furnished with the utmost elegance and closed, to be used hardly at all. Mrs. Winchester and her niece live alone in the great residence, and its doors are closed to all but a few. The tap, tap, tapping of the carpenters' hammers never disturbs them in their many and luxurious quarters, which are far removed from the sound as if it were somebody else's house that was being built.

Whether Sarah was driven by a grief-fueled frenzy or simply fiddling with house projects is open to debate. Regardless, she was just a bit more fanatical about it and had more disposable income to indulge in it. It's said that she fired her first two architects and then began drawing the blueprints herself. Her enthusiasm might have overtaken her skill, however, providing logical, non-supernatural reasons why there might be an oddly misplaced door or stairway.

The house was severely damaged in the 1906 San Francisco earthquake and some argue this is another reason behind the home's present misshapen appearance. The top three stories of the seven-story building collapsed altogether, which could explain the "nowhere doors" and "nowhere staircase"—they may have once led to floors that no longer exist.

Sarah died in 1922, passing away peacefully from heart failure. Construction on the Winchester house immediately ceased. Sarah left everything to her niece, who auctioned off the house and furniture. Five months later, the Winchester Mystery House opened to the public as a tourist attraction. Rumor has it that a "family of carnies" bought the property and the rest is history. (According to Mary Jo Ignoffo's biography of Sarah, *Captive of the Labyrinth*, a man named John Brown purchased the house and, while he wasn't technically a carnie, he had indeed worked in amusement parks designing roller coasters.)

▶ *The "nowhere staircase"*

Smart marketing created a house that became a legend, one filled with tales of ghosts and guilt. But this odd mansion, with its twisting passageways and doors to nowhere, might have been a source of comfort and purpose to an elderly woman rather than a labyrinth in which to hide from her demons. Ignoffo states that Sarah was in love with architecture, not ghosts or secret societies. Her father manufactured decorative architectural pieces and Sarah grew up next door to his factory. Perhaps building was simply in her blood.

In *Ghostland: An American History in Haunted Places*, Colin Dickey asserts that Sarah Winchester wanted to pursue the study of architecture at a time when social convention dictated that this was a subject suitable to men alone, so she decided to experiment on her own house, for better or worse.

This provokes the question: Was Sarah Winchester just more eccentric than your average homeowner? Or were her efforts an architectural example of naive art, or outsider art—art that is created by someone without formal training?

Lone wolf builds, like the Winchester Mystery House, are rare but not unheard of. Every so often, someone somewhere will buy or inherit a house and decide to keep adding or expanding the buildings on the property in an amateur, haphazard fashion until their home becomes a well-known local oddity.

In the late eighteenth century, the Lord of Fonthill, William Beckford, spent years building Fonthill Abbey (see page 14)—a cavernous Gothic building with a 300-foot tower. The project devoured his wealth and, some say, his sanity. "Some people drink to forget their unhappiness," Beckford wrote, "I do not drink, I build." One feels that he and Sarah Winchester would have had much in common.

Here are a few more compelling examples of lone wolf architecture:

Palais Idéal

HAUTERIVES · FRANCE

Reading this book, one could be forgiven for thinking that secret places are the domain of the very rich. But the poor and anonymous keep secrets as well and have rich inner lives seeking expression. Often a lack of time and money prevent these worlds from taking shape, but some, against all odds, are built, not with money and armies of workers, but with hard-bitten tenacity and determination.

In the vegetable patch of a country postman in Hauterives, France, stands a palace, albeit a small one.

Joseph Ferdinand Cheval was forty-three, with three living children, when he tripped over a stone on his way to work. His life had been difficult. His eldest daughter, Alice, had died at the age of fifteen and his days were marked by illness, poverty, and grief. But when he saw the stone, he was reminded of a dream he'd had long ago. In it he "had built a palace, a castle or caves, I cannot express it well. . . . I told no one about it for fear of being ridiculed, and I felt ridiculous myself."

But not so ridiculous that he did not try to realize his vision in secret. For the next thirty-three years, Cheval worked to make the palace a reality, building a bizarre amalgamation of styles, turrets, corridors, and statues. He picked up stones during his daily mail round and took them home to build the Palais Idéal. At first, he carried the stones in his pockets, then switched to a basket. Eventually, he used a wheelbarrow. He often worked at night, by the light of an oil lamp.

The palace is covered with cryptic messages carved by Cheval. One word comes up over and over again. *Travail*. Work.

"One man's work," one of his carvings declares, another one, rather practically, "Do not touch anything," and a third proclaims, "God's designs are impenetrable."

Cheval's own designs are no less impenetrable. The building displays a wild mishmash of influences, from Southeast Asian to

baroque. Hundreds of niches pockmark the walls, many of them holding small stone figures or animals. The palace's facade contains architectural elements of a Hindu temple and a Swiss chalet, as well as spires and battlements.

"By creating this rock, I wanted to prove what the will can do," Cheval was quoted as saying in the later years of his life. After his daughter's untimely death, his own end seemed to loom more darkly. He wanted to matter, to mark the earth with something of his own.

Time and time again in this book, we see people confronted with death, then retreating into their own world, building it from scratch and hiding inside. Perhaps this is one of the most natural responses to death, to build a receptacle for one's soul in the hope it will remain there forever. The palace was Cheval's beautiful, strange attempt to stand up to his own mortality.

The House on the Rock

SPRING GREEN • WISCONSIN

Have you ever had a nightmare where you were trapped inside a carnival fun house, hounded by the thunderous, ear-bleeding whine of automated instruments drumming out Ravel's poisonously catchy *Boléro*? And when you woke up, did you think, "Oh, if only I could relive this hellish, claustrophobic experience"?

The House on the Rock in Spring Green, Wisconsin, is a grand 17,630 square feet and contains more than two miles of winding exhibits, including the world's largest carousel (which does indeed play *Boléro*, on repeat), a monstrous sculpture of a squid fighting a whale, a re-creation of a Victorian street, and massive collections of guns, armor, dolls, model airplanes, crowns, swords, and self-playing instruments. At least two music videos have been filmed at this

◄ *The World's Largest Carousel at the House on the Rock plays* Boléro *until your ears bleed.*

location and Neil Gaiman (who once lived part-time in Wisconsin) featured it in his book *American Gods*.

Alex Jordan Jr. began building this architectural wonder in the 1940s on a sandstone formation known as Deer Shelter Rock. It initially served as his weekend retreat, but he kept building rooms upon rooms to house his many collections. The house garnered so much attention that it finally opened in 1959 to the public and became a successful tourist attraction. Jordan sold the house in 1988 to an associate, and it remains a private business.

A lot of the items showcased in the House on the Rock are fake, and visitors are warned of this, though this wasn't always the case. Like the Winchester Mystery House, the early marketing team for the attraction wasn't overly burdened with a sense of honesty and rather shamelessly advertised that the house contained authentic Tiffany lamps and music machines that had been owned by royalty, none of which was true.

Author Jane Smiley wrote about the house in 1993 for the *New York Times*, referring to its creator as a single-minded eccentric. She commented on the dust, the cracked windows, the water-damaged books, the collections that are "massed together" with no order, or curation, all of which leads to an inviting but overwhelming experience.

The House on the Rock is a living manifestation of one man's dream—to single-handedly build the largest, most random collection of fake items anywhere in the midwestern United States and put it in a house on a rock. A noble goal.

Smith Mansion

WAPITI VALLEY • WYOMING

In the early 1980s, a man named Francis Lee Smith decided to build a home for his family on ten acres in the wide-open Wapiti Valley of Wyoming, on the Buffalo Bill Cody Scenic Byway, halfway between Cody and Yellowstone.

Smith used locally harvested lodgepole pines. After he finished with the essentials—the bedrooms and kitchen—he kept on building for the next ten years, tacking on staircases and extra floors until the structure soared seventy-five feet into the air and included several porches as well as a crow's nest. The house took on a bizarre, slap-dash, rabbit warren appearance that quickly turned it into a local landmark.

The Smith "mansion" featured a dining room table hewn from a tree stump, a swing that served as a bed on hot summer nights, and an indoor basketball court. A single woodstove provided the only heat for the entire house—there was no plumbing and limited electricity. Despite this, the family lived in the house for several years, but eventually Smith's obsession led to a divorce. His wife and children moved into town, and he was left alone with his masterpiece.

According to a *New York Times* article, legends about the home are plentiful. Some say Smith saw the house in a vision, others that he built it as a lookout tower in case the now sleeping volcano in Yellowstone erupted.

Smith worked on his house with no ropes or tethers and in 1992 he fell to his death while constructing an upper balcony. The house has sat empty ever since.

Smith's daughter, Sunny Larsen, hoped to raise funds to open the house to the public as a museum, but in 2019 it was sold to an unnamed buyer.

Sunny claims her father followed no blueprints and that he built the house "off the cuff," in a fashion similar to that of Sarah Winchester. She asserts that he wasn't a madman, as some locals maintain. Instead, she thinks of him as an artist.

9

The Initiation Well, the Knights Templar, and the Freemasons

SINTRA • PORTUGAL

The blindfold is drawn tight, the silk pressing into your eyelids. The darkness that comes is so thick you could choke on it.

You feel a hand on your shoulder. It steadies you. You are stripped to the waist, buttons popping—you hear them skittering across the stone floor. You shiver in the dank air and goosebumps break out across your skin.

You breathe slowly and try to stay calm. One gasp of protest, one uncontrollable shiver, and you could be rejected, thrown out of the society.

◄ *The mysterious Initiation Well at Quinta da Regaleira was the likely location of many secret ceremonies and rituals.*

Someone presses a metal hilt into your hand. You clutch the sword to your bare chest and walk forward. You descend the 135 steps slowly, inching your way down the moss-covered spiral staircase, deeper and deeper into the earth. You must not trip. You must not fall.

What seems like a long, long time later, you reach the floor of the well. You can sense the other members surrounding you. You feel their warmth, their breath on your cold skin. Strong hands take the sword and hot lips kiss your naked spine, your stomach, your mouth.

A cheer echoes off the stone walls— "Welcome your new brother! Huzzah!"

You reach up and remove your blind-fold. You are in a circular chamber. The marble floor bears an image of a compass and a cross. Candles flicker atop several small tables. Despite the damp air, the room feels inviting, almost cheerful.

Someone hands you a white robe and you slip it on. A skull is passed to you, filled with something dense. Red.

Blood? You take a sip. No, wine. You drain the skull and are given another.

You smile and your shoulders relax. You are an initiate. A fully fledged brother. It wasn't so difficult, in the end.

At least, this is what you are thinking right up until you are handed a dagger and shoved down a tunnel leading off from the base of the well. . . .

▶ *The intensely Gothic Regaleira Palace features five floors, gargoyles, and an octagonal tower.*

The Initiation Well at the Quinta da Regaleira is an eighty-eight-foot-deep stone pit of mystery. It has never held water, never quenched the thirst of a single soul. Rather, it is a ritualistic enigma involving a secret society with roots in alchemy, the Freemasons, tarot, the Knights Templar, and the Rosicrucians.

António Augusto de Carvalho Monteiro, nicknamed Monteiro the Millionaire, was a successful Brazilian businessman who lived from 1848 to 1920. His interests were broad, ranging from entomology to secret societies and mysticism. Born into a wealthy family in Rio de Janeiro, he sold coffee and gems to increase his already healthy fortune. Eventually he moved to Portugal, received a law degree, and earned a reputation as an eccentric.

In 1904, Monteiro hired Italian architect Luigi Manini to help him build a magnificent quinta (estate) near the city of Sintra. Never one to hold back, Monteiro desired the grand palace at Quinta da Regaleira to include several architectural styles, including Renaissance, Roman, and the lavish Portuguese late Gothic, known as Manueline.*

The result was surprisingly harmonious, and the palace seems to have sprung straight from the pages of a dark, enchanting fairy tale. It boasts five floors, an octagonal tower, a "floating library" with a mirrored floor, turrets, and an ornate facade, complete with gargoyles.

Quinta da Regaleira's Roman Catholic chapel, with its exquisite stained glass windows and frescoes, is also worthy of a storybook. Of particular note is a large red Order of the Christ Cross (the symbol of the Knights Templar) picked out in mosaic on its floor, along with several pentagrams.

The magnificent grounds surrounding the palace are no less mysterious. The park brims with swampy grottoes, statues, elaborate

* This was a wild, uniquely Portuguese version of the Gothic style, characterized by swirling traceries of stone foliage, pillars twisted like lengths of rope, maritime elements such as shells and pearls, and a somewhat lackadaisical approach to symmetry.

stone benches, caves, ponds, and fountains. A system of tunnels weaves underground throughout the estate as well, labyrinthine passageways with many entrances that connect various features, like the chapel and two Initiation Wells.

While the smaller is merely a simple staircase connecting circular floors (it's known as the Poco Imperfeito, or Unfinished Well), the main Initiation Well, Poco Iniciatico, might be the most intriguing and ominous of all the quinta's structures. It has been described as a tower built in reverse, with spiral stairs leading downward, ending in a floor featuring the Masonic compass overlaid on a Knight's Templar cross.

The spiral staircase, with its carved columns, has twenty-two niches and nine landings, each separated by fifteen steps. The significance of the nine landings and the number of steps is widely debated. Most believe they link to various mystical aspects of the Freemasons, tarot, and the Knights Templar. (For example, the number nine possibly symbolizes the nine founders of the Templar order, while the number fifteen is, according to Masonic tradition, the sacred

▼ *A rather ominous depiction of an assembly of Freemasons for the initiation of a master, 1733.*

numeral representing God.) Others claim the number of landings is a reference to the nine circles of hell in Dante's *Divine Comedy*, while those with a metaphorical bent assert that a walk down the dark spiraling staircase is meant to represent a journey into the earth and a return to Mother Nature's womb.

The bottom of the well contains a baptismal font and two tunnels that lead to other parts of the estate—one to the Waterfall Lake, with its dainty stepping-stones, and one to the Poco Imperfeito.

No one knows what Monteiro did in his Initiation Well. No documentation exists on its purpose, beyond its name and the symbols on its floor. But if Monteiro had been engaging in mystical initiation rituals, then the hidden passages were perhaps a way for other members to come and go without being seen by the palace staff. This would be particularly important if the men's robes were splattered with the blood of a freshly slaughtered lamb. (The secretive nature of these rituals tends to lead one to wild speculation.)

Need a secret society refresher to help appreciate Quinta da Regaleira's arcane symbolism?

Knights Templar

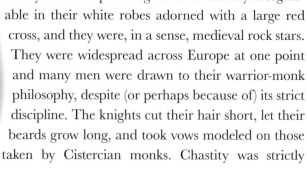

The Knights Templar, also known as Temple of Solomon, was a military religious order of knights founded during the Crusades in the twelfth century. The Templar knights were instantly recognizable in their white robes adorned with a large red cross, and they were, in a sense, medieval rock stars. They were widespread across Europe at one point and many men were drawn to their warrior-monk philosophy, despite (or perhaps because of) its strict discipline. The knights cut their hair short, let their beards grow long, and took vows modeled on those taken by Cistercian monks. Chastity was strictly enforced and the knights were not permitted to kiss another human being, not even their mothers.

The Templar vows had two notable monastic exceptions: Fighting was permissible (and encouraged) and all ceremonies were rigidly kept secret. (This secrecy later led to their downfall, as rumors about their order were hard to disprove.)

The Templars believed it was their duty to protect Christians visiting the Holy Land and to fight in the Crusades. Aristocrats throughout Europe donated land and gold to fund the Holy War that the Templars waged in Jerusalem. In fact, so much coin flowed through their ranks that they were forced to devise a system of accounting—one that later became the foundation for current-day banking.

The Grand Master of the Knights Templar ruled from Jerusalem, obeyed none but the pope, and had inconceivable power. Naturally, the Templars' extraordinary wealth and influence eventually also brought jealousy and enmity. They were blamed for the later failures of the Crusades, and the knights were falsely accused of blasphemy, depravity, and worshipping false gods (and cats—King Philip IV of France charged the Templars with idol worship involving a a cat). It was said they used an ointment concocted from murdered babies and practiced ritual magic.

The allegations didn't stop there; their accusers claimed that at the secret Templar initiation ceremonies new members spat on the crucifix and then kissed one another on the mouth, spine, and belly button.

These outlandish claims were made by the Templars' enemies (witches, heretics, and political dissidents received similar accusations). On Friday, October 13, 1307, King Philip IV ordered the arrest of all Templars in France and the seizing of their property. (This specific date later fueled an urban legend claiming this event was the origin for Friday the thirteenth superstitions.) Pope Clement V ordered the suppression of the order in 1312 and confiscated the knights' wealth and property throughout Europe.

A group of the Knights Templar who had moved to Tomar, Portugal, in 1122 fared somewhat better. The King of Portugal did not believe the allegations, and offered the knights protection. He changed their name to the Order of Christ, and demanded they take vows of poverty and chastity, thus helping them escape the worst of the Templar persecution. If any of the Templars managed to secretly hold onto their wealth, they were likely part of this Portuguese branch.

Numerous conspiracy theories exist about the Knights Templar. The most well known is the one exploited by Dan Brown in his best-selling *The Da Vinci Code*—that the Knights Templar were secretly dedicated to protecting the bloodline of Christ. Another is featured in the Nicholas Cage film *National Treasure*, which purports that the Knights Templar hid a vast treasure somewhere in America.

The Knights Templar also play a large part in the popular *Assassin's Creed* video game franchise, which features a fictional thousand-year feud between a secret brotherhood of assassins and Templar knights.

Indeed, the Templar reach is long. The Temple district in London is so named because the area was once a Templar strong-hold. The surname Templeman was originally given to a person who lived on a Templar property. And the temperance movement took this name in honor of these knights, who supposedly drank sour milk instead of alcohol. The Templars are still invoked in books and film to instantly create a sense of dangerous zealotry, ancient secrets, powerful wealth, or noble causes.

Perhaps Monteiro had ancestral connections to these Templars and chose to continue their legacy of secret rituals at his estate. Perhaps he buried ancient Templar treasure somewhere on his prop-erty. In the final scenes of *Indiana Jones and the Last Crusade*, a 700-year-old Templar knight guards the ultimate treasure, the Holy Grail. One wonders what might be under the red-tipped cross at the bottom of the Initiation Well, or beneath the second cross on the floor of the chapel. A secret tunnel leading to a Templar burial site?

Rosicrucians

Not to be confused with the Illuminati, another mysterious sect, the Rosicrucians are a tricky lot, hard to pin down. Are they a religion? A brotherhood? A cult? A secret society? According to Rosicrucian legend, the order was founded in 1403 by Christian Rosenkreuz, who is likely fictional. The order's name comes from their signet, which is a rose superimposed on a cross. Their beliefs are broad, encompassing alchemy, Jewish mysticism, occultism, gnosticism, and Hermeticism (based on revelations from the Egyptian god Thoth).

The Rosicrucians claim to possess ancient wisdom, which is just vague enough to be wildly interesting. Popular lore about the Rosicrucians include: the current members secretly govern Europe, they can turn lead into gold, they created the roots of Freemasonry, their founder was a magician and an alchemist, and the original brotherhood never actually existed and the early Rosicrucians texts were a medieval hoax. The popularity of the Rosicrucians has ebbed and flowed, following cultural trends. When alchemy was fashionable in sixteenth-century Europe, the Rosy Cross brotherhood flourished. Their star faded a bit during the logical days of the Enlightenment in the eighteenth century but revived during the occult movement in the nineteenth century, eventually spawning many offshoot brotherhoods, including the Hermetic Order of the Golden Dawn in 1887. Known as a "magical society," the Hermetic Order of the Golden Dawn is believed to have had a profound impact on twentieth-century occultism, as well as Wicca and Thelema (a new religion founded by Aleister Crowley, see page 161). Certain ancient Rosicrucian rituals are also said to survive among the Freemasons—the Golden Dawn was not Masonic but its members were often devoted Freemasons.

Both men and women are allowed to join the modern-day Rosicrucian society, which currently claims to trace "its roots in the mystery traditions, philosophy, and myths of ancient Egypt dating back to approximately 1500 BCE." Today, its members "are a community of philosophers who study and practice the Natural Laws governing the universe." Vague. So very vague.

Freemasons

Freemasons hold the dubious honor of being one of the world's most famous secret societies. They've been accused of covering up murders, of being a cult, controlling the government, having ties to the Knights Templar and a Templar treasure, of starting the American Revolution, embedding countless Masonic symbols and codes into the streets of Washington, DC, of forcing members to drink wine from a skull while performing secret handshakes, the list goes on.

If you are a man, can prove you have good character, and believe in a "Supreme Being," you can approach a Masonic temple and request to join.

One of the oldest and largest international brotherhoods in existence (the first Grand Lodge was established in London in 1717), the Freemasons describe themselves as a charitable society and social organization. The roots of Freemasonry date back to a guild of medieval stonemasons who built many of the cathedrals and castles of Europe. Eventually the guild became a community of men from all professions, meeting in secret, discussing god knows what, and performing mysterious rituals. It didn't take long for conspiracy theories to bloom.

If you are a man, can prove you have good character, and believe in a "Supreme Being," you can approach a Masonic temple and request to join. A few notable Freemasons include: Napoleon Bonaparte, Wolfgang Amadeus Mozart, Ludwig van Beethoven, George Washington (and thirteen subsequent American presidents),

Harry Houdini, Winston Churchill, Mark Twain, Oscar Wilde, and John Wayne. Despite this illustrious list, the Catholic Church forbid Catholics from becoming members in 1738, threatening automatic excommunication. This has been modified since Vatican II in 1983—membership is still prohibited, but instead of being excommunicated, Catholics who join the Masons may not receive Holy Communion, as they are viewed as being in a state of grave sin.

There are about one and a half million Freemasons in the United States, which is around a quarter of the membership it held in this country in the late 1950s . . . and why so many Masonic temples in small American towns appear unused, repurposed, or abandoned.

According to rumor, initiation rituals involve blindfolds, half-naked men baring their chests to prove they are not women, and ancient stone-working tools such as an apron, a square and compass, and a trowel. The most common symbol of the Freemasons is a compass depicting a 90-degree right angle, with the letter "G" in the center. One can find this image carved onto any number of gravestones in nearly every cemetery in America. It is a symbol of the Freemasons' stone-working roots, though what the letter "G" represents is widely debated. (God? Geometry?)

The all-seeing eye is another Masonic motif (and its inclusion on the dollar bill has sparked endless conspiracies). But while this image has been around since antiquity (it is based on the Egyptian Eye of Horus), it started appearing in Masonic literature around the mid-1700s. The ceiling of Monteiro's church has an all-seeing eye carved into a pyramid shape, overlaid on a Templar cross.

The pentagram is also a common Freemason design and it too has ancient roots. (It wasn't until the nineteenth century that the pentagram began to be connected to the occult.) The pentagrams on Monteiro's chapel floor and the one on the door to the basement are undoubtedly a nod to the millionaire's Masonic ties.

The god Dionysus is often connected to the Freemasons and pops up in various forms in Quinta da Regaleira, from marble statues to murals. The cult of Dionysus was an ancient Greek society that worshipped the Dionysian Mysteries—a ritual where participants used intoxicants, music, and dance to free inhibitions and return to a "natural state." One can easily picture Masonic initiates being blindfolded and led down the steps of the Initiation Well, given copious amounts of wine, and encouraged to free themselves through dance alongside their fellow brothers.

The Tarot

Tarot originated in Italy, the first decks appearing between 1440 and 1450. And while tarot mysticism may seem the odd man out in this secret society mix, it has ties to Freemasonry. Antoine Court de Gébelin, born in 1725, was a pastor in southern France and a Freemason (his lodge brother was none other than Benjamin Franklin). While his writings mainly focused on Masonic-themed civilizations, de Gébelin published an essay on tarot around 1781, in which he maintained that the images represented on the cards were a distillation of the secrets of the Egyptians as put forth in the ancient *Book of Thoth*. This had entirely no basis in fact. Nevertheless, the article was hugely popular and many believe the first use of tarot decks for cartomancy (fortune-telling) can be traced directly back to this essay.

If you were to go looking for tarot symbolism at Quinta da Regaleira, you would find it at the Initiation Well, which seems to be a clear representation of the much-maligned Tower card.

A tarot deck consists of four suits (wands, pentacles, cups, and swords) plus twenty-one additional illustrated cards—known as the major arcana—as well as a card numbered zero, titled The Fool.

The major arcana includes medieval archetypes, as well as depictions symbolizing death, destruction, karma, spirituality, dreams, nightmares, sex, love, hope, free will, etc. Tarot cards were first used as divinatory devices in France in the early 1780s, the most popular deck being the Tarot de Marseille, which was based on the original Italian deck and is still in print today. It was controversial at the time for its depiction of La Papesse—a female pope—possibly based on the legend of Pope Joan. (Pope Joan was a woman who disguised herself as a man and supposedly served as pope for a number of years in the Middle Ages, her gender only being discovered when she gave birth. Most scholars believe this story to be untrue, and modern-day tarot decks generally title this card The High Priestess.)

Many images in the Marseille deck are considered to have Hermetic elements, including alchemy and astrology, and the deck would later become a basis for the bestselling Rider-Waite deck that later replaced it in popularity. (Aleister Crowley, see page 161, designed his own set of tarot cards—known as the Thoth deck—that wasn't published until 1969, years after his death.)

A September 18, 1919, edition of the *Washington Times* announced that fortune-telling had become a fad in England, stating that: "Amateur fortune telling is obtaining an increasing vogue at afternoon tea and evening parties in England." The paper advised readers that if they "wish to convince completely the half credulous . . . [he or she] will have a pack of Tarot cards, mystic, picturesque, and wonderful, employed by golden-faced necromancers in old Egypt."

THE TOWER.

Alas, aspiring tarot readers are warned against charging for these readings, for while using tarot cards will make someone popular, "She is not a professional. She does her soothsaying to please herself and other guests." Tarot reading has seemingly never gone out of fashion since it swept through British tea parties in the early twentieth century and then experienced another surge in popularity during the COVID-19 pandemic. There are now hundreds of decks to choose from, with illustrations featuring everything from *Alice's Adventures in Wonderland*, art nouveau, ancient Egypt, angels, *Game of Thrones*, tattoo art, the Day of the Dead, manga, cats, and crows. There is even a deck highlighting Masonic symbolism.

If you were to go looking for tarot symbolism at Quinta da Regaleira, you would find it at the Initiation Well, which seems to be a clear representation of the much-maligned Tower card. It is often interpreted to mean danger, crisis, sudden change, but also liberation—all of which might apply to the search for immortality and enlightenment at the heart of so many secret societies. Also, the twenty-two niches in the Initiation Well could represent the twenty-two major arcana cards.

It's entirely possible that António Monteiro lit candles and sat with his Freemason friends on the floor of the Initiation Well, burning palo santo and gravely pulling cards from the Tarot de Marseille. But such things are hard to prove. More likely he was a rabid admirer of absolutely everything esoteric and had his estate built to feature every single one.

Perhaps Monteiro was a Grand Master Freemason, and his estate held a secret Templar treasure. Perhaps he hosted shadowy initiation rites that involved drinking wine from skulls and nude dancing. Perhaps his ancestors were part of the Portuguese branch of the Templar knights, and Monteiro was privy to secrets that had been kept since the order was disbanded in 1312.

One can hope. But why all the secrecy, Monteiro? Was he really hiding something deeply shocking and taboo on his estate? Or was he just echoing the secret societies of which he was such a fan? It's hard to say if these brotherhoods of knights and Masons genuinely hid terrible secrets, or if their mysterious practices were part of their appeal. It hurt the Knights Templar, in the end, and allowed unfounded rumors about their rituals to spread like wildfire. But modern-day Freemason initiates have asserted that their interest in the society was partly fueled by the enigma surrounding the ceremonies.

The key to the front door of Monteiro's Quinta da Regaleira's palace allegedly also opens the door of his Lisbon tomb, which lies in the Prazeres Cemetery, in western Lisbon, and is a Masonic temple in miniature, facing east. The tomb is carved with more motifs: bread and wine symbolizing body and spirit, owls representing wisdom, bees for industriousness, and poppies for eternal sleep. In the years since his death, perhaps someone has used this palace key to open Monteiro's tomb and take note of its contents. But if so, they are keeping it a secret. For now, Monteiro has taken his mysteries to the grave. ◈

▶ Monteiro's symbolism-laced tomb in Lisbon's Prazeres Cemetery.

ADULT FAIRY TALES

Poring over images of the Quinta da Regaleira, you may find your-self reminded of the dark, teeming world of Guillermo del Toro's post–Spanish Civil War fairy tale, *Pan's Labyrinth*. Moss, twisted creatures, secret passageways, lichen-laced stairs spiraling down into the earth, it's all there. While the movie was filmed in the Guadarrama mountain range, a six-hour drive from Sintra, del Toro confirmed on social media that he was indeed inspired by the estate's mysterious atmosphere and used its inverted tower in the design of his opening shots. In the film, the well's staircase leads to a shadowy, underground paradise "where there are no lies or pain."

Roman Polanski's film about rare book dealing and the occult, *The Ninth Gate*, was also filmed largely in Sintra.

THE GARDEN OF MONSTERS
VITERBO · ITALY

Fifty-seven miles north of Rome lies a monstrous garden, forgotten for hundreds of years. Stone demons, nymphs, and dragons rise from the vegetation, moss-covered and eroded by centuries of rain and neglect. It is called the Sacred Grove (Sacro Bosco) and was built in the 1600s by a mercenary and nobleman named Pier Francesco Orsini after the death of his beloved wife. Grief-stricken, Orsini had a wild garden planted and ordered the vicious beasts carved from the bedrock of the hillside. The garden is at first glance deliberately chaotic, a rebuke of the carefully trimmed gardens that were fashionable during the Renaissance. Its many strange features include obelisks, Latin quotes carved into plinths, and a tilting, "twisted" house, which is particularly disorienting to enter and only allows you to regain your bearings when you look from its unglazed windows at the sky and the world outside.

Wander deeper into the garden and you will encounter a stone tortoise, sirens, and a statue of Cerberus, the two-headed guardian of

▶ *The inscription above this doorway translates to: "Every thought flies," providing insight into the tongue-shaped stone altar that lies inside.*

the underworld. At the top of its winding paths stands the eight-sided Temple of Eternity, dedicated to Orsini's wife.

Much like the newer gardens at the Quinta da Regaleira, the sacred grove hides arcane symbolism galore. Had Monteiro stumbled upon this forgotten garden during his travels? It is unlikely. The garden languished in a state of overgrown oblivion until it was rediscovered in the 1950s. But perhaps Monteiro had the necessary connections to know of it. Certainly in the latter part of the 1900s the garden inspired many, including Salvador Dalí and Niki de Saint Phalle, who later created her own bizarre Tarot Garden full of tentacled trees and massive, glistening mosaic serpents.

While Orsini's garden is purposefully mystifying and difficult to interpret, there is a pattern. Much of it is carefully arranged to be "read," a sort of book in garden form, its paths and sculptures inspired by poets both famous and obscure, from Dante and Petrarch to the little-known Francesco Colonna and his hallucinogenic *Hypnerotomachia Poliphili*, a medieval forebear of *Alice's Adventures in Wonderland*. Written in 1499, it tells of a man who, in search of his lost lover, wanders a frightening wood, falls asleep, dreams of strange beasts, wolves, and nymphs, sinks into a deeper layer of dreaming, and eventually arrives in a perfect garden, strewn with odd monuments and ruined temples. There, he is reunited with his lover, only for her to vanish as soon as he embraces her. In one of the earliest it-was-all-a-dream endings, the main character wakes up to find that his travels, accomplishments, and victories were figments of his imagination.

MASONIC CAVES FILLED WITH OTTOMAN GOLD

JERUSALEM

Zedekiah's Cave, under the Muslim quarter of Old City Jerusalem, is a five-acre limestone quarry brimming with legends. According to lore, King Zedekiah used the cave to flee Jerusalem on his way to Jericho. There, he was captured by King Nebuchadnezzar of Babylon and had his eyes plucked out after watching Nebuchadnezzar slaughter his sons. Drops of water that trickle into the cave are called "Zedekiah's Tears."

The cave is also known as Solomon's Quarries and many believe that King Solomon used stones from this man-made cave to build the First Temple.

Suleiman the Magnificent—the longest reigning sultan of the Ottoman Empire—sealed the quarry in the sixteenth century to keep out invaders and it wasn't reopened until 1854, when an American missionary discovered it with the help of his dog. Soon afterward, a group of Freemasons held their first ceremony in the quarry. King Solomon is said to have been the first Grand Master Freemason and the group felt a strong connection to the location. Israeli Freemasons still hold a ceremony in the cave each year.

Perhaps the most exciting legend of Zedekiah's Cave is that somewhere within lay buried three ancient Ottoman trunks of gold, still waiting to be discovered.

YALE SECRET SOCIETIES

NEW HAVEN · CONNECTICUT

Most people have heard of the Skull and Bones senior society at Yale. It was founded in 1832 by William Huntington Russell and Alfonso Taft, father of President William H. Taft. It has powerful alumni and is also known, ominously, as the Brotherhood of Death. The internet teems with conspiracy theories about its hypermysterious rituals, its hunger for world domination, its ties to the Illuminati and the CIA. But Skull and Bones is not the only secret society at Yale. There are several: Scroll and Key, Spade and Grave, Wolf's Head, Book and Snake, Berzelius—these are just a few of the recognized clubs. It's likely that there are also many underground societies that have not been officially accepted or identified.

Each of the secret societies at Yale gathers in soundproof clubhouses located around New Haven, all with walls so thick and a presence so foreboding that they have come to be known as "tombs."

According to David Alan Richards, author of *Skull and Keys: The Hidden History of Yale Secret Societies*, the first wing of the Skull and Bones tomb was built in 1856, with an ancient Egyptian theme. The other societies soon followed suit, each bringing their own architectural preferences. Scroll and Key hired Richard Morris Hunt to design their tomb—Hunt had designed the Biltmore House for the Vanderbilts (see page 218). Hunt's tomb featured a heavy Moorish revival design. Book and Snake built their clubhouse as a Greek Temple, as did Berzelius, but Wolf's Head went in a different direction: Dutch Ratskeller. The Manuscript Society, which claims both Jodie Foster and Anderson Cooper as members, was focused more on artists and built its tomb in a humble modernist style, barely noticeable with its simple white brick walls. The front of the building has no doors or windows. Its only decoration is a faint circle worked into the bricks, which could symbolize omega, the full moon, the sun, a saint's halo, the Round Table, or alchemical gold, i.e., a state of perfection.

What lies inside these tombs is anyone's guess. Someone did manage to break into the Skull and Bones tomb in 1876 and the thief later published a description of its floor plan—meeting rooms, a kitchen, a library. Fairly sedate stuff. Perhaps the thief missed the secret passageway that led to the marble chamber with the sinister, bloodstained slab holding the bound, writhing, sacrificial victim.

◄ *The ivy-covered tomb for the Brotherhood of Death, 1879.*

10

The Gateway to Hell

PARIS · FRANCE

You dodge the gendarmes, the heels of your waterproof boots hitting the cobblestones with a hard *clack-clack*. You aim for the abandoned stairway in the old train tunnel.

Two of your experienced cataphile friends were supposed to join you on this expedition, but they never appeared, so you are on your own today. And perhaps this is better. You will be able to prowl the bone-deep silence of the ossuary without their chatter. You will be able to shake hands with your own mortality and then laugh in its face.

You drop down into the secret opening and the gruesome darkness hits you like a slap.

◄ *The bones of six million Parisians fill 200 miles of tunnels in the Catacombs of Paris, France.*

You flip on your flashlight and begin to worm your way through Paris's clammy intestines.

You wade through inky, knee-deep water and ruminate on why you keep coming back to the bones. Why do they pervade your dreams?

You breathe in the humid air, which smells of coffins, oozing mud, and wet stone. You stumble upon the remains of burnt red candles and other rubbish—a small black cauldron and a few glass vials filled with unknown liquids. You spy a pentagram drawn in chalk.

You see a smattering of graffiti, the most haunting being a Herman Melville quote, written in blood-red paint: "To the last, I grapple with thee; From Hell's heart, I stab at thee; For hate's sake, I spit my last breath at thee."

You suddenly wish for your friends' chatter, yearn for it. Their cheerful tones would cut through the dense, endless silence.

Your legs are dripping wet. You sit down near a pile of brittle-looking femurs and shiver.

"They tried to hide hell by shoving it underneath this city," you think, "but these bones cry out in anger."

You can hear their screams, the shrieking of the bones. You put your hands to your ears, but it doesn't block out the sound.

The bones miss the soil, they miss having their own six feet of dirt, they miss the nobility of being whole, instead of stacked among other scattered pieces of skeletons to form geometric designs that are pleasing to the living human eye, but horrific to the dead.

You know you are lost.

Your flashlight dies. You pound the base on your palm and it flickers to life for a few more minutes.

The rescue team will come and the dogs will sniff you out. But it could be days.

Days of hunger and cold and darkness.

Days of howling, shrieking, seething bones.

From Dante's *Inferno*, to Auguste Rodin's massive sculpture *The Gates of Hell*, to modern-day cataphiles burrowing through off-limits underground crypts, to the endless string of Hollywood films featuring "hell portals," our fascination with the underworld persists.

Why are people now drawn to the idea of a hellish gateway? What is at the root of this endless allure, the ancient attraction of all things sunken, buried, subterranean?

In his book *Underland: A Deep Time Journey*, Robert Macfarlane writes that "to understand light you need first to have been buried in the deep-down dark." Macfarlane attempts to unlock our yearning toward the underworld by descending into caves, shafts, burial chambers, and glaciers. He battles claustrophobia as he slithers through crevices and squeezes into tight passages, all in an effort to discover the eternal charm of what lurks beneath.

"HALT! HERE LIES THE EMPIRE OF DEATH," reads the ominous inscription at the doorway to Les Catacombes de Paris. The bones of six million Parisians lie under the city in these tunnels of the dead. Despite this, and the ghastly epitaph, the catacombs are one of France's most popular tourist attractions, drawing in half a million people a year to view the artfully arranged skulls and femurs. Tourists are permitted to wander just a small fraction of the approximately 200 miles of tunnels, but this eighteenth-century Parisian boneyard is notorious for its "cataphiles"—urban explorers who illegally sneak into the pitch-black caverns through off-grid openings, occasionally resulting in rescue teams being sent in to recover lost risk-takers.

"Parisians do not ask to see the catacombs. But tourists run to them in crowds." So states a French underground inspector in a 1922 article in the *New York Herald* about the ossuary—proof that the popularity of these caverns dates back at least a hundred years. "That bone pit is a disgrace to Paris," states another Parisian. "Why do they all come sightseeing into the bowels of the earth? What do they expect to find?"

Twenty-nine miles north of Prague, in an isolated forest, the well-preserved Houska Castle perches in all its Gothic glory atop a steep cliff. Built by King Otakar II of Bohemia in the latter half of the thirteenth century and currently owned by the heirs to the Škoda Works fortune, its vaulted halls boast murals featuring demons and strange animal/human hybrids, dozens of taxidermied rams' heads, and a green chamber painted with faded scenes of hunts and twisting vines. But these are not what attract the curious visitors who come poking about with cameras and drones. That would be the castle's gateway to hell.

⚷ **The chapel was supposedly erected to prevent demons from spilling into the human realm, and to protect us from whatever lurks in the deep.**

Houska's chapel was built over a large sulfurous hole that was believed to be so deep it led all the way to the underworld. The chapel was supposedly erected to prevent demons from spilling into the human realm, and to protect us from whatever lurks in the deep. In what will prove to be a common practice throughout this section, Otakar II thought he could hide hell by throwing a church on top of it, hoping it would keep out all the terrors of the unknown. According to Houska lore, when the castle was being built, convicts at the local prison were offered pardons if they would volunteer to tie a rope around their waist and let themselves be lowered into the hole. Down, down, down they would go, until they reached the border of hell, wherein they would be pulled back to the surface so they could give a report of what they'd witnessed in the netherworld. When the first prisoner was lowered into the hole, his screams brought the other prisoners to their knees in terror. When he was again pulled back to the surface, he looked like he had aged thirty years and his hair had turned white.

▶ *The Gothic Houska Castle looms menacingly over the surrounding landscape, Blatce, Czech Republic.*

And then there are the rumors about the Nazis. Houska Castle was occupied by the Wehrmacht (the unified armed forces of Nazi Germany) during World War II. While there, the Nazis purportedly experimented with the occult. Locals assert that the Germans used the power emanating from Houska's hellish gateway to aid in their studies, though what they achieved remains a mystery.

The Houska gateway legend has slowly begun to creep into the public consciousness and the speculation that the castle was built to cover a portal to hell is a good hook for travel shows and graphic novels. What was once an element of terror has now become a draw for tourists and Houska sees its fair share every year.

A certain Irish portal to hell is believed to be the root of modern-day Halloween. The Celtic celebration of Samhain is a time when the dead walk the Earth, when evil spirits, gods, and demons break free from hell for a night and cause diabolical mischief. And where was one of the largest Samhain celebrations held? Rathcroghan.

Rathcroghan translates to "fort of Cruachan." It is approximately 5,500 years old and is referenced in many early medieval manuscripts, such as *Lebor na h-Uidre*, also known as *The Book of the Dun Cow*, a twelfth-century tome containing, among other things, purported visions of heaven and hell. Rathcroghan was also the seat of Medb (Maeve), a Connacht queen who might have been the inspiration for Shakespeare's fairy queen Mab. Her stronghold was famous for its great medieval fairs and for having one of Ireland's three great cemeteries.

It was also famous for its portal to a nether realm.

Legend states that the narrow, 120-foot-long limestone cave in Rathcroghan leads to the Celtic Otherworld. The Irish believed that this portal opened on Halloween (Samhain) every year, as the veils between the worlds grew thin, allowing dead souls to reenter the mortal realm. Along with dead souls, the hell cave also had a habit of leaking monsters from the deep, such as a triple-headed beast called

Ellen Trechen, flocks of poisonous red birds, a herd of demonic pigs, and broomstick-clutching witches.

Irish pagans were advised to dress as ghouls or demons during Samhain festivals to trick the witches and evil spirits, for fear that innocent humans would be dragged down into the Otherworld. People carved faces in turnips or beets and lit them with candles to scare away these hellish monsters, and carried treats in their pockets to bribe them, if necessary.

Some Irish immigrants brought these ancient Celtic rituals to the United States in the 1800s and Rathcroghan, with its underworld gateway, became the origin of every costumed reveler taking to the streets on October 31 for trick-or-treating.

Other underworld gateways across the globe include:

Sibyl's Cave

MONTE DI CUMA · NAPLES · ITALY

A fabled entrance to Hades—the ancient Greek underworld—lurks in Sibyl's Cave near Naples in Cumae. (Cumae was the first Greek colony on the mainland of Italy.) In *The Aeneid* (19 BCE) Virgil described this cave as a place where:

> *The gates of hell are open night and day*
> *Smooth the descent, and easy is the way:*
> *But to return, and view the cheerful skies,*
> *In this the task and mighty labor lies.*

According to *The Aeneid*, the Cumaean Sibyl was an oracle who prophesied from the confines of this cave and served as a guide to Hades. Sibyl wrote her prophecies on oak leaves and, many centuries later, the author Mary Shelley penned an introduction to her novel *The Last Man*, in which she claimed that she discovered prophetic writings on leaves in Sibyl's Cave. According to Shelley, she used these "prophecies" to write her dystopian novel about a man living at the end of the twenty-first century, 250 years after her own death.

> *At length my friend, who had taken up some of the leaves strewed about, exclaimed, "This is the Sibyl's cave; these are Sibylline leaves." On examination, we found that all the leaves, bark, and other substances were traced with written characters. What appeared to us more astonishing, was that these writings were expressed in various languages: some unknown to my companion, ancient Chaldee, and Egyptian hieroglyphics, old as the Pyramids. Stranger still, some were in modern dialects, English and Italian. We could make out little by the dim light, but they seemed to contain prophecies, detailed relations of events but lately passed; names, now well known, but of modern date; and often exclamations of exultation or woe, of victory or defeat, were traced on their thin scant pages. This was certainly the Sibyl's Cave.*

Fengdu Ghost City

CHONGQING · CHINA

Fengdu, called "The City of Ghosts," sits on the banks of the Yangtze River and is renowned for its statues of ghosts and demons, as well as its monasteries, shrines, and temples devoted to the afterlife. In fact, all the architecture in Fengdu relates to the underworld and hell. The site itself is 2,000 years old and mentioned in classic Chinese literature.

"The Ghost King" is the name of a giant face on a hill in Fengdu. At 138 meters (453 feet) tall, it holds the Guinness World Record for the largest sculpture carved on a rock.

According to legend, the dead must pass three tests in Fengdu before moving into the next life. The first is to cross the "Bridge of Helplessness" in less than nine steps. The second, to laugh before a statue of the King of Hell in order to frighten away his demons. And finally, balance on one foot on a rounded stone for three minutes. Apparently, only the virtuous can manage this last feat.

Boca do Inferno

CASCAIS • PORTUGAL

The Boca do Inferno chasm (translation: Hell's Mouth), near the town of Cascais, Portugal, was originally a sea-cave. When it collapsed, it left a chasm and a sea-arch. During storms, the waves crash so violently against this arch that the water shoots volcanically upward, giving some viewers a sensation of being at the mouth of hell.

The Boca do Inferno is notorious as the place where Aleister Crowley faked his death in 1930 (see Twelve Kings and Dukes of Hell, page 161). With the help of a poet friend, Crowley pretended to have jumped into its churning waves, either as a publicity stunt or to annoy his mistress. His friend released his steamy suicide note to the press: "Can't live without you. The other mouth of hell that will catch me won't be as hot as yours." Three weeks later Crowley turned up at a gallery in Berlin for an exhibition of his works. Cocky.

Pluto's Gate

DENIZLI MERKEZ • TURKEY

Pluto's Gate, also known as Ploutonion, was an ancient temple built in 190 BCE with a passage that was said to lead to the underworld. This hell portal is actually a small cave that emits lethal carbon monoxide. Because of these deadly vapors, ancient Greeks believed the cave belonged to Pluto, god of the underworld. Temple priests used to lead cows into the cave during religious rituals and then dramatically retrieve their corpses a few minutes later, after they perished in the fumes. (Cows would die more quickly than humans, as their noses were closer to the ground, where the heavy gas collected.)

The temple was destroyed by Christians (and possibly a series of earthquakes) in the sixth century, but in 2013 the ruins of Pluto's Gate were rediscovered. Francesco D'Andria, professor of classic archaeology at the University of Salento, said he found the site by "reconstructing the route of a thermal spring," which originates in the cave. D'Andria attested to the gate's poisonous gases, still present today: "We could see the cave's lethal properties during the excavation. Several birds died as they tried to get close to the warm opening, instantly killed by the carbon dioxide fumes."

Actun Tunichil Muknal

SAN IGNACIO • BELIZE

Actun Tunichil Muknal is also known as the "Cave of the Stone Sepulcher" (which sounds like the title of the next Indiana Jones film). At the far back of the cavern, more than a mile past the entrance, sits the thousand-year-old remains of sacrificial victims. The ages of the skeletons vary from infants to adults. All were killed brutally. The most famous victim is known as the Crystal Maiden; her bones having calcified, they now have a sparkling, "crystal" effect.

While some experts believe these ancient victims were slain by the Maya for being witches, many others think they were ritualistic sacrifices to the Maya gods of the underworld, and the locals call this cave Xibalba, or underworld.

▶ *The Crystal Maiden*

Hekla, the Mountain of Hell

ICELAND

One of Iceland's most active volcanoes, Hekla, is noted both for its eruptions and the folklore that surround it. *Hekla* means "hooded" or "short-hooded cloak" and may refer to the clouds that hover around it or the snow that wreaths it when it is sleeping. After Hekla erupted in 1104, rumors spread across Europe that the volcano was a gateway to hell. The Cistercian monk Herbert of Clairvaux wrote of it, "The renowned fiery cauldron of Sicily, which men call Hell's chimney . . . that cauldron is affirmed to be like a small furnace compared to this enormous inferno."

Icelanders claim that witches dance on the volcano during the pagan holiday of Beltane (a celebration that traditionally begins on

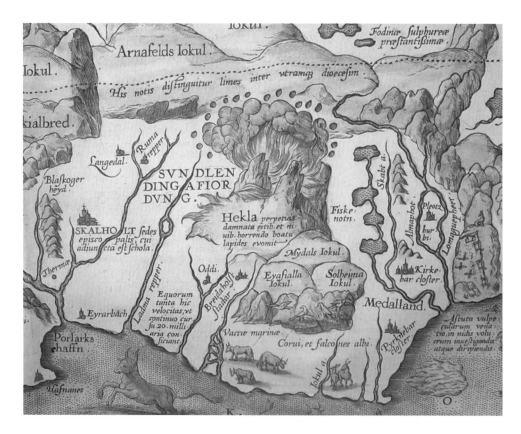

the evening of May 1 and heralds the return of summer—revelries often include a giant bonfire).

Macfarlane asserted in his book that he wanted to have the hell literally scared out of him. He wanted to go somewhere hidden, somewhere foreboding, perhaps even mythological. Once you have seen hell, wormed under the surface of the great unknown, or gone into the dark woods and lived to tell of it, can you truly fear it? Many humans have craved this catharsis, for nearly every culture has created an underworld and spent vast portions of their literature and art describing it, or ritualizing it, or imagining places through which it might be reached. There are legendary caves, volcanoes, and bottomless pits in almost every corner of the globe—places that traditional folklore claims are opening to nether realms, as if the earth is just a pincushion laid over hell, with entrances every few miles. ◈

TWELVE KINGS AND DUKES OF HELL

Once upon a time, near Loch Ness in Scotland, there sat a manor called Boleskine House. It was a very, very cursed house indeed.

Some of the folklore that surrounds Boleskine includes tales of how it was built on the ruins of a thirteenth-century church that burned down with the congregation still inside, and how a seventeenth-century wizard raised the dead in the nearby graveyard, and how the head of a beheaded Jacobite can still be heard rolling around on its floors.

But none of these legends outshine the fact that Aleister Crowley, often called the "wickedest man in the world," allegedly used Boleskine House to summon underworld royalty.

Crowley was a British occultist and writer. He attended Trinity College at the University of Cambridge, and in 1898 he joined the Hermetic Order of the Golden Dawn, a secret society that studied magic and the occult. He soon founded his own religion, Thelema,

◀ *Abraham Ortelius's map of Iceland from 1585 depicts Hekla erupting, incinerating all dancing witches.*

which promoted "do as thou wilt." Crowley's dark deeds are legion and his ties to Boleskine are no less grim. He bought the house in 1899 so he could practice a summoning spell from *The Book of Sacred Magic of Abramelin the Mage*, translated by S. L. MacGregor Mathers. This spell claimed it could conjure twelve kings and dukes of hell and required six months of celibacy and abstinence to perform it.

Some assert that Crowley left without completing the spell and others avow he succeeded but departed without banishing the twelve kings and dukes back to the inferno. Crowley himself confessed at one point that the spell had gone awry.

Jimmy Page of Led Zeppelin bought Boleskine House in 1971 and owned it for more than twenty years. Though the house was dilapidated, he was a fan of Aleister Crowley's writings and knew of his connection to the building. Page hired his friend Malcolm Dent to take care of the place and Dent, in an interview with the *Inverness Courier*, claims to have endured his share of odd experiences.

"I arrived a total skeptic, to a degree I still am, but there are things at the house you can't explain . . . doors would be slamming all night, you'd go into a room and carpets and rugs would be piled up."

Despite this, Dent said Boleskine was a lovely place to raise his children, with marvelous views of Loch Ness.

Boleskine Manor also served as the inspiration for "Skene," in Somerset Maugham's 1908 book *The Magician*. The title character, Oliver Haddo, is clearly based on Aleister Crowley, who Maugham had met earlier in Paris. In the book, Skene is the name of Haddo's ancestral home, where he performs a magic ritual and sacrifices his wife (who later is raised from the dead long enough to point to him as her murderer). The protagonist, Arthur, then kills Haddo and burns Skene to the ground.

Like every self-respecting cursed house, Boleskine itself burned down in 2015 and again in 2019. It now lies in ruins.

◀ *Aleister Crowley*

EVIL RIGHT ANGLES AND
THE THINGS THAT SKULK IN CORNERS

Portals to hell aren't the only place to find demons. In 1924, Harry Houdini visited Sarah Winchester's house while on a spiritualist lecture tour. Afterward he would claim that while there he saw a curious room without corners, entirely round. Why round? So that when the devil came for Sarah Winchester's soul, he wouldn't be able to find it caught in a corner. Houdini claimed that Winchester's séance room was built in the same fashion, so the spirits could move freely. Houdini even alleged that Winchester wore a different-colored robe for each spirit she invited into her home.

The truth is that there are no round rooms in the Winchester Mystery House (with the possible exception of the conical Witches Cap) and, as you can read in the chapter on her house (page 109), Sarah never had a séance room and almost certainly never had variously hued spirit robes, nor entertained notions of evil right angles. But the idea that spirits can be caught in corners is not a new one and is perhaps founded in an ancient Chinese folk belief that evil spirits only travel in straight lines.

In fact, corners seem to be fairly crowded. It was once believed that germs lingered there (apparently bumping elbows with spirits and fighting over legroom), and for a time hospitals were noted for their curving architecture. The New York Cancer Hospital on the Upper West Side, built in 1884, owes its design to this belief. Its unique round brownstone towers were erected so germs (along with spirits?) couldn't get stuck in any godless corners and breed maladies. The now abandoned hospital on Ellis Island, designed by Florence Nightingale and in operation from 1902 to 1930, has curving hallways for similar reasons.

11

The Weird History of Labyrinths

VARIOUS

You make your way carefully down the steps, feeling ahead with your toes in the dark. You carry nothing but a sword and a ball of golden thread that you have secured at one end to the entrance and are carefully unspooling as you walk.

You notice the stench first, then the bones of those who came before you, rattling under your feet. Up ahead are the hallways, the turns, the fear thick as rot in the air, and, eventually, it: the one you are to be sacrificed to, the horned beast at the center of it all, the Minotaur.

◄ Sixteenth-century oil painting in the Palazzo dei Diamanti in Ferrara, Italy, depicting a labyrinth, a mysterious symbolic construction that has appeared in many cultures across millennia.

But you will not end up like the others. Above you, in the palace, is a princess who loves you passionately. She has revealed to you the secret of the labyrinth. Her love will save you.

At least, that is your hope. But surely these bones beneath your feet were once loved too. And yet they all ended the same, alone in the dark.

No. No! You will not be like them. Ariadne waits for you and, as you inch along the passageway, you cling to that tiny thread of hope with every shred of your being. You move among groves of stone pillars and under painted stone lintels, twisting and turning until you are utterly lost. And then you hear it, up ahead. No snorting, no animal stench, only the swish of a richly hung robe, soft footsteps, the sound of a knife slipping from its sheath. It is coming for you, feet quick and soft on the tiled floor. You are not afraid. You hold the thread tightly in your fist and move toward the monster.

Labyrinths* have existed across the globe and throughout every age and culture. They have been found in Etruscan tombs and prehistoric caves in India. Sweden has more than 300 labyrinths dotting its fields and glens, some dating back to 3000 BCE. In Nepal there is a little-known manuscript from 1740 that recounts how traveling monks from the Vatican came upon a lost fortress city deep in the jungle, designed in the shape of an impenetrable labyrinth (see The Lost Labyrinth City of Scimangada, page 180). In the medieval cathedral of Chartres, France, another labyrinth dating to the thirteenth century is imprinted in the marble floor of the nave. On El Brujo, the Hill of the Wizard in Peru, the mummy of a sorceress was discovered in 2006 bearing mazelike tattoos across her fingers.

What makes the labyrinth so mysterious is that it is uniquely human, an insignia particular to the mind of Homo sapiens, linking tribes and cultures that could never have crossed paths. Why were these structures built? What did they symbolize and what secrets do they hide?

One of the most famous references to a labyrinth is the tale of Theseus and the Minotaur. When Queen Pasiphae of Crete bears a monstrous child with a bull's head, King Minos commissions the architect Daedalus to design a dungeon for it to live in, a prison-maze that would be impossible to escape from. The Minotaur is fed fourteen tributes every year, seven boys and seven girls, until the young hero Theseus, aided by the king's daughter, Ariadne, faces the monster at the heart of the labyrinth, destroys it, and is able to escape by following the thread back to the entrance.

When Arthur Evans uncovered what he believed to be the palace of King Minos in 1900 on the island of Crete, he found countless coins bearing the symbol of the labyrinth, but no labyrinth. Desperate to make his name and possessed of a vivid imagination, Evans decided

---

*"Labyrinth" and "maze" are often used interchangeably, but scholars give them two distinct meanings. Labyrinths have only one entrance and one path that winds toward a central goal. Mazes can have any number of passageways, false turns, and dead ends.

to conjure up the labyrinth himself. He insisted that the palace itself was the structure from Ovid's myth. He even had it partially rebuilt from concrete and commissioned a Swiss painter to "restore" (some might say "completely invent") the murals visible on its walls today.

Like Sarah Winchester's California mansion (see page 109), savvy marketing and improbable legends brought the crowds rather than soundly researched reality. Thanks to Evans's enthusiastic peddling of his theories, the idea that the palace at Knossos is the labyrinth ingrained itself in popular consciousness—and not without reason. Consisting of more than a thousand interlocking rooms and rising up to five levels high in places, its floor plan is gloriously convoluted.

And the Minotaur? Some historians believe it was a high priest in a bull's mask who stalked through the palace, killing youths in a sacrificial ritual. Others think it was simply an animal and the entire tale is a mythologized version of the Minoan bull cult, which involved young people leaping over bulls' horns or killing them in a symbolic taming of nature.

As to whether the labyrinth ever actually existed, hundreds have tried to find it. Pretty much any cave on the island has been made a candidate, including the Gortyn caves twenty miles away from the palace. When researchers entered them in the 1960s, they found German weaponry from World War II, fifteenth-century graffiti, and evidence of a modern-day Minotaur cult, including tangles of string lying on the floor, as if someone had been playing Theseus.

The most convincing theory is that the labyrinth was always only a symbol, a metaphor spun into a physical structure for dramatic effect by ancient storytellers. The real question, then, is not where is the labyrinth but what is it? What does it mean? Why does it exist in so many places around the world and on cave walls predating the myth of the Minotaur?

A hundred interpretations have been put forward: The labyrinth represents the womb, human viscera, the neural pathways of the mind, or it's a map marker for a mythological city or castle, a prison.

It may have represented all of these things at various times in history. What is certain is that the labyrinth has undergone a fascinating evolution over the millennia, in tandem with the evolution of humanity, and that it began as a place of confusion, fear, and evil.

The Labyrinths of Bolshoi Zayatsky Island

Bolshoi Zayatsky Island is an utterly isolated spot in the White Sea, off the shore of northern Russia. It features a massive, onion-domed monastery, a number of distinctive rock piles, and little else.

▼ One of fourteen turf labyrinths on the remote Zayatsky Island, Russia.

Certainly nothing suggests its bleak and bloody history. In 1923, the monastery was repurposed as a gulag, a forced labor camp where enemies of the Russian state were brought by the thousands. It was termed a "Special Prison," a place where inmates were sent for execution. Hundreds were shot among its rocky hills, including many female writers and intellectuals.

But should you walk along its craggy shores, you will encounter something older than gulags and bloodthirsty regimes, older even than the monastery. Over and over, you will find ancient labyrinths along its shores: about fourteen in total, built of stone and turf, ranging from simple spirals to more complex designs.

In ancient times, life was terribly perplexing. Storms, diseases, forests, the dark, all of it was unknown and uncontrollable. Danger could arise at any moment and mortally wound loved ones. Because there was no concrete science as to how these dangers worked, they were often personified as evil spirits.

The labyrinths on Bolshoi Zayatsky Island are believed to have been built by fishermen to catch these evils; every morning, before setting sail, the men would perform the ritual of walking the labyrinth. Troublesome spirits were thought to follow them, intent on mischief. But, while the fishermen could retrace their steps, the spirits would become hopelessly lost in the labyrinth's spirals.* In reality, the labyrinth might simply have been a helpful meditation, calming the minds of the fishermen before they set out into the icy waves.

*This seems to directly contradict the superstition laid out in Evil Right Angles and the Things That Skulk in Corners (see page 163), that evil spirits are best trapped in corners and rounded spaces allow them freedom of movement. However, the superstitions may be more closely linked than they appear. No corners mean no stopping, which means the spirit is forced to wander endlessly. If ancient labyrinths were used as ways to confuse spirits, then there is a direct line to the nineteenth-century notion that round walls and curving pathways were a way to immobilize evil and fight disease.

Turf Mazes

Knossos is only one of several ancient cities associated with labyrinths. Another is the legendary city of Troy, best known as the city defeated by a wooden horse hiding Greek soldiers in its belly. Its walls were said to be arranged in a mazelike pattern so complex that to try to enter as an outsider would be folly. In another of the Trojan myths, a victory dance is described whose steps are likened to the complexity of the labyrinth. This legend spread throughout Europe, all the way to Scandinavia and parts of England. To this day, locals refer to the labyrinths found across their fields as Troy Towns.

Troy Towns are generally turf mazes, like many of those found on Bolshoi Zayatsky Island— winding dirt paths separated by low, grassy mounds. In pre-Christian times they were used as sites for ceremonial dances meant to beg for good harvests and to coax nature to be kind.

Even then, these labyrinths lurked at the edge of public consciousness, offering fertile ground for horror writers to turn them into places of ancient witchcraft and dastardly spells.

By Shakespeare's day turf mazes had already started to disappear. Through the character of Titania in *A Midsummer Night's Dream*, he laments, "The quaint mazes in the wanton green, for lack of tread are indistinguishable."

By Victorian times these labyrinths had taken on an occult tinge. In Arthur Machen's influential horror story "The White People," a young girl is brought by her governess onto the moors where they play "an old game" in a Troy Town. The girl has already been inducted into a forbidden world teeming with witchcraft and the Fair Folk. She has learned to perform strange ceremonies called the Scarlet Rites and the Yellow Rites, all of them hauntingly described in her diary. In this particular game she writes of how *one had to dance, and wind in and out on a pattern in the grass, and then when one had danced and turned long enough . . . you could be turned into anything you liked. . . . You could take a person out of himself and hide him away as long as you liked, and his body went walking about quite empty, without any sense in it.*

Note that this was in the age of industry, with steam engines cutting across the country and factories spewing coal smoke into the air. Even then, these labyrinths lurked at the edge of public consciousness, offering fertile ground for horror writers to turn them into places of ancient witchcraft and dastardly spells.

Turf mazes can still be found hidden in forest clearings and along shores. Many of them are in the process of fading away, just as they were in Shakespeare's day. So, should you find "a quaint maze on a wanton green," do not treat it as a relic to be admired from a distance. Follow its paths in the waning light and think of life and where it's led you. The best way to preserve a turf maze is to walk it.

Cathedral Labyrinths

Early Christians were quick to incorporate the pagan symbol of the labyrinth into their own rituals. By the Middle Ages, the fear of nature and evil spirits had been somewhat replaced by a fear of hell and the fate of one's eternal soul. The labyrinth grew to accommodate this, coming to represent a symbolic pilgrimage toward God. These are the labyrinths still found on church floors, such as in the cathedral at Chartres, France. Supplicants would kneel on the path, inching along and praying their way slowly toward the center. You were not actually expected to meet God once you got there, rather, the path represented an inner journey, away from the hardships and wickedness of the world and then back again into one's own skin. Through the

Christian lens, the Minotaur was the devil and Theseus was Jesus, the one who conquered evil. To walk, or kneel, along the labyrinth's coils was to meditate on this and find hope in salvation. (In a development from the pagan labyrinths, cathedral labyrinths were often designed so that their passageways formed a cross at their centers.)

Ironically, cathedral labyrinths were deemed a distraction in later centuries and many of them were torn out.

Hedge Mazes

As life's workings became marginally better understood, the labyrinth morphed into a place of delight, a diversion to be explored. Italian architects began designing pleasure gardens, as early as the fourteenth century, forming intricate patterns out of shrubs, herbs, flower beds, and pathways. In Elizabethan times, these gardens made the leap to England, where they were called knot gardens (named so for yet another version of the labyrinth, the Celtic knot) and were planted in the parks of palaces and country houses. The shrubs were seldom more than ankle high, certainly not meant to get lost in. In fact, the gravel paths were usually too narrow to be walked at all due to the voluminous costumes of the time. Instead, the mazes were meant to be viewed from upper windows,

In the ruined courtyard of Sudeley Castle in Gloucestershire stands a particularly striking knot garden. Pale roses climb the pitted stone and thread the unglazed windows. The castle itself has stood in partial ruins since its destruction by Cromwell's troops centuries ago, but the intact part is inhabited to this day, and the grounds are meticulously maintained. The elegant, looping forms of Sudeley's knot garden are said to be based on the fabric pattern of Elizabeth I's dress, which she wears in the famous painting *An Allegory of the Tudor Succession: The Family of Henry VIII*. (The painting is a brazen dig at all things Catholic. It depicts Elizabeth standing on a carpet, representing the newly formed Church of England, flanked by the goddesses of Peace and Plenty, while her Catholic brother-in-law Philip, is squarely off the carpet and has the god of war running toward him with a club. Not exactly subtle.)

Later, Louis XV would have a proper hedge maze built at Versailles, the shrubs coaxed to heights well over thirty feet. Though the Versailles labyrinth looked rather simple from the sky, its towering hedges made it suitably confusing to those inside and its cool green alleys became a popular escape from the stifling protocol of the court. It was in every way a modern evolution of the ritualistic prehistoric labyrinths and the religious medieval labyrinths. While the pagan labyrinths were built as wards against the dangers of the unknown and cathedral labyrinths as paths toward God, the labyrinth at Versailles had no central goal. Instead, its paths were asymmetrically arranged, leading to thirteen little courtyards. At the center of each courtyard stood a statue featuring a scene from *Aesop's Fables*' "The Parrot and the Ape," "The Mice in Council," "The Swan and His Owner," and so forth. The metaphor was clear: Instead of a single moment of epiphany, a destination to make the journey of life worthwhile, wanderers achieved brief, sparkling moments of moral clarity upon reaching a statue and reflecting on its meaning.

The concept for Versailles's labyrinth was devised in part by famed chronicler of fairy tales Charles Perrault, who could not help himself and added one more puzzle piece to this garden of delight. At the labyrinth's entrance stood two statues, Aesop and Cupid, the god of love. Recorded on their gilded signs was this brief repartee: "Yes, I can now close my eyes and laugh; with this thread I'll find my way," says Cupid, holding a ball of thread much like Theseus's in the legend of the Minotaur.

▶ *A map of Versailles's labyrinth (technically a maze) taken from a 1677 illustrated guide, intended to lead wanderers on a chronological path to the various fairy-tale sculptures scattered among the hedges. The guide also contained the accompanying stories for each sculpture.*

PLAN DV
LABIRINTHE
DE VERSAILLES.

Aesop retorts, "My dear, that slender thread might get you lost: the slightest shock could break it."

The point would have been clear to any pleasure-obsessed nobles darting in and out of the labyrinth's green folds to conduct their amorous affairs. To successfully navigate life, Perrault insists, one must have both wisdom and love, with a slight favoring of wisdom over love.

The labyrinth at Versailles was hugely popular for many decades, but toward the latter half of the eighteenth century it began to fall into disrepair. It was fiendishly expensive to maintain, and by the 1770s it had begun to resemble one of the true labyrinths of yore, wild and unkempt, eldritch statues peering pale-eyed from among the foliage. In 1775, 110 years after its planting, the labyrinth was destroyed to make space for Louis XVI's orchard of exotic trees.

Mirror Mazes

What could be more gleefully disorienting than a maze? One made of silvered glass, where every turn brings you face to face with your own confusion, and every disoriented step is repeated into infinity.

The earliest surviving design for a space made completely of mirrors was sketched by Leonardo da Vinci in one of his notebooks. The drawing, called "The Mirror Chamber," depicted a mirrored, octagonal cabinet where you could see all of yourself at once—a mind-boggling concept in the fifteenth century, when mirrors cost a fortune and tended to be quite small. Even hundreds of years later, when the Galerie des Glaces (Hall of Mirrors) was built at Versailles, it was considered an extravagance of massive proportions, something never before seen in the world. Due to Venice's monopoly on mirror makers, it was also a struggle to manufacture. France had to entice mirror makers away from their home city and once Venetian officials caught wind of this, they forbade mirror makers from leaving on penalty of death. Though the Hall of Mirrors isn't a maze, it had a dizzying, dazzling effect on visitors, sending ripples through the aristocracy and inspiring many later structures.

(An oft-repeated myth states that the earliest mirror maze was built in New Amsterdam, later Manhattan, in 1651, twenty years before Versailles's Galerie des Glaces. The "House of Mirrors" was supposedly built by Peter Stuyvesant as an attraction, with admission of one Dutch guilder. Historians have roundly rejected the notion.)

In the late nineteenth century there was a veritable boom of mirror mazes. Expanding on the idea of a maze as a recreational enjoyment, a "Moorish Maze" was built on the third floor of the Panopticum, a palace of amusements in Berlin, quickly followed by the Labyrinth of Pillars in Constantinople, and the Crystal Maze in New York.

The oldest surviving mirror maze stands on Petřin Hill in Prague, overlooking the steeples and jumbled rooftops of the Lesser Town. Built for the Jubilee Exhibition in 1891, the maze is housed in a curious wooden building built to look like a medieval gateway. The maze itself was designed by local architect Antonín Wiehl and features a series of Gothic archways stretching away in seemingly infinite corridors. It was designed to lead to a diorama of the Battle of Prague, fought between the Swedes and the Bohemians, an expansive moment of wide-angle vision after the confusion of the mirrors.

Labyrinths in the Modern Day

Many secrets in this book grew out of necessity, or a desperate want, before morphing into places of curiosity and pleasure. These days, we delight in dark secrets. We search out obscure locations, explore abandoned places, travel to lands that seem suitably distant and mysterious, climb cloud-wreathed mountains or burrow into caves, aided by high-tech equipment and a coterie of guides, all for just

a taste of something wild. Labyrinths offer us that same thrill. We want to find them, to wander their paths and become lost (but only a little lost, and only for fun).

Today we have corn mazes, trellis mazes, the artsy immersive madness of Meow Wolf in Santa Fe, New Mexico, and the relatively new piece of internet folklore called "The Backrooms," an endless, silent expanse of abandoned corridors, indoor water parks, and fun houses meant to elicit simultaneous feelings of nostalgia and unease. In pop culture, Guillermo del Toro's dark fairy tale *Pan's Labyrinth* exchanges the Minotaur for the nature god Pan (who proves to be quite as bloodthirsty, offering the young heroine Ophelia the gift of eternal life in return for the blood of an innocent). A hedge maze is used prominently in Stanley Kubrick's *The Shining*, representing a path toward madness instead of enlightenment. (The maze motif even appears in the patterns on the carpets inside the haunted hotel.) And in *The Name of the Rose*, the library in the fourteenth-century abbey is laid out like a labyrinth, illustrating the tortuous nature of the medieval quest for knowledge.

The labyrinth is still here, all around us. It is a symbol of life itself, a shape for the shapeless, an attempt to describe the inde-scribable. Like the splendid dollhouses in the chapter "Doll's Eye View," the labyrinth is a distillation, a miniaturization of life, a way to compress the confusion of existence into a man-made design. But unlike dollhouses, the labyrinth never seeks to render life movable or manageable. If anything, it allows us to revel in our lostness, to acknowledge that there is a beauty to wandering, a thrill to being unsure of one's direction. ◈

◀ A modern-day labyrinth built of neon-lit acrylic panels in Hainan, China.

THE EGYPTIAN CITY OF CROCODILES

One of the four great labyrinths of antiquity mentioned by Pliny the Elder in his *Natural History*, published in 77 BCE, is the Egyptian city of the crocodiles, Crocodilopolis. Today it is only ruins, in the modern-day city of Al-Fayyūm. In its heyday, this structure was a necropolis of huge proportions, filled with winding corridors and burial chambers, as well as temples to the crocodile god Sobek.

According to the early Greek historian Herodotus, the labyrinth was enclosed by a great wall. Inside were twelve courtyards and 3,000 chambers, 1,500 of them aboveground and 1,500 below. Herodotus wandered in the upper chambers but was not allowed to go into those below, as he was told they housed the tombs of the kings and the mummified bodies of the sacred crocodiles. Today only the building's foundations survive, unearthed by British archaeologist Sir Flinders Petrie in 1888. Altars in two of the temples were discovered to have small doors hidden in their sides. Beyond the doors were tiny rooms, just large enough for a priest to sit and make mysterious utterances on behalf of his god to any unsuspecting supplicants praying outside.

THE LOST LABYRINTH CITY OF SCIMANGADA

In 1703, the Vatican decided to stretch its tentacles of influence into Central Asia, sending missionaries to the remotest corners of the Himalayas over a period of about seventy years. One such missionary was Father Cassiano da Macerata, who traveled through Nepal in 1740 and wrote of encountering vast and ancient ruins in the jungles there, which he later learned were the remains of the ancient city of Scimangada. He goes on to describe the city as being built in the form of a labyrinth so large that its walls enclosed "pleasant fields and small streams that watered them." He added that the plan of this city could be found wrought in stone in the royal palace of Batgao, in modern-day Bhaktapur.

According to Father Cassiano's account, Scimangada was an impenetrable fortress that, like Troy, was only finally able to be defeated through treachery. A turncoat gave up the city's secrets, informing the enemy of the city's defenses. The enemy staged a distraction at the main gate while breaking through a distant point in the wall, massacring the inhabitants within.

EMPEROR YANG'S PERPLEXING PALACE
A Chinese Labyrinth

The Chinese term for *labyrinth* is *migong*, literally "a perplexing palace." Emperor Yang of the Sui Dynasty is thought to have constructed a labyrinth palace, which he dubbed the "Perplexing Multistoried Structure," in the sixth century. According to a ninth-century fictional work called *Milou ji*, the palace took a year and an army of workers to build and was designed as a sort of prison to hold several thousand of the emperor's concubines. A wonderland of painted balustrades and interlocking chambers and levels, it had thousands of windows and doors, and was said to be so confusing that even the concubines who lived there were unable to find their way out. This was not the main purpose for the confusing layout, however. The emperor found excitement in being lost, and the palace's labyrinthine design was concocted to titillate and inflame his appetites. He would wander through the maze of corridors and chambers, never knowing which of his concubines he would meet on the other side of the doors. In the legend, the palace is described in admiring terms, though it seems horrific today, the emperor not unlike the mythical Minotaur, wandering his lair in search of fresh meat.

12

Marie-Antoinette's Secret Escape

VERSAILLES · FRANCE

The Duchess of Polignac is the first to flee, slipping away by carriage on July 16, 1789. The Duke of Bourbon and the Count of Vaudreuil follow shortly after. By the end of summer, Versailles is all but deserted. The great galleries, once ablaze with light and crowded with peacocking nobles in vivid finery, are cold and dark. But the king remains, as does his wife, Marie-Antoinette, waiting anxiously for news from Paris.

◄ *Restoration of Marie-Antoinette's private library at Versailles, featuring a disguised jib door.*

On the night of October 5, 1789, it rains. Water drums on the vast tin roofs and rattles along the stone balustrades. It is loud enough to disguise the distant strike of an actual drum, lonely and far-away, but drawing closer. No one in the palace hears it.*

They do not hear the rumble of angry voices rolling through the gardens, either, nor the sound of many feet tramping through shadowed groves and up the broad marble steps to the palace. It is only when the mob is at the palace proper, their sputtering torchlight dancing in the glass, that the meager collection of royal guards is alerted to what is about to happen. . . .

In her bedchamber, the queen opens her eyes. Had she dreamed it? No, there it is again. The unmistakable clash of weapons, then an ear-piercing scream. It is a ragged, desperate sound, clogged with blood. "Save the queen!"

*The royal couple knew that a crowd of some 7,000 Parisians—led by market women and fishwives—had marched the thirteen miles from Paris to Versailles to demand bread. Tense negotiations had taken place between government officials and the mob all evening. But by midnight, the worst was thought to be over and most of the palace's inhabitants had retired to bed. They were unaware that a portion of the mob was still very much intent on entering the palace by any means necessary.

◄ *The Petit Trianon, hidden among high hedges about two kilometers away from the main palace, was Marie-Antoinette's refuge from the intrigues at court.*

She sits up with a start. A moment later, a guard bursts in and urges her up. A crowd of women has marched from Paris, dragging a cannon and a mass of anger and frustration. Two of her Swiss Guard have been decapitated, their heads now on spikes in the court below.

The queen gathers up her nightdress and her lady-in-waiting puts a shawl over her shoulders. The mob is running through the halls, shouting for her, jeering, threatening to tear out her heart, fricassee her liver, stitch her intestines into ribbons for their hats and bonnets.

The queen takes one last look at her room, at the delicate bundles of flowers and pink ribbons in the cream-colored silk wall-paper. She has spent years of her life loathing them. She is not sad at the thought of leaving them. But there are other corners of Versailles—a little library, a theater disguised as a plain country house, a magical grotto, a miniature village, places where she was happy and among friends—that she will miss terribly. She wishes she could say goodbye to them, not only the rooms but the friends, who are all far away now. The mob has reached the doors to her apartments. The guard and her lady-in-waiting are calling for her, whispering through an open panel in the wall. She goes to them and closes the panel behind her. And just as the mob bursts into her rooms she is gone, the palace swallowing her, the floral wallpaper closing over her, like water over a drowning body.

"My dear daughter," Holy Roman Empress Maria Theresa wrote to her child, who, at the age of fourteen, had just been packed off to marry the dauphin, the eldest son of the king of France. "Do not take any recommendations; listen to no one, if you would be at peace. Have no curiosity—this is a fault which I fear greatly for you."

Maria Theresa's fear was well-founded. She was aware that she had more or less thrown her daughter to the gilded wolves of the French court as a political sacrifice and she was beginning to see that perhaps her daughter was not prepared for the task.

Marie-Antoinette had been raised amid the informality of Schönbrunn Palace in Vienna, surrounded by a passel of siblings, a doting, overprotective mother, and an affectionate if philandering father. She was a curious, charming child, who had learned to trust easily and to think of everyone as her friend. But Versailles was nothing like Schönbrunn. In fact, no place on earth was quite like that decadent, dangerous French court.

What began as a hunting lodge in 1624, where the king could escape the overcrowded stench of Paris, had, by Marie-Antoinette's time, grown into a sprawling city beneath a single roof, housing thousands of aristocrats, servants, cooks, courtiers, and animals. And it was a place of secrets and lies.

Such a vast building could hardly help but cast a great shadow and, indeed, Versailles practically drips secrets. Today, fifteen million people visit it every year, but the tour along its crowded hallways gives only the briefest glimpse of the structure's most obvious glories. Of its 2,300 rooms, 67 staircases, and 679,784 square feet of marble, tile, and oak parquet floors, only a fraction is open to the public.

What of the rest? What of the room secreted behind a crimson panel in the King's Bedchamber, where the young, shy Louis XVI kept his gadgetry and collections of coins? And the staircase his father used to meet his mistresses, as well as the spiked gate Louis XVI blocked it with to keep said mistresses out? All are locked away.

Escaping Paradise

Two generations before Marie-Antoinette was disgorged onto the steps of the palace, a cult had grown up around Louis XIV, not unlike the sorts encouraged by Egyptian pharaohs to cement their place in history. Louis was called the Sun King and, like the sun, he was the giver of all wealth and power in the French court. The national fortune was his to do with as he pleased. One's rank was determined by proximity to him and so the lesser nobles orbited him like planets and moons, hoping for grace and favor to be bestowed upon them. In a bid to centralize his power and keep his nobles in line, Louis XIV decreed that the governmental seat of France would be at Versailles, in an enormous palace like none the world had seen before.

O—🗝 While Versailles was stunning to look at, it was not a pleasant place to live. It was hollow, shallow, and exhausting, its days filled with endless waiting for the king or an adjacent noble to pass by.

In 1682, the entire French court moved to the sleepy village outside Paris and the palace was transformed into the equivalent of an enormous gilded stage, where the royalty and aristocracy performed a carefully choreographed dance of politics, protocol, and debauchery.

The palace was an incredibly public place. Anyone who was suitably well-dressed could gain entrance and almost every aspect of the royal family's life was meant to be watched, from childbirth to death. From the moment Marie-Antoinette woke up, she was surrounded by courtiers and ladies-in-waiting. (The gilded cattle fence in her and the king's bedchamber was constructed to hold back the mass of people who would congregate there every morning.) During dinner a cavalcade of people watched the queen and king eat their

▶ *The Hall of Mirrors was built to demonstrate France's superiority to all who visited Versailles. Its 357 mirrors were larger than any made before.*

cold meals. (The kitchens were far away, in a building adjacent to the palace; the dishes never arrived hot.)

While Versailles was stunning to look at, it was not a pleasant place to live. It was hollow, shallow, and exhausting, its days filled with endless waiting for the king or an adjacent noble to pass by. In 1760, Bengt Ferner, a Swedish tutor visiting the court with his young, aristocratic ward, wrote in his diary, "Versailles is a boring retreat; everything I saw here is dead and sad." Another Swedish tutor wrote (cover your ears if you're French), "Brilliance and dirtiness are the distinctive characteristics of the Frenchmen: they are elegant in their dressing and their residences, everything visible is fine, but there is so much dirt behind the gold."

In Versailles's case, the dirt was literal. Toilets were few and far between, and where they did exist, they were often hidden behind difficult-to-discern panels. Even the king was sometimes forced to do his business behind curtains or the hastily held-up coat of a servant. Courtiers defecated in fireplaces and behind drapes, as did the dogs the aristocracy kept as pets. All of this turned the grand halls of the palace into little better than the alleyways of Paris.

There was plenty of metaphorical dirt as well. Gossip and scandal were rampant. Nobles were forever being shipped off to their châteaus in disgrace, or pardoned, or sent to worse apartments for being tiresome, or allowed better ones for being amusing. Every position of privilege was closely monitored by a chorus of those hoping for its holder's downfall and criticism was relentless. One powerful lady was venomously described in the Duke de Saint-Simon's memoirs as "a tall creature, meager, and yellow, who laughed sillily, and showed long and ugly teeth . . . who needed only a broomstick to be a perfect witch."

It is little wonder people wanted to escape. Those of lower ranks did so in the hedge labyrinth, on boats in the man-made lakes, or in the hidden servants' passages in the palace walls. But the young queen, Marie-Antoinette, shaped the palace around herself and carved out spaces within its parks and outbuildings. Hidden away from the watchful eyes of the court, she built little pockets of true wonder and beauty. Behind the gold was not only dirt, as the Swedish tutor uncharitably suggested, but also a sort of honesty, a truth revealed only in hiding.

The Rebel Queen

While revolution was growing its first cautious buds in the slums of Paris, the same was happening on a more personal level for the young queen. Her refusal to wear a corset when she first arrived caused a minor scandal and resulted in many anxious letters between her mother and her mother's spymaster at the French court. In one of these letters, the Austrian empress worried that her daughter's lack of a corset would cause her waist to become misshapen and her shoulders off-kilter. In another letter to her daughter, she admonishes her to "lavish caresses" on her frigid husband to finally produce an heir. It is little wonder that Marie-Antoinette began to look for ways to assert herself.

To begin with, she roundly ignored her mother's warning about trusting no one and soon gathered around her a close circle of friends and confidants. She began to flout protocol and increasingly spent her days at the Petit Trianon, a cozy palace about ten minutes by carriage from the main palace of Versailles. Those who were invited to visit her there considered it a great honor. Those who were not made up tales of the supposed debauchery and wickedness that went on in the queen's private quarters. With each new scandal, the queen retreated further and spent more.

There was an emptiness, a recklessness, to the final years at Versailles and the frantic way in which pleasures were pursued. As France and the world dragged itself toward the modern age, Versailles froze in a mad fantasy, with the queen at the heart of it all.

Still, Marie-Antoinette's choice to withdraw into make-believe is a sympathetic one. What began as a quest for extravagant distractions morphed into a tragic grasp for privacy. Over and over, she tried to build for herself places where she could speak and act without some twisted version of the action appearing in cheap gazettes in Paris the next morning. The queen was a slattern, her enemies said, who enjoyed wandering about in farmer's clothes. She was an adulteress in love with a Swede, a fool obsessed with nothing but clothes and jewels. She was a Machiavellian schemer intent only on benefiting her native Austria and driving France into ruin.

What was the truth? Let us step back in time, and follow her, quietly, down gilt corridors, behind cleverly disguised doors, and out into the gardens, where we will see who she truly was.

The Secret Library

Though her enemies liked to portray Marie-Antoinette as a pleasure-obsessed airhead, she was actually a curious and intelligent woman. The foremost evidence of this is that she kept a large and interesting library. Off the Queen's Bedchamber, behind the secret panel through which she would later escape on that blood-soaked October night in 1789, lies a warren of small rooms, invisible to the crush of tourists outside. They include a bathing chamber, a beautifully decorated sitting room called the Méridienne Room, and a small library covered floor to ceiling in glass-fronted bookshelves. (The door to the library is convincingly disguised as a bookshelf, painted with volumes of gold-stamped leather-bound books so realistic you might reach out to take one; they even sport dangling green silk bookmark ribbons.)

In her early letters, Empress Maria Theresa not only warns Marie-Antoinette to avoid bad people, she urges her to avoid bad books. Bad books, according to the empress, included novels, romances, and anything of low morals. Marie-Antoinette assured her mother she was reading a hefty tome on history (which perhaps she was) but failed to mention the wide array of "bad books" she was also enjoying. Published catalogues of her library reveal that she owned *Les Liaisons Dangereuses (Dangerous Liaisons)*, along with a volume of anti-Catholic jokes, some Voltaire, and a number of frothy plays. In a move that would no doubt have shocked her mother, she also collected a sixty-volume set of romance novels. Many of them featured female protagonists who marry for love, quite the opposite of what Marie-Antoinette had been forced to do and no doubt a beautiful fantasy to her.

Though Marie-Antoinette was hardly a political radical, she did have an unconventional streak, a hidden enjoyment of things deemed daring by the old guard. At the height of the French Revolution, when she and her family were placed under house arrest in the Tuileries Palace, she requested that her books be sent to her. And when she was later imprisoned, her most constant request to her jailers was for something new to read.

The Ornamental Farm

During the late 1700s, a move toward naturalism was sweeping the noble classes. It was the very beginning of the Romantic movement, which would later influence so much gloriously emotive art and architecture. At least some of its rise can be credited to Marie-Antoinette.

In 1783, she decided to have a small model village built as part of the Petit Trianon gardens. Called the Queen's Hamlet, it was likely inspired by Prince Louis Joseph of Condé's hamlet at his château in

Chantilly, built around ten years earlier, but even that was not the first. The idea of a ferme ornée, or ornamental farm, had already cropped up in England and elsewhere. It was Marie-Antoinette's version that endured, however.

The Queen's Hamlet was built to look old, the cottages built in the Norman style, their stucco and beams artificially aged. The windmill did not work and was never equipped for milling anything, but it was all part of the illusion: The farm and its surroundings were meant to offer a path back to simpler times, a place where the queen and her friends could go for a carefully sanitized dose of nature. Adding to its appeal to the queen, cows brought in from the Swiss Alps and ducks and chickens wandered the paths and scratched in the herb beds. Close by, the queen had her private gardens planted, not imprisoned in greenhouses or labyrinthine hedges like the green areas of her old-fashioned relatives but laid out in the style of the so-called English garden—wild and seemingly untended, with little paths leading toward a hidden grotto.

The Grotto

Little is known of the purpose of Marie-Antoinette's grotto, a dim, cave-like chamber near her hamlet, empty except for two stone benches and what Count Félix d'Hézecques describes in his memoir as "a bed of moss." What is known is that the grotto was designed to obscure. Its waterfall masked any sound of conversation from within (should any ruthless courtiers be lurking in the shrubbery outside), and its two entrances were barred, one by a wooden lattice, the other by a metal grate. It also had a large, strategically placed crack that one could look out of and see who was approaching down the path. Gossiping tongues would claim all of this pointed to the queen using

▶ *Restored interior of Marie-Antoinette's private theater, disguised from the outside to look like an unassuming farmhouse.*

the grotto to meet her lovers, but academics suggest it was a place for a different sort of intimacy, a cool, dark sanctuary where the queen could go and rest, enveloped by nature, far from the falsehood of court.

Even this naturalness is a carefully constructed facade, however. The grotto's massive stones are artificial, poured from concrete. Marie-Antoinette was very specific as to her wishes for the hill in which the grotto was placed, asking for fourteen wax models before she accepted one. The grotto, like the farm and all its gardens, is a false world, a caricature of real life, but an earnest one.

"Here I am not queen," the queen reportedly said of her private domains. "I am myself."

The Incognito Theater

Tales of Marie-Antoinette dressing up as a milkmaid and wandering around her hamlet in arcadian bliss have survived to this day. In truth, Marie-Antoinette could be a bit of a snob. (When her

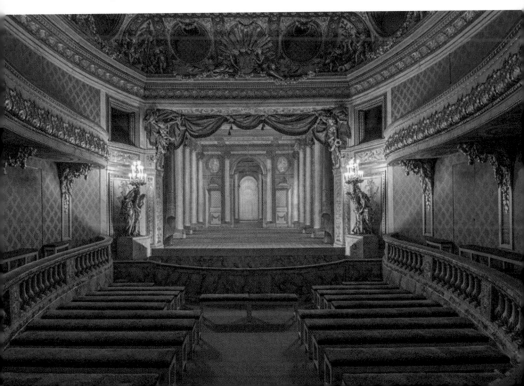

husband brought her to a château he fancied in the countryside, she declared it to be a "gothic toad-hole" and refused to set foot inside.) But the popular myth may have grown from a confusion with another of the queen's favored pastimes: theater. She loved music, opera, and playacting, and even enjoyed stepping onto the stage from time to time, playing small roles for her close friends and favorite servants.

Tucked away among the trees of what was once the orangery, hiding in plain sight inside what looks like an outbuilding for servants or staff, is the Queen's Theater. It began as a temporary stage, a thrown-together construction in a wilder, untamed corner of the park. Eventually, Marie-Antoinette decided she wanted a more formal setting where she could show off the art and music that she had commissioned, and yet someplace still far enough away from the enormous theater of the main palace (which was almost too expensive to use, requiring 3,000 candles for a single performance). Thus, in the same space where the makeshift stage had been, a little theater was built.

From the outside, it is rather plain. The church disapproved of theater at the time, especially one where the queen of France intended to take the stage herself. Theater was considered a rather scandalous pastime, reserved for those of the lower classes. Marie-Antoinette would not have wanted the building to announce itself to a wandering cardinal or cleric.

Considering that Versailles was already a huge stage, it may seem odd that the queen chose to escape it by fleeing to another stage or to an ornamental farm. And yet if Shakespeare is to be believed and "All the world's a stage," then perhaps the struggle lies not in escaping the stage altogether but in finding a stage where one feels comfortable. Marie-Antoinette's theater was artifice, but it was an artifice she had chosen herself. In her theater, a performance was nothing but a performance, a brazen bit of make-believe.

The theater was flimsily built, the sculptures not made of marble but of papier-mâché. And yet, ironically, it has survived to this day relatively unscathed. Rarely seen by anyone not willing to wander off the beaten paths of the modern-day park, the theater is kept mostly closed, though it has been restored. Particularly wondrous? Some of the original stage scenery has survived from Marie-Antoinette's day, including the set of a forest and a rustic town.

Gardens of Mysterious Delights

Once, in the heart of Paris, there stood a garden of amusements called the Jardin de Monceau, a peculiar eighteenth-century precursor to Disney World, where well-heeled aristocrats could stroll past dozens of different cultural oddities in the space of a single walk. It was built by the eccentric Duke of Chartres, a libertine and Freemason Grand Master, who would later vote for the execution of his cousin the king during the Revolution and was eventually guillotined himself.

The Jardin de Monceau is no longer standing, but at the time it contained sixty themed areas, including a miniature Egyptian pyramid, a Roman colonnade, a Chinese merry-go-round, a pond of water lilies, a Dutch windmill, a temple of Mars, a minaret, an Italian vineyard, an enchanted grotto, a trio of hedge mazes called the Geometric Gardens, and, as the duke himself described it, "a Gothic building serving as a chemistry laboratory."

At some point, Marie-Antoinette may have visited the park and been enamored of its Chinese merry-go-round because she had a similar one installed in her gardens in 1777. Her carousel was surrounded by a half-crescent colonnade and three brightly painted pagodas. Ladies rode on peacocks, gentlemen sat on dragons, and the contraption was powered by servants who set the whole thing to spinning with ropes. The carousel did not survive, and was dismantled sometime during the revolution. As for its counterpart in Paris, by the 1860s, only a few remnants of the Jardin de Monceau remained, the false landscapes and ruins having been swallowed up by the city. However, some features can still be seen today, such as the Venetian bridge, the rotunda, and the Egyptian pyramid, its scabbed green door hiding a murky chamber where, according to an 1861 article in *Le Siècle*, the Duke of Chartres once held tea parties and mysterious rituals, his guests and him inhaling the fumes of mind-altering herbs and reciting poetry around a statue of the goddess Isis.

The Mirrored Boudoir

While the Galerie des Glaces might have been the grandest mirrored oddity in the queen's general vicinity, it was not the only one. In the Petit Trianon, where Marie-Antoinette chose to spend as much time as possible during her last years at Versailles, an extraordinary room was built whose mirrored walls could slide up out of the floor, covering the windows and rendering the room suddenly and utterly private. In the kitchen below, the mirrored panels offer an odd sight, hanging rather forlornly in the plain stone room, like forgotten bits of set-dressing. But once they fly up through the floor, the room above is instantly transformed. A gloomy winter day might suddenly be shut away, replaced by candlelight and laughing reflections. Nosy, possibly hostile onlookers could be elegantly shut out.

The mirrors were commissioned two years before the French Revolution, during a time when the queen was beset by endless rumors and scandal. As the aristocracy became less popular, "the Austrian," as Marie-Antoinette had been dubbed, was made the lightning rod for public hatred, much more so than her husband or her peers. The Petit Trianon became her place of escape after Versailles became too insufferable. The smaller palace was off-limits to all, even her husband at times, and the technologically advanced devices she had constructed speak to her increasingly desperate need for a place where she could escape the relentless scrutiny.

Similarly techy, though existing only in blueprints, her dining room table was supposed to rise up through the floor from the kitchens below, fully set and laid with food, eliminating the need for nosy servants (or enemy spies) to hang about while she ate.

The Queen's Secret Panel

Both the king and queen's bedchambers featured access to hidden rooms, passageways, and multiple staircases. Their apartments were, however, on opposite sides of the main palace, with the enormous Hall of Mirrors between them. In the early morning hours of October 6, 1789, when the guard burst into the queen's bedchamber warning her of the mob outside, a secret panel to a hidden passageway may well have saved her life.

Making her way through the panel with the guard and her lady-in-waiting, Marie-Antoinette fled down a short corridor, then through another door disguised as a mirror in the Salle des Glaces. From there, she tiptoed barefoot down the great, empty gallery until she came to her husband's apartments at the opposite end. It took five minutes of pounding desperately at the door before a manservant came to unlock it.

> Making her way through the panel with the guard and her lady-in-waiting, Marie-Antoinette fled down a short corridor, then through another door disguised as a mirror in the Galerie des Glaces.

Once reunited with her husband and children, Marie-Antoinette and her family climbed into a carriage and hurried to Paris. "Try and save my poor Versailles," the king said to his minister of war, thinking they would return. They never did. Marie-Antoinette would live for four more years, each one progressively worse than the last.

The French Revolution put an end to the extravagance of the French court. Though Marie-Antoinette's secret panel allowed her an initial escape from the stage on which she had been an increasingly unwilling actor for the past twenty years, there was nowhere for her to go. After Versailles was breached during the Women's March of 1789, she and her family were placed under house arrest in the Tuileries Palace in Paris. All attempts to flee the country failed. In 1792, the monarchy was abolished. Marie-Antoinette was stripped of her title. Her husband was beheaded and her children taken from her. She was imprisoned in the Conciergerie, a grim medieval fortress in the center of Paris. On October 16, 1793, she was brought to the guillotine, dressed simply in a cap and white gown, hardly recognizable as the extravagant creature of yore, the daughter of an empress, the wealthiest woman in the world— except that she sat very straight and regally inside her cart.

Back at Versailles, her hamlet had fallen into disrepair. Her beautiful chambers were looted, the furniture auctioned off to fund the revolution. And yet, remarkably, much of Versailles remained preserved. Even tiny details from Marie-Antoinette's day were visible centuries later, with a 1986 *New York Times* journalist writing how, in the Queen's Bedchamber, ". . . workers found 18th-century hairpins that had fallen between the cracks of the parquet floor."

To this day, Marie-Antoinette's character lingers in dozens of chambers and structures across the grounds of Versailles. (Her presence is so strong that in 1901, two visiting Englishwomen claimed to have seen her sketching close to her hamlet, as well as a number of other ghostly figures in fashions from the late 1700s.) Her sanctuaries are what is left of her. And yet Marie-Antoinette understood that her extravagant architectural feats were only shells, pretty set-dressing to hold what was truly precious.

In Marie-Antoinette's final letter, to her sister-in-law, written at 4:30 in the morning on the day of her execution, she tried to lay

◄ *The Queen's Bedchamber at Versailles. The normally difficult-to-discern jib door is open and visible on left.*

out all that was important to her, including a few sentences of advice for her children, whom she missed bitterly. "In a word," she wrote, "let them both feel that in whatever situation they may be placed, they will not be truly happy but by being united. . . .[I]n prosperity, happiness is doubled when shared with a friend; and where can one find a friend more tender, more dear, than in the bosom of one's own family?"

Her sanctuaries at Versailles had been built out of a desperate wish for privacy, but never solitude. The library, the village, the theater, and the mirrored boudoir were all places where she wished to be surrounded by her dearest friends and family. They also offered her space to rebel, in small ways, against a life she had not chosen, to read books her mother had forbidden her, to commune with nature, or to pretend, on the stage of her private theater, that she was not a queen at all. It was those fleeting moments of joy and laughter, not the sumptuous architecture surrounding them, that she treasured most in her final hours.

In the last lines of her letter, she writes, "I had friends! The idea of being separated from them forever . . . is the greatest grief I feel in dying; let them know at least, that to my latest moment, I thought of them." ◆

FLYING CHAIRS
or "How to Reach Your Mistress as Quickly (and Stealthily) as Possible"

Louis XV, Marie-Antoinette's grandfather-in-law, was a master of finding ways to swiftly transport himself to his lovers' chambers. Initially, he built a private staircase up to Madame de Pompadour's apartment, with a secret doorway that opened directly next to her bed. Not quite satisfied with this, he ordered one of the first-ever passenger elevators to be installed in Versailles. Called "flying chairs," they soon became all the rage and were added to several mansions around France. (Versailles's flying chair no longer exists, having been dismantled in 1754.) Much like the elevators of today, they were prone to malfunctions. Louis de Rouvroy, the Duke of Saint-Simon, recounts an amusing story in his book *Mémoires* about a duchess who became trapped in her elevator and could only be freed after workers demolished the walls of the elevator shaft and plucked her from the rubble.

WYNTOON
an American Ferme Ornée

Should you be a skilled kayaker making your way along the remote McCloud River in northern California, you may be surprised to come around a bend and be confronted with an incongruous collection of half-timbered Bavarian houses butted up against the riverbank. The houses sport turrets and leaded windows and are nestled, almost hidden, among the trees. You are seeing Wyntoon, the remains of a grand estate once owned by famed newspaperman William Randolph Hearst. His castle at San Simeon gathers 750,000 tourists annually, but Wyntoon is visited by no one and is not open to the public.

Hearst's mother, Phoebe, originally commissioned a Gothic-style castle for the property, inspired by one she had seen in the Rhine Valley. It featured a central tower seven stories high and a great hall but burnt down after only thirty years. No sooner had the ashes cooled

◄ *Wyntoon was William Randolph Hearst's very own wilderness playground, deep in the woods of northern California.*

than Hearst ordered a fairy-tale village built, a gathering of rustic chalets that were something of a spiritual successor to the Queen's Hamlet at Versailles.

Hearst initially wanted another castle, like the one that was destroyed by fire. His chief buyer even went to war-torn Spain to snap up a twelfth-century monastery for its stonework, which Hearst had disassembled and shipped to San Francisco at a cost of $1 million. However, the Great Depression hit and Hearst was forced to downscale his plans, resulting in the small village.

The half-timbered homes are painted with fairy-tale motifs and have names like the Cinderella House and Bear House. While they may look quaint and rustic, they are each miniature mansions, most more than four stories high and each capable of housing up to twenty guests. One features a movie theater, one a banquet hall. Another was called "the nerve center" and had telephone operators on call around the clock.

Plagued by bankruptcy and fearing a Japanese invasion, Hearst and his mistress Marion Davies retreated to Wyntoon to wait out World War II. It is still in the family's ownership today.

THE AFRICAN VERSAILLES

Versailles has twins, little sisters, and out-and-out wannabes in dozens of countries across the globe, from Schloss Herrenchiemsee, Ludwig II's unfinished replica of the palace on a remote island in a Bavarian lake, to a gaudy villa in Florida, also unfinished, whose McMansion-style porticos and red lacquered staircases have little to do with the French palace but whose owners insist on calling it "Versailles" because it's big and expensive. But one of the most intriguing copies lies abandoned in what is now the Democratic Republic of Congo (then Zaire), almost entirely forgotten. Built by President Mobutu Sese Seko and meant to be the grandest of its kind on the continent, the palace (as well as a brand new town) was coaxed out of a remote portion of the jungle in just a few years. President Mobutu's palace was said to have cost $400 million to build, and featured two swimming pools, countless bedrooms for visiting dignitaries, and even a nuclear fallout shelter able to house up to 500 people.

Once completed, the palace, called Gbadolite, continued to be the site of vast expenditures. French chefs were flown in on the Concorde. The pope visited, as well as the king of Belgium. In a surreal echo of France during the revolution, impoverished citizens watched a dictator spend millions on decadent pleasures and eventually rose up. Opposing troops ransacked Gbadolite in 1997 and it was later abandoned.

Investigations later revealed that President Mobutu had misappropriated up to $15 billion in public money to fund his personal Versailles as well as the purchase and construction of many other mansions around the world. Interestingly, the ruins are still watched over by a small group of loyalists who hope that one day President Mobutu's children will return and restore the palace to its former glory.

13

The
Krazy Kat Klub
Speakeasy

WASHINGTON · DC · USA

Henry David Thoreau once wrote, "Live in
each season as it passes—breathe the air, drink
the drink, taste the fruit, and resign yourself
to the influence of each."

You muse over this quote as you walk down
the narrow Washington, DC, alley near No. 3
Green Court. Your eyes scan the brick walls,
searching for a small sign with a black cat.
It's after nine o'clock, but languid rays of the
midsummer sun caress the seedy backstreet.

◄ Patrons of the Krazy Kat Klub (including the owner Throckmorton) lounge in its notorious tree house
discussing art, smoking, and sipping illegal booze in teacups.

You look to the left, and spot the hand-painted words, "Syne of ye Krazy Kat," along with a drawing of a cartoon cat being hit by a brick. Jackpot. You pull open the wooden door, enter an old livestock stable, and climb a winding staircase. Suddenly you are in a dark dining room, enveloped in a murmur of happy voices and the scent of beeswax candles. You pause to admire several of the abstract paintings that hang on the walls, then head out back, to the courtyard.

Cleon Throckmorton, the artist and theatrical designer, is giving an impromptu art lesson. He finds you a canvas and you join in, letting your brush dance through paint until the sun goes down. You set the canvas in a corner to dry, and then ascend the ladder to the Kat's famous tree house.

You loaf for an hour, maybe longer, lighting cig after cig, the smoke curling up toward a perfect summer night sky—midnight blue, with violet-gray clouds. Your feet are up on the table, your chair leaning back. Your skin and clothes are covered in dried paint. You feel like a part of the art, a part of the world, a living canvas.

You hear the jazz music begin, descend the ladder, and make your way

◀ *Five artistic thrill-seekers loiter outside the secret, back-alley entrance to the Krazy Kat Klub speakeasy.*

back inside. Two glittering silent film stars, sleek and sweaty, dance in the middle of the floor. You press yourself between them and let the music take you.

When the musicians stop to catch their breath, the crowd pushes toward the bar. You let it sweep you along. You grab a stool and peruse the menu: home-brewed wine and sweet and sour cocktails—bee's knees, gin rickey, sidecar, old-fashioned, Mary Pickford, hanky panky, corpse reviver. . . .

You gaze across the room while you sip a brightly crimson negroni. The music starts up again.

The thrill of the rowdy crowd and the wild jazz, the bracing swigs of bootleg liquor—these are not the main draw of the Kat. No, it's the defiance, the disobedience, the flouting of the law. You are drunk, not on illegal liquor, but on freedom, the freedom to dance, drink, and sing, whatever you want, with whoever is willing. You are young, and lithe, and raw. Life is short. "Carpe diem!" you shout into the crowd, into the buzzing heat.

The shrill wail of sirens cuts through the brassy jazz song that's pounding through your body. The people near you hear it as well and freeze, their cocked heads twisting toward the sound. A few seconds pass. They shrug and go back to the dance. You hop off the stool and join them.

"I breathe the air," you cry, as you whirl across the room, sweat beading across your forehead, your lips red with Campari, your cheeks flushed with warmth. "I drink the drink."

In 1918, the prohibition of alcohol crept into the United States through the back door, with a temporary act meant to save grain for the war effort. At the time, many saw it as a necessary response to political events. In reality it was the result of more than a century of pressure from the powerful temperance movement. Founded in 1826 in Boston, the American Temperance Society soon gathered more than a million members. Alcohol, they argued, was the devil's drink. Victorian London was sinking into a mire of gin shops and debauchery. America, they insisted, must not go down that path.

On October 28, 1919, Prohibition was officially passed by Congress, as well as the Volstead Act, which defined liquor and outlined the punishment of producing it for commercial sale.

In reality the American government didn't have the capacity to enforce such a catastrophically far-reaching act and the Prohibition years were a wild, dark time of police raids, Mafia shoot-outs, and the rampant illegal production and sale of liquor. Secret establishments selling alcohol boomed in the 1920s. The best ones provided a safe haven for people of all genders, orientations, races, and economic backgrounds to meet, party, listen to music, and, of course, drink. Many were frequented by celebrities and many were run by the Mafia.

The underground liquor served in these establishments was notorious for being brewed in bathtubs—hence the phrase "bathtub gin"—or in secret stills. The unregulated moonshine often tasted terrible and could be downright dangerous. During Prohibition, as many as 100,000 people died from drinking liquor that had been made from a base of industrial alcohol. That said, many rural families kept their own stills, including this author's ancestors. They drank what they could and sold the rest. Very few were ever caught or prosecuted.

Because this bootleg liquor lacked regulation, quality, and flavor, bars began mixing in lemon juice, lime juice, honey, bitters, sugar syrup, Coca-Cola, and fruit to mask the taste. These cocktail concoctions were also easier to drink quickly, in case the bar was raided.

Experts claim that there were between 20,000 and 100,000 speakeasies in New York City alone during Prohibition. The name originated from the necessity of the patrons having to "speak easy," or softly, to avoid unwanted attention from the police. The phrase dates back to 1823, when Britain was undergoing efforts to curb its "gin craze," a British slang dictionary listing "speak softly shop" as denoting the house of a smuggler. In 1844, a British naval memoir used the phrase "speak easy shop" for places selling unlicensed liquors, and in 1837 the *Sydney Herald* referenced "speakeasies" as being slang for grog shops.

Speakeasies were also known as "gin joints" and "blind pigs," the latter term resulting from establishments that would charge customers to see an attraction, such as a blind pig, and then serve a "complimentary" alcoholic beverage on the side, thus dodging the law.

Speakeasies usually boasted hidden doors that required a secret password to gain entry, which only added to the spirit of exclusivity and rebellion. Jazz music, already widely popular, became even more beloved and fashionable as it spread through this new, illicit world.

This rebellious, hedonistic fervor was captured in books like F. Scott Fitzgerald's *The Great Gatsby* (the film adaptation by Baz Luhrmann depicts a seductive, high-octane speakeasy hidden at the back of a barber shop).

▶ *A customer seeking illegal liquor gives the secret knock, and a hidden panel in the door slides open.*

Bootlegging was the source of the title character's wealth and his grand parties on Long Island exemplified the Jazz Age culture. Flappers shimmied through the pages of Agatha Christie's early mysteries. Ernest Hemingway focused on the "Lost Generation" of the 1920s in his book *The Sun Also Rises*, presenting his ex-pat contemporaries not as debauched, war-damaged loafers, but as disenfranchised freedom seekers.

Manhattan had many famous speakeasies. Chumley's in Greenwich Village drew the literary crowd—Hemingway, Fitzgerald, Willa Cather, E. E. Cummings, Edna St. Vincent Millay. It was a converted blacksmith's shop and had two unmarked doors that exist to this day. The walls were covered with the dust jackets of books that the establishment claimed had been worked on by authors who had visited there, from the Lost Generation to the Beat Generation and beyond. Sadly, Chumley's closed in 2020 as a result of the pandemic lockdown and its green barstools, plush leather booths, and literary memorabilia were all put up for auction.

The Back Room sells cocktails in teacups and beer in paper bags in homage to its gin joint roots, when people used these methods to disguise their liquor consumption.

On Norfolk Street on the Lower East Side there was a speakeasy behind Ratner's, a kosher restaurant, known simply as "The Back of Ratner's." Gangsters like Meyer Lansky and Bugsy Siegel met there, as well as film stars like Groucho Marx and Fanny Brice. It's still in operation today. The Back Room sells cocktails in teacups and beer in paper bags in homage to its gin joint roots, when people used these methods to disguise their liquor consumption. The Back Room has been featured in several film productions, including HBO's *Boardwalk Empire*, and has a trick bookcase leading to a secret lounge for VIPs only (celebrities and/or friends of the owner).

Cousins Jack Kriendler and Charlie Berns opened what ultimately became the 21 Club in 1922. It was first the Red Head (on Washington Place), then Club Fronton. When it moved uptown to 42 West 49th Street in 1926, it became the Puncheon Grotto. Its final move was to 21 West 52nd Street. "Jack and Charlie's 21" was known locally as "21" or the "21 Club." The speakeasy section was often raided by the police, but—in something that feels like it was ripped straight from the cinema—the cousins devised a disappearing revolving bar, faux staircases, and a clever scheme of levers that tipped the bar shelves so the liquor bottles were funneled into the city's storm drains and sewers. The speakeasy is now a secret wine cellar, entered through a camouflaged door in a brick wall.*

In 1926 the members of the Algonquin Round Table, which included such luminaries as the writers Noël Coward and Dorothy Parker, and comedians Harpo Marx and Robert Benchley, began meeting at the 21 Club. Rumor has it that Dorothy and her friends were at the 21 on October 29, 1929, the night of the stock market crash. People lost millions, but the "Vicious Circle" drank and partied as if nothing else mattered . . . which is one way to handle this kind of devastating loss. There is something so admirably cocky in it, so brash and defiant. It encapsulates the very spirit of the Roaring 20s, and is a fitting response to the end of that wild, rebellious decade. Alas, although the 21 Club was an NYC institution, and had been featured in a host of classic films including *Rear Window* and *All About Eve*, it also closed its doors in 2020 as a result of the COVID-19 lockdown.

While the 21 Club was one of the premiere speakeasies in New York City, the Krazy Kat Klub held this honor in Washington, DC. Founded in 1919 by artist, architect, producer, and theatrical designer Cleon Throckmorton in the Latin Quarter, the speakeasy's name came from the androgynous feline character of the

---

*This vault has held the private wine collections of Mae West, Frank Sinatra, John F. Kennedy, Marilyn Monroe, Gloria Vanderbilt, and Elizabeth Taylor, to name just a few. When the celebrities came to dine, they could request their own bottles of wine to be brought to the table—the ultimate swagger.

popular comic strip Krazy Kat by cartoonist George Herriman. It ran from 1913 to 1944 in the *New York Evening Journal* (owned by William Randolph Hearst, a fan of Herriman). Krazy Kat's gender remained ambiguous throughout its publication and Herriman referred to his character as both "he" and "she."

▲ *Cleon Throckmorton*

Throckmorton saw the Krazy Kat Klub as a bohemian haven, a safe space for artists, musicians, and playwrights. He even offered painting classes in the courtyard. This not-so-secret watering hole quickly achieved notoriety for its top-notch jazz music as well as its rowdy ambience and reputation for chaos and mayhem. But its fame originated in something else as well: its cheerful tolerance of all types of love and its welcome embrace of all forms of sexuality. While city authorities officially referred to the Kat as a "den of vice," many government employees frequented the speakeasy, and it became one of the most fashionable places in DC.

A 1919 article in the *Washington Times* described the Krazy Kat as "a smoke-filled, dimly lighted room that was fairly well filled with laughing, noisy people, who seemed to be having just the best time in the world, with no one to see and no one to care who saw." Besides the dining room, there was also a floor for dancing and an outdoor courtyard that featured a tree house reached via stepladder. The newspapers reported several raids on the club, with the *Washington Post* remarking that many of its patrons "worked for the government by day and masqueraded as Bohemians by night."

Clearly, 1920s Washington, DC, ached for a place where both artists and uptight nine-to-fivers could mingle and be themselves, as well as flout the very laws the government employees spent their days upholding. Throckmorton's Krazy Kat, with its wild, welcoming approach, filled this niche perfectly.

The Krazy Kat closed its doors just months before the stock market crash in 1929. Throckmorton remarried and moved to

▲ *Open the refrigerator at the back of this garage in Los Angeles to find the 1970s-themed speakeasy Good Times at Davey Wayne's.*

New Jersey. He began designing sets for Broadway plays and, by the time Prohibition was repealed in 1933, his Greenwich Village apartment had become the new refuge for actors, artists, and intellectuals—a homier, gentler sanctuary in this new Depression-era world, a place where alcohol was no longer outlawed, but also no longer carried the glittering allure of danger and drama. Literary elites like E. E. Cummings, Eugene O'Neill, and Noël Coward continued to meet at Throck's after-hours salon, raising money for leftist causes but mostly reminiscing about their days as Jazz Age rebels.

Speakeasies might no longer be a haven for thirsty flappers and rebellious youths, but nor have they vanished altogether. In fact, the concept of "secret bars" has swung into the modern age with a vengeance, proving that people still long to sip cocktails in hidden locations, if only to regain some whiff of those mysterious, illicit years.

In Brooklyn, you can visit Le Boudoir, a Marie-Antoinette-themed speakeasy in an abandoned nineteenth-century subway tunnel, only reachable through a faux bookshelf in the restaurant Chez Moi. Also in Brooklyn, in the Greenpoint neighborhood, a fully functioning laundromat unassumingly called the Sunshine Laundromat Pinball hides a secret bar and pinball venue behind a panel disguised to look like a washing machine stack. (Sadly, both of these Brooklyn establishments have closed.)

At a hot dog joint named Crif Dogs in the East Village, diners can enter a vintage phone booth, pick up the red receiver, and slip into a speakeasy through a hidden panel.

Enter the broom closet on the third floor of McMenamins Old St. Francis Hotel in Bend, Oregon, turn to a wall of brooms, and push on the right panel to find a secret bar. (The hotel features several secret "art" rooms as well.)

Every weekend in the Hollywood neighborhood in Los Angeles, people line up outside what looks like a private garage in the midst of a rummage sale. Why? If you walk through the refrigerator at the back, you will find a retro '70s-style bar. Good Times at Davey Wayne's has a record-spinning DJ and a backyard featuring an Airstream trailer that sells barbecue.

Head to the back of the Pizzeria Da Vitto in Paris and locate the walk-in freezer doors. Push through to the speakeasy Moonshiner and imbibe cocktails while listening to jazz tunes on the vintage gramophone.

To find L'Épicier, also in Paris, enter a Middle Eastern deli on rue Notre-Dame de Nazareth. If you manage to locate the right item on the proper shelf, a passage will open to reveal the cozy, Moroccan-decorated speakeasy.

Backdoor 43 in Milan, Italy, lies on a canal-side street and is said to be one of the world's smallest bars—only 43 square feet. A key and a secret password are required to enter this lilliputian speakeasy.

Prohibition was extremely unpopular in its day, despite the positive impact it might have had on alcohol-induced deaths and diseases in the United States. History has proven time and again that forbidding human desires simply tends to make them flourish in secret. Some would argue that alcohol is as American as Johnny Appleseed, who, according to Michael Pollan in *The Botany of Desire*, planted apple trees not because the Lord was good to him but because he wanted to provide American settlers with something they desperately needed: liquor in the form of hard cider.

In *America Walks into a Bar*, Christine Sismondo states that watering holes are as vital to American life as they are controversial.

From the Puritans quaffing a good "beere" in a New England tavern to saloons, grog shops, gin joints, and modern-day microbreweries, alcohol and the establishments that serve it are here to stay.

The Eighteenth Amendment was finally repealed on December 5, 1933 (not without opposition—two-fifths of Americans in the 1930s wished to have Prohibition reinstated). There are still many "dry" counties in the United States that restrict alcohol, and a poll by CNN in 2014 revealed that 18 percent of Americans "believe that drinking should be illegal." The debate continues. ◆

THE BILTMORE'S HALLOWEEN ROOM
ASHEVILLE • NORTH CAROLINA

As is the custom with laws, Prohibition mainly affected the poor. Meanwhile, the very wealthy did more or less exactly as they pleased. The grand 250-room Biltmore Estate was built in Asheville, North Carolina, between 1889 and 1895 by George Washington Vanderbilt II and, at 175,000 square feet, is the largest privately owned residence in the United States. For a time, it was also the largest and most exclusive speakeasy in the country.

Today, this Gilded Age mansion offers popular public tours of the house and extensive grounds and is known for its secret passageways. The building's enormous library features a secret door on the second-story balcony that hides a clandestine reading nook. The billiard room also has a hidden door by the fireplace that opens to a smoking room. Other secret treasures include a trapdoor in the winter garden, a concealed closet in one of the bedrooms, a camouflaged door in the breakfast room, and an underground tunnel that leads from the old dairy barn to the winery.

But it is the Biltmore's basement that is most interesting. It is here that lavish, alcohol-fueled bashes were held. Its brick walls are covered in bright but eerie murals featuring black cats, bats, witches, and soldiers, causing it to be nicknamed the Halloween Room, despite the fact that it was painted for a New Year's Eve party held by Vanderbilt's only daughter, Cornelia, in 1925. The inspiration for the art is thought to be an avant-garde Russian theatrical troupe called La Chauve-Souris, which translates to "The Bat." Cornelia and her husband, British aristocrat John Francis Amherst Cecil, were apparently fans.

Undoubtedly liquor poured freely at Cornelia's celebrations throughout the '20s, but her grand mansion was never bothered by the police. The Volstead Act protected private residences from being raided unless they were selling the liquor that they were serving—and, of course, the cocktails at Cornelia's parties were always on the house.

Cornelia was said to be quite eccentric and she soon grew bored throwing cocktail-drenched basement bashes at her estate. She left the Biltmore Estate, studied art in New York City, and, according to newspapers at the time, dyed her hair pink, changed her name to "Nilcha," moved to Europe, and married twice more. She never returned to the United States.

THE HIDDEN DOOR
TO THE KNICKERBOCKER HOTEL BAR

Buried in the Times Square subway station in Manhattan is a white door with a worn metal sign that says, simply, KNICKERBOCKER. It once led straight to the bar of millionaire John Jacob Astor IV's glittering, lush Knickerbocker Hotel. Built in 1906 in the Beaux Arts style, the hotel featured red brick facades and a mansard roof. It possessed 500 rooms and enough space for 2,000 people to dine, drink, and party.

The Knickerbocker was the hub of Times Square during the Gilded Age (1870–1900). John Jacob Astor was so in love with the fantastical, fairy-tale art of Maxfield Parrish that he commissioned the artist to paint a mural of Old King Cole as the centerpiece

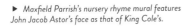
▶ Maxfield Parrish's nursery rhyme mural features John Jacob Astor's face as that of King Cole's.

for the hotel's bar, which Parrish rendered as a triptych. (Parrish's iconic triptych hung in the hotel for two decades before being moved to another Astor hotel, the St. Regis.)

John Jacob Astor was aboard the *Titanic* in 1912 and went down with the ship. His son Vincent inherited the Knickerbocker; by the time Prohibition came into effect, the hotel's popularity had waned and it was closed in 1920. The building was subsequently converted into office space, then added to the National Register of Historic Places in 1980 and designated a New York City Landmark in 1988. In 2015 it reopened as the Knickerbocker Hotel, but the secret entrance from the Times Square subway remains closed.

BUCKET OF BLOOD

SEATTLE · WASHINGTON

The historic Louisa Hotel in Seattle, Washington, built in 1909, stood empty and forgotten for fifty years before construction work in 2018 brought to light a speakeasy hidden in its basement. Known as the Club Royale, it operated during the 1920s and '30s. To gain entrance, patrons would knock on a door, show a membership card, and then walk down a steep, muraled staircase into the club. Nicknamed the "Bucket of Blood" for its giant cups of beer, it was said to have been raided once in 1931 but the music was so loud and the imbibers so raucous that no one noticed until the pianist was handcuffed and pulled off the stage. (Also noteworthy: Jimi Hendrix's mother worked as a waitress and sometimes sang there.)

Thanks to the renovation the glorious murals decorating its staircase were rediscovered, hidden underneath wallpaper. The art echoes the progressive nature of many speakeasies—same sex couples and a dapper, diverse clientele. The building, which stands in Chinatown, has been owned by the Woo family since 1963. They are seeking to preserve the murals as markers of Seattle's rich and wild history.

AND THE STREETS RAN RED
WITH WINE

Mary Foote Henderson was certainly *not* one to "breathe the air, drink the drink, and eat the fruit." A wealthy supporter of temperance during the early twentieth century, she and her husband lived ensconced in privilege in Washington, DC, in a mansion so grand and ostentatious that it was known locally as Henderson's Castle and apparently modeled after a castle Mary saw while traveling in the Rhineland.

In 1904, Mary Henderson published a book on temperance and vegetarianism titled *The Aristocracy of Health: A Study of Physical Culture, Our Favorite Poisons, and a National and International League for the Advancement of Physical Culture*—sounds like a riveting read, no? Henderson was the kind of woman who let her actions speak as loud as her words. When her husband died in 1913, she made headlines by emptying his extensive collection of wine into the gutter. She was aided by her morose butler, who sang grim, somber hymns while she smashed bottles on the front lawn of the castle.

Sadly the thirty-room Henderson Castle, with its battlements and crenelated towers, no longer exists. After Mary died in 1931, it was put up for auction and turned into a "tennis and swimming club" and the old ballroom was turned into a bar. The patrons were young, wild, and rambunctious. A neighbor bought the castle in 1946, solely in order to watch it be torn down three years later so peace could return to the neighborhood.

COLOSSAL GREEN GRANITE BEETLE
KN OF KHEPERA A FORM OF THE SUN GOD
SYMBOL OF CREATIVE POWER AND RENEWED LIFE

14

The Shocking Things in Cupboard 55

LONDON · ENGLAND

You straighten your tie and brush a piece of lint from your brother's best Prince Albert frock coat. You feel beads of sweat forming at your temples, underneath the wig you used to hide your long hair.

The thin, bespectacled curator glares at you then returns his gaze to the special permit you forged from the head professor of medieval history at Oxford.

The curator frowns.

You believe everyone should have the right to access the British Museum's notorious Cabinet of Obscene Objects, but this has been outlawed since the Obscene Publications Act.

◄ The British Museum, London. Not pictured: the Secretum—a room created by the British Museum in 1865 to store the items deemed "obscene." Men had to apply for a special permit to view the art. Women were not allowed entrance.

Finally the curator stamps your special permit and, with a sigh and a flick of his chin, motions for you to accompany him.

You follow him through locked doors and down a dark set of stairs to the museum basement. You are led past dusty windows and gloomy offices, over threadbare carpets, through another set of locked doors, and then, at last, you arrive.

"You have thirty minutes," the curator whispers. "Don't touch anything and, for god's sake, don't make any drawings of what you see here or you will be publicly escorted from the museum and banned."

You nod and try to look studious and puritanical. The curator leaves.

With a soft whoop of joy, you start to wander through this secret collection of art. You have the room to yourself and can roam at will.

Your eyes linger on scenes from myth. You see a seventh-century Sri Lankan gilt bronze statue of Tara, an important figure in Buddhism, but consigned to the Secretum because of her voluptuous breasts. You see a terra-cotta lamp depicting a woman standing on the back of a crocodile and you laugh when you realize what exactly the woman is doing.

Many of the things you witness seem to have a lightness, a sense of humor. It's an approach to sex that is entirely foreign to you. You had bamboozled your way into the British Museum's Secretum out of curiosity and in protest of the strict restrictions keeping the public from seeing such art. Yet you are surprisingly transported by the freedom of expression.

You hear footsteps. The grim curator has returned to drag you away from the erotica and shove you back into the safe arms of the public portion of the museum.

A secret museum is a bit of an oxymoron. The very definition of "museum" indicates a public exhibition, something available for everyone to visit and experience. And yet the contents of some museums were deemed so scandalous, so shocking, that they were kept under lock and key for centuries or never opened at all. So how do secret museums happen?

In the case of the Vatican's Dan-Brown-famous archives, it's really more of a private church depository (see The Not-So-Secret Archives, page 262). Or it was always only meant for a select few, such as the vast spillover of museums that is kept in locked warehouses and basements, treasures from bygone days enjoyed only by researchers and the occasional janitor.

The British Museum's Secretum, however, was a public collection forced into hiding with the passing of the Obscene Publications Act in 1857.

The British Museum is currently the United Kingdom's most visited museum, receiving approximately seven million visitors a year. It was founded in 1753, when Sir Hans Sloane* offered the British Parliament the opportunity to buy his personal collection, which included 50,000 books and prints, 32,000 coins and medals, and 334 volumes of dried plant specimens from around the world. It opened to the public in 1759.

The main building of the museum was designed in the Greek Revival style and built between 1823 and 1852. A round reading room with a copper dome (inspired by the Pantheon in Rome) was added in 1857 and frequented by such notable figures as Oscar Wilde, Bram Stoker, Sir Arthur Conan Doyle, Virginia Woolf, Thomas Carlyle, Vladimir Lenin (who signed in under a false name), and Karl Marx.

---

*He was, by all accounts, a cruel, wealthy royal physician who, in his spare time, invented a modern form of drinking chocolate (he was the first person to start mixing sugar and milk into chocolate, to reduce the bitterness, and he introduced the concoction to British society).

◄ This statue of Tara (Sri Lanka, seventh century) would likely have stood in a temple. The British Museum considered it too erotic and kept it locked away for decades.

In 1881, selections from the British Museum were partitioned off to form the Natural History Museum and, a century later, books from the British Museum were used as the basis for the British Library. Though its tomes are gone, the Reading Room is still occasionally open to the public. It has been embellished with the Great Court, a two-acre enclosed space that encircles the Reading Room and boasts a stunning glass roof. Its original blue, gold, and cream color scheme has been restored as well.

The British Museum is known for its outstanding archaeology and ethnography collections and holds more than eight million items, including the Rosetta Stone and many more wondrous items, all available to the public since it opened—with one notable exception. A tiny corner of this colossal collection once held items considered "antique porn."

The Secretum, which is Latin for "private," has also been called the Cabinet of Obscene Objects. Like the Secret Cabinet in Naples, it was only available for perusal to "gentlemen of mature years and sound morals." What proof a gentleman of such sound morals could give to gain access to such a room is outside this author's scope. Did he show letters of reference? Or indicate that he was a student, or a professor, or a member of the clergy?

The off-limits collection of the Secretum held some 200 items, described by an early museum curator as: "abominable monuments to human licentiousness." Many had been locked away for years before the Obscene Publications Act, but they weren't wrangled into an official collection until 1865.

What sorts of items were displayed in the Secretum? Here are a few:

- a Roman terra-cotta lamp depicting a naked woman riding a crocodile's tail shaped like a human phallus
- a sculpture of a satyr making love to a goat (a popular Roman theme)

- a piece of a temple wall from India featuring two lovers engaged in agile oral sex
- wax candle phalluses
- a reproduction of a medieval chastity belt
- animal membrane condoms
- a seventh-century Sri Lankan gilt bronze statue of Tara, an important figure in Buddhism but consigned to the Secretum because of her voluptuous bare breasts
- a vase from 440 BCE with a woman spreading seeds in a garden of phalluses

Curators continued to add items to the Secretum up until the 1950s, but the freewheeling 1960s swept in and locking such items away suddenly seemed very old-fashioned. During that decade, large portions of the Secretum's artifacts were dispersed to other sections of the British Museum and the Secretum disappeared, with the exception of the handful of items that still remain locked away in Cupboard 54 and Cupboard 55 of the Department of Medieval and Later Antiquities.

The author Tony Perrottet visited the last remaining section of the Secretum in 2008. He described "gloomy stairs," "shabby corridors," "grimy windows," and one sad wooden cupboard marked with a bronze plaque with the number 55. When opened, it contained mainly items of Judaica, because, as the curator put it, "There was no logic to the Secretum." Luckily for Perrottet, Cupboard 54 proved more stimulating. It held several wax phalluses.

The Secretum was by no means the only secret museum collection in existence during the last few centuries. Here are a few more:

Gabinetto Segreto

NAPLES · ITALY

The archaeologists who excavated Pompeii and Herculaneum in the eighteenth and nineteenth centuries weren't prepared for the frequent representations of sex and genitalia in the art and objects they found there. They included phallic wind chimes, phallic oil lamps, phallic amulets, phallic tintinnabulums*, and mythological illustrations featuring pink-bottomed nudes and lusty satyrs.

All art of a suggestive nature was locked away by Charles III in 1752 when he was King of Naples (he became King of Spain in 1759 and resigned the crown of Naples to his son Ferdinand I). Ferdinand allowed visitors to see these items with special permission, and in the early 1800s a French booklet about the Pompeii excavations, complete with saucy illustrations, began to circulate in Europe. Most copies were destroyed by government officials and the few that remained became rare collector's items.

But in 1819, when King Ferdinand brought his wife and daughter to the museum, he was horrified by the erotica. As a result, everything that was deemed pornographic was ordered to be locked away, made accessible only to men "of mature age and respected morals."

The erotic frescoes that remained in Pompeii? They were covered with metal shutters and viewable only by men, for a small fee. This gentlemen-only practice endured in Naples until the 1960s.

Unsurprisingly, all this secrecy only made this cabinet ("cabinet" here refers to a locked bookcase) all the more popular and many gentlemen of wealth and education sought out this restricted section

---

*This word, which means "little bell" in medieval Latin, is currently used to describe the sound of bells ringing and is also applied to the bell mounted on a pole that is used in Catholic mass. However, a tintinnabulum in ancient Rome was an object—usually a giant carved phallus—that had bells attached to the, er, tip. It was thought that these items kept away evil spirits and brought good luck.

of the museum when doing their grand tours of Europe. Possibly the most famous of the Pompeii and Herculaneum erotica trove is a piece carved from a single block of Italian marble known colloquially as The Goat. The sculpture is alarming even to modern sensibilities—it is a carving of a handsome bearded faun, possibly the half-human, half-goat god Pan, making graphic love to a female goat as she gazes at him adoringly. It once stood in a nobleman's garden.

Scholars speculate that these kinds of depictions were commonplace among the first-century Romans and statues featuring sex (and violence) were basically the equivalent of modern garden gnomes or gazing globes. With emperors like Caligula and Nero, this isn't terribly surprising. Public sentiment toward erotic art would shift with the crowning in 324 CE of Constantine I, the first Christian Roman emperor.

▲ *Polyphemus caressing Galatea, erotic fresco from Pompeii, 50–79 CE, Secret Cabinet, Naples National Archaeological Museum*

Civilizations rise and fall, and social conventions fluctuate like the moods of a mercurial emperor. Nothing lasts.

The Gabinetto Segreto remained hidden from women and children for the next 180 years, finally opening to the public in 2000. The tide turns once again.

The Hellish Secret Library

PARIS · FRANCE

Prior to the French Revolution, it is believed that there were only fifty or so "scandalous works" in the Bibliothèque Nationale. However, the book collections of slain aristocrats and shuttered monasteries added greatly to the bibliothèque's volumes in the 1790s and brought in a surge of morally questionable texts (or so they were deemed at the time). In the mid-1800s the word "enfer" came into use to classify works that might be deemed erotic. ("Enfer" means "hell" in French and has a long history of being used to denote books that certain people find dangerous—books that might put you on the path to hell.) L'Enfer collection in the Bibliothèque Nationale currently contains approximately 2,600 volumes and restrictions on entry have loosened considerably in the last forty years.

> "Enfer" means "hell" in French and has a long history of being used to denote books that certain people find dangerous—books that might put you on the path to hell.

The British Library's Private Case was established within a few decades of L'Enfer, and it was a collection of books that, in the 1850s, were pulled from public view because they were deemed obscene. Many items have, over time, been removed from the Private Case and placed back on the public shelves. The current collection holds just 2,500 books, much reduced from its original 4,000 volumes, but even the few that remain are now available for patrons to view in the Rare Books & Music Reading Room.

Such private case collections of erotica exist in many libraries and are often referred to by a symbol. The New York Public Library uses three asterisks for its Triple Star collection of erotica and for many years these three stars meant that librarian supervision was required for viewing. According to a *New York Times* article in 2016, *Playboy* was once classified as a triple star, as were playing cards with illustrations of naked women.

This collection is considered a bibliophilic treasure. Former NYPL librarians fondly recall feeling like pioneers when they were sent on missions in the 1970s to buy the new books being sold in the Time Square pornography shops. Subsequently, the library boasts one of the finest collections of mid-century American erotica in the world. Other notable items in the New York Public Library's Triple Star collection include William Faulkner's pencil drawings depicting sex with his mistress, Henry Miller's typewritten manuscript of *Tropic of Capricorn*, a first edition of Nabokov's *Lolita*, and a pornographic cartoon drawn by Jack Kerouac.

Crime Museum

LONDON · ENGLAND

Not all secret museums feature erotica. The Metropolitan Police of London are guardians of a private museum that is most definitely not open to the public. The only way to get in? You have to be a member of the country's police force. The Crime Museum (formerly known as the Black Museum) is a teaching museum, intended to help police officers study criminals and their behavior.

Sources can't even agree where it's currently located. Some say it's in the basement of the Curtis Green Building; others claim it's located on the first floor of the Metropolitan Police Headquarters, and some say that it can be found in Room 101 at New Scotland Yard Headquarters in Westminster. (A brief bit of research proved that these all are the same building.)

The Crime Museum was founded in 1874 and started as a collection of confiscated prisoner property and items used in criminal acts. The museum has never officially opened, but it maintains a steady stream of police academy students who have been instructed to view the collection as part of their training. It now holds more than 500 exhibits, including many weapons that have been used to commit murder, like swords disguised as walking sticks and shotguns disguised as umbrellas. The museum also boasts letters from Jack the Ripper, hangman's nooses, and several exhibits featuring serial killers.

An 1877 edition of Minnesota's *The Worthington Advance* had this to say about this secret museum: "The Black Museum is a room at the London Police Headquarters in which during the last three years *pieces of conviction* have been arranged and labeled, forming a ghastly, squalid, and suggestive show."

The *London Spectator* goes into further detail, describing the weapons stored at the museum: "Several of the pistols, mostly beautiful weapons, are the instruments of suicide . . . almost all among the higher classes of society . . . and when a visitor asks how a pistol with which a gentleman of wealth and station shot himself has come into the keeping of the Museum, he is told: 'the family mostly do not like to have it; so they ask the police to come and take it away.'"

The *London Spectator* rather joyously continued to detail the bloodstained clothes of murderers, their brutal murdering tools, letters written by serial killers, and the correspondence of convicted criminals such as baby-farmer Margaret Waters: "How much sin, shame, sorrow, and cruelty that small dusty bundle (of letters) represents!"

On a lighter note, this weekly British magazine also mentioned forged betting tickets ("a curious and ingenious example of perverted cleverness") and a large assortment of tools used by burglars.

Certain artifacts from this museum have been displayed in other galleries, such as the Museum of London, or loaned out as part of other exhibitions, but the public is still barred from entry into the Crime Museum itself.

The Secret Libraries of Timbuktu

MALI · AFRICA

Timbuktu is a city of myth. Legends of its extraordinary riches and inaccessible location have sparked imaginations across the globe, and the word "Timbuktu" has evolved into a metaphor for a faraway place.

But the city actually exists and it teems with secrets. Founded some 1,100 years ago in what is now Mali, it was once a thriving commercial center hidden in the middle of the desert dunes, twelve miles north of the Niger River. The main trade during the city's golden age was ivory, salt, gold, and enslaved people and it was an important meeting place for caravans traveling across western Africa.

The book trade also boomed during the city's heyday, as many Islamic scholars traveled through Timbuktu. (The University of Sankore, located in the city, is thought to be one of the first institutions of higher education in the world.)

The city began to decline in the 1600s, as new trading routes developed, and by the 1800s it was a barren outpost. But the bibliophiles did not die with the town. Its

> Experts estimate that there are still dozens of private libraries in Timbuktu and that thousands of ancient manuscripts are held in secret by families who have watched over them for centuries and are reluctant to hand them over to an uncertain government.

ancient manuscripts were hidden by caring civilians, away from the dangers of a shifting political landscape. Books were buried in cellars, or hidden in walls, until the day they were finally collected into Timbuktu's several libraries, which now hold around 700,000 works.

In Joshua Hammer's book *The Bad-Ass Librarians of Timbuktu*, he writes about Abdel Kader Haidara, an archivist from Timbuktu who collected thousands of books and manuscripts from desert shepherds (they had been secretly guarding the books for generations). Haidara, a sort of "noble book smuggler," managed to secretly relocate 350,000 medieval texts to a safe location.

Experts estimate that there are still dozens of private libraries in Timbuktu and that thousands of ancient manuscripts are held in secret by families who have watched over them for centuries and are reluctant to hand them over to an uncertain government.

If we truly are what we hide, then the people behind the secret libraries in Timbuktu hid books only to preserve them from destruction and are thus those most beloved of all creatures: bibliophiles. ◈

BE AFRAID! OUR MUSEUMS ARE HAUNTED!

Like, really, really haunted.

Before the Louvre was a museum, it was a fortress, originally built in 1190—giving the location plenty of time to accrue its share of ghouls. The most famous Louvre ghost is Jean L'Ecorecheur, or Jack the Skinner, who was a butcher by trade and the personal assassin of Catherine de' Medici. Eventually she had him murdered and his ghost is said to still haunt the museum's galleries. He is known as the Red Man of Tuileries because he is dressed in crimson and likes to lurk in the nearby Tuileries Garden. Even Napoleon III claimed to have spotted him in 1815.

A giggling ghost girl is said to run down the hallway of the Luce Center for the Study of American Art at the Metropolitan Museum of Art in New York City, and most night guards have seen the ghost of the Smithsonian's first curator, Spencer Fullerton Baird, wandering the halls. Meanwhile, the bell tower of the San Francisco Art Institute has been so plagued with ghostly activity in the form of screams, footsteps, smashed furniture, and flickering lights that the school has hired psychics to perform séances.

The British Museum might actually lay claim to the most spooks, unsurprising as it contains nearly 6,000 human remains in the form of Egyptian mummies and bog bodies. Sudden temperature drops,

◄ *The private library of Mamma Hairdara in Timbuktu, Mali, containing books that had been hidden for generations, some dating back to the twelfth century.*

songs played on ancient instruments, and ghostly orbs are all familiar to the museum's employees. One security guard describes being shoved backward by a ghostly hand, another tells of her encounter with a spirit that reached into her body and grabbed her "by the spine."

Shudder.

FLESH-EATING MUSEUM BUGS

Chicago's Field Museum is one of the largest field museums in the world and receives about two million visitors a year. It has many wonderful exhibitions, including its rare book room, Bird Egg Collection, and Inside Ancient Egypt display. It also boasts a library with more than 275,000 volumes.

But the most gruesome corner of the museum? The secret flesh-eating beetle room on the third floor, with its drying racks, tanks, and millions of dermestid beetles (also known as hide beetles). Beetles have been used to clean bones since at least the nineteenth century and museums rely on these insects for their collections. The bugs won't feast on moist flesh, so the beetle room is filled with drying carcasses. It's definitely not for everyone, with its grisly sights, smells, and *sounds.* Yes, the chewing of a million insects is audible and horrifying.

The beetle room is sealed off from the rest of the museum behind a double set of thick doors, which is lucky for visitors, as the stench of putrefying flesh is rather alienating. The industrious bugs can clean a small carcass in a few hours, a larger one, like that of a medium-sized bird, in a few days.

Using beetles to clean bones in museums seems to be the universally approved method. There is always a fear that the insects will escape from the beetle room, find their way to a collection, and

◀ *A flesh-eating beetle.*

destroy it, but overall these bugs appear to be worth the risk. So the next time you are roaming the Field Museum, consider the fact that somewhere nearby, behind closed doors on the third floor, millions of hide beetles are chewing, and chewing, and *chewing*.

A FEW QUICK BRITISH MUSEUM FACTS:

1. The British Museum was one of the first buildings to install electric lighting in 1879. Up until this point, it used daylight as its only source of light—gas lamps and candles being too dangerous—and often had to close early during foggy winter days.

2. Many films have been shot in the British Museum, beginning with *The Wakefield Case* in 1921, right up to *The Mummy Returns* in 2001, *Possession* in 2002, *Night at the Museum: Secret of the Tomb* in 2014, and *Wonder Woman* in 2017.

3. Mozart visited the British Museum as a child in 1765 and dedicated his composition "God Is Our Refuge" to the institution.

4. The museum was the subject of an art hoax in 2005 by art prankster Banksy, who has hidden joke items in other galleries as well. Banksy carved a caveman using a modern shopping cart on a rock, snuck it into a display, and hung a sign indicating that the art depicted "early man venturing toward the out-of-town hunting grounds."

The most popular exhibit at the British Museum was the King Tutankhamun display in 1972, the fiftieth anniversary of the tomb's discovery. The exhibit received almost two million visitors. The most beloved item? King Tut's golden death mask.

15

The Bone Chamber

LEUK · SWITZERLAND

The town is not easily reached. You were called
on a matter of urgency—something disturbing
has been found in the basement of an old
church—but an hour from your destination
the road ends at a small depot with nothing
but snowbound peaks ahead. The only way
through is by train, so you drive your car onto
a rusting railway carriage and rattle into a
seemingly endless, pitch-black tunnel. The
weight of the mountain crushes down on you,
the pressure popping your ears. When you
finally reach the other side, you must take a
winding road down into the valley and back
up its flank. Only then do you see the town of
Leuk, clinging to the barren hillside above the
Rhine River. It is a bleak place this time of year,

◄ In 1982, a wall of bones was discovered hidden in a small town in the Swiss Alps. Many of the skulls
contained mysterious, round punctures.

severe stone buildings with small windows, ancient scrollwork, a grapevine with a blue tin sign under it proudly declaring it to be more than 400 years old. The village is dominated by a massive church with a square tower, its visage strangely forbidding.

A group is already gathered in the small graveyard below the church. They show you into the basement room, speaking excitedly in their musical mountain dialect, so different from the tones of Zürich in the north. They point you to a cupboard in the corner of the room, the back of which has been broken out. Behind it is a dark, cramped space. A strange smell emanates from within. You ask for a flashlight and, when you shine it through the opening, your breath catches. A thousand skulls are grinning out at you. The narrow space beyond the cupboard is filled floor to ceiling with bones.

You shift the beam of your flashlight and see a wall made of skulls extending around a corner, into blackness. You ask the workers question after question, but the answers are always the same. No one knows how far the bones go. No one knows who the dead are. There is no historical record of the room, not even in village lore. But that's what you're here for and so you crawl through the cupboard and step down among the bones.

Leuk, at the height of the pandemic, is practically deserted. No cars, no people in the streets. Next to the church, an old piece of clockwork ticks away behind glass. Down the crooked lanes, miniature mansions and derelict castles rise above the old farmhouses, harkening back to more prosperous days. Inside the church's nave lies a sixteenth-century female mummy wearing good leather shoes. It is all rather Tim Burton–esque, but not by design. You don't get the impression that the town cares who comes here or what they see. There is certainly nothing pointing visitors toward its greatest curiosity, a bone chamber discovered in the church's basement in 1982.

Stepping into the chamber today, little suggests what it might have looked like when the room was first uncovered. It has been cleaned and dusted, decked out with folding chairs and red wall hangings, and adorned with a crucifix so realistic it borders on the stomach churning. Only the strange smell lingers, something damp and heavy and vaguely disquieting. The smell comes from the skulls. They are ancient, dirty. Some have conspicuous holes in their foreheads, perfectly round, like bullet holes.

For many years, no one in the town knew of the room's existence. For as long as anyone in Leuk could remember, the chamber in the basement of St. Stephan's Church had been small and whitewashed, with nothing but a few well-maintained gravestones embedded in its walls. Then, in 1982, the church decided it would like to turn the space into a community room. Workers were hired and they immediately noticed that the room was far smaller than it should be. The walls on two sides were thin, not the massive stone of the church's foundations. What was behind them? In one corner was a wooden cupboard and here the workers decided to break through and see what was on the other side. And see they did.

The skulls behind the false walls were layered six feet deep. Thousands of them filled the space, the estimate lying between 15,000 and 20,000. The floor was a mess of femurs and tibias. Who

▲ *The Sedlec Ossuary chapel in the Czech Republic features a chandelier made of human bones.*

did they belong to? It was only the first of many questions. Another mystery was waiting just a little farther in.

Ewald Grand, one of the workers on the site in 1982, was handing load after load of bones through the cabinet opening when he discovered he was holding an old wooden cross. He didn't think much of it. In fact, he thought so little of it that he took it home as a gift for his mother, who washed the artifact in her bathtub. Upon hearing that there might be objects from the thirteenth century in the bone chamber, Ewald brought the artifact back and remembered the archaeologists marveling at its cleanliness.

As workers made their way deeper into the chamber, they next came upon a fresco: a so-called Totentanz, or dance of death, dating back to medieval times, as well as twenty-six wooden statues, all of them arranged carefully among the bones. There were two pietàs, multiple St. Sebastians, a knight, and an unknown female saint. No one had any idea what they were looking at or why someone might bury statues with the dead. Overnight this quiet, local renovation project became a subject of national interest.

There are many ossuaries and bone chambers across the world, from Europe to the Maya temples, places where skulls and human skeletons were arranged to often quite sumptuous effect. In Sedlec, Czech Republic, there is one with a chandelier made from thigh bones, its ceilings and archways festooned with femurs, like some sort of macabre Christmas garland. In Cologne, Germany, a basilica contains a chamber known as the Goldkammer, or golden chamber, its vaults covered in Latin inscriptions, the words spelled out in human bones said to have come from 11,000 virgins murdered by the Huns.*

The Catholic church insists these traditions aren't meant to be grotesque. They are memento mori, reminders to all who enter that life is short and must be cherished.

What makes the bone chamber in Leuk so special, however, is not its appearance, which pales in comparison to the grisly extravagance of other ossuaries. Far more interesting is the oddness of its rediscovery and the three mysteries the chamber presents. First, why were the statues given a funeral along with the bones of the dead? Second, why were the bones walled up and hidden away, forgotten by even the villagers themselves? And finally, who do the bones belong to?

The mystery of the statue burial offered the most clues. All but one of the pietàs was found to be covered in a layer of soot, suggesting they had been kept in a place damaged by fire and were moved to the bone chamber. All of them, even the fourteenth-century cross (despite its excursion into Madame Grand's bathtub), were in excellent condition and still retained their original paint, meaning it was unlikely they were in use in a church, where they would have been constantly handled, kissed, and exposed to sunlight.

Switzerland has long been split between the austere, art-hating Calvinists, and the Catholics with their baroque, gold-filled

*The 11,000 virgins are thought to be a translation error; in several early versions of the legend, the Latin "M" was interpreted as the Roman numeral 1,000, when it was likely an abbreviation for "martyr." It is possible there were only eleven virgins.

churches. At some point during one of the countless power shifts, the art pieces are thought to have been hidden in the church's attic or in another part of the village to avoid destruction. As time passed and the region's Calvinist fervor cooled, they would have been brought forth again and found to be utterly out of fashion.

An old tradition, its origins in a 1623 decree from a local bishop, stated that one was to respectfully bury devotional items that were no longer in use, from the linen towels that wrapped the communion bread, to porcelain, to old prayer books. One was even supposed to perform funeral rites for the items. As consecrated, formerly sacred elements, the statues could not be destroyed. Thus, when the room was sealed in the nineteenth century, the artifacts were placed among the bones of the townsfolk and given a burial as if they were tiny humans themselves.

The second mystery—why did the church decide to hide the skulls in the first place?—provided fewer leads. It may have been done out of superstition or simply so that the room beneath the church could be used without having to stare at rows of skulls. Roger Mathieu, the town historian, has an amusing theory: The nineteenth century was a time of grand gestures, romantic ideals, and a slightly bizarre fascination with the morbid. It was the century of Byron, Shelley, and Keats, a time when young scholars kept skulls on their desks to signify just how deep and interesting they were. And where was an aspiring young romantic to procure such a skull? The basement of the church in Leuk, of course! Mathieu claims that students from the upper classes would steal the skulls for their personal collections and also occasionally bowl with them, punting them across the graveyard in midnight games. This disrespect prompted the parish to wall the bones away and forget they ever existed.

In the end, the mystery of the origin of the bones was solved as well. Remember the statues of St. Sebastian found among the dead? St. Sebastian is sometimes called the "plague saint" and was prayed to for protection against the black death. He was particularly popular in Renaissance art, for both aesthetic (he was usually portrayed as handsome and half naked) and practical reasons (there were a lot of plagues going around). As it turns out, many of the bones belonged to victims of a pestilence that swept through Leuk in the seventeenth century. The church's graveyard was originally farther down the mountain but was moved in 1836 to make way for a road, the remains put in the church basement for safekeeping. As for the puzzling holes in many of the foreheads, they were either from the pickaxes of the gravediggers who first unearthed them, or indeed bullet wounds. A number of the skulls are thought to belong to soldiers killed in battle when Napoleon's troops invaded Switzerland in 1798.

But some riddles persist. No known record exists of the names of those buried. Furthermore, the backmost layer of the skulls remains untouched, and one of the bone chamber's primary researchers, Walter Rupp, believes there may be Roman remains in the oldest portions of the walls.

So far, no one knows. The bones don't seem to mind. They wait in the dark below the church, watching the few who enter and the few who leave. They know you'll be back. In the words of the Totentanz painting, "What you are, we once were, and what we are, you soon will be." ◆

THE HIGH-TECH BONE CHAMBERS OF TOKYO

Charnel houses are still in use, though they have little in common with the gruesome crypts and bone walls of yore. Today, in Japan, they hide inside sleek, spaceship-like high-rises where parking garage-style systems deliver the ashes of loved ones to visiting relatives at the push of a button and burial walls look like neon-lit honeycombs. Temple Byakurenge-do is a state-of-the-art ossuary near Shinjuku

Station in Tokyo with a floor dedicated to the dead, kept locked and off-limits to anyone but families of the deceased. (Owners are afraid the technology will be copied by competitors.)

The desire to live on, even if only in organized, climate-controlled anonymity, has not disappeared in our modern world. At the Kōkoku-ji Temple near Shibuya Station, a flickering glass wall of thousands of tiny Buddhas guards the ashes of the dead. Family members are given a smart card that, when swiped, lights up their loved one's tiny box so they can find it among its 2,044 identical neighbors. Land is expensive in Japan, so burial plots are an extravagance and locals find the idea of communal death comforting. "All these glass Buddha statues are like your compatriots," one of the temple's priests told *Vice* in 2016. "You'll be there with them once you die. If you can think that you're going to be with your friends once you're dead, you won't be sad."

In a city where increasing numbers of people live in isolation, it's a sort of heaven. You will be with strangers but never alone, not buried out in the cold but warm and dry, always well-lit and carefully dusted as long as the bills are paid.

THE SIX CRYPTS OF THE CAPUCHINS

Beneath the church of Santa Maria della Concezione dei Cappuccini in Rome lies a collection of six crypts connected by narrow passageways, and once considered so terrifying that, ridiculously, for a year in the nineteenth century, women were not allowed to enter them for fear they would faint. The crypts contain the skeletal remains of more than 3,600 bodies, some of them with their clothes and matted beards still intact. The bodies are believed mostly to be those of Capuchin friars. As burial space became scarce, and fresh corpses refused to stop arriving, the bodies began being repurposed for decorating the walls, altars, and ceilings.

The six chambers are: the Crypt of the Resurrection; the Mass Chapel (which does not contain bones, but does contain the heart of Maria Felice Peretti, the grand-niece of Pope Sixtus V); the Crypt of the Skulls; the Crypt of the Pelvises; the Crypt of the Leg Bones and Thigh Bones; and the Crypt of the Three Skeletons, which contains the skeletons of three unknown children. In the final crypt, a placard in five languages declares the same sentiment as was found on the painting in the chamber in Leuk: "What you are now, we used to be; what we are now, you will become."

The Capuchin crypts have been visited by many personages, including Mark Twain and Marquis de Sade, who found the desiccated corpses of the monks more impressive than all the splendors of Rome. In his journal de Sade writes: "In each of the niches or under every arcade there is a well-preserved skeleton, placed in varying attitudes, some reclining, others in the act of preaching, others at prayer. All these skeletons are dressed in the Capuchin habit: some are bearded. Never have I seen anything more impressive."

Nathaniel Hawthorne also imparted a biting observation on the crypts in his 1860 novel *The Marble Faun*: "There is no disagreeable scent, such as might have been expected from the decay of so many holy persons . . . The same number of living monks would not smell half so unexceptionably."

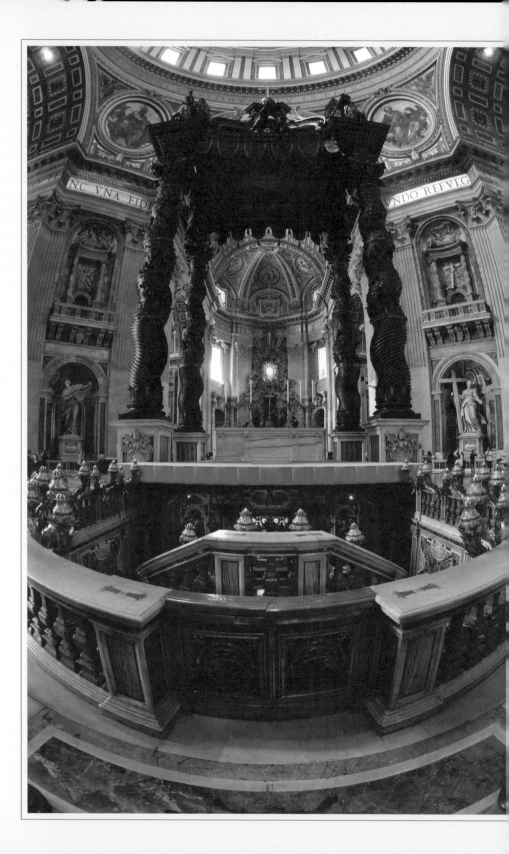

16

Saints Below

THE VATICAN · ITALY

You follow the road out of the city to the place where the saint is buried. When you arrive among the weeds and tombs beyond the walls you find a silent crowd has gathered—an anxious mass of the devout, clutching wooden crosses and oil lamps. You smell sweat in the hot night air, juniper and incense, and no small amount of fear.

None of you should be here. The emperor does not approve of the cult that has sprung up around the fisherman saint. To be caught could mean confiscation of property, even execution. But that was not enough to stop you, any of you, from making the journey tonight. You all have prayers and desperate wishes. You all hope they will be answered here.

◄ *The Baldacchino, St. Peter's massive baroque altar, is purported to mark the exact resting place of the eponymous saint. But what is really sealed away beneath it?*

You push through the throngs to get a glimpse of the saint's tomb. It is relatively simple, a small, gray building embedded in a red wall. The body inside is said to bestow miracles. The dead saint has the ear of God, you have heard, and your husband is with God now, gone up to heaven after a sudden bout of fever. All you want is to speak with him one last time.

The doorway to the tomb is jammed with people. You want to get inside, to touch the sarcophagus and whisper your secret prayers. But there are too many people. And then, in the distance, you hear a murmur of anxious voices. The rattle of a harness? You must be quick.

You sidle closer, closer, and then you realize you will not get in. You realize your husband is gone and that no prayers or offerings will bring him back. And in that moment you feel relief, a strange, sad sort of peace. You make a decision: While the people jostle around you and the sounds of the guards draw closer, you take a sharp rock and scratch a few words into the outer wall of the saint's tomb.

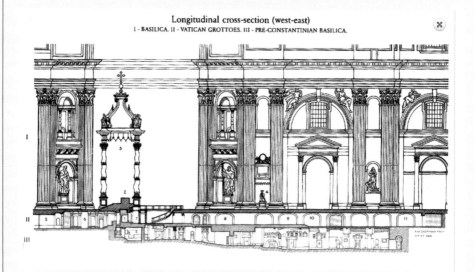

Longitudinal cross-section (west-east)
I - BASILICA. II - VATICAN GROTTOES. III - PRE-CONSTANTINIAN BASILICA.

▲ Cross-section showing the underbelly of St. Peter's Basilica. The pink layer shows the sleek, marble Vatican Grottoes, including many tombs of popes. The blue layer shows the ancient necropolis, buried until only the last century, a Roman graveyard town hiding one very special set of bones.

You sink back into the crowds, and into history, but your words linger. For nearly 2,000 years they remain etched in the wall. Rome expands and swallows the tombs that once stood outside its walls. The old necropolis becomes entombed itself, consumed by the massive foundations of a new church. The place where you stood sinks deeper and deeper underground, covered by layers of dirt and stone, until it is fifty feet beneath the earth. And then, in 1940, your message comes to light again.

The old scratches must be decoded, painstakingly translated. But in the end, your words survive: "To Renatus, an excellent husband."

Scholars in later years examine your marks and notice a strange detail: From the vertical stroke of the "T" in "Renatus" three small parallel lines extend to the right, producing a combination of "T" and "E." The letter "E," in the shorthand of the early Christians, stood for the Garden of Eden—for paradise, heaven, eternal peace. You have accepted that your husband is gone to the realms above.

Ironically, two millennia later, there is indeed a realm above the place you stood. It is not heaven, though it does its utmost to convince you of its proximity to God: Michelangelo's roiling clouds and saints cover the ceilings. Crowds from across the globe wander the marble floors. Gold leaf, relics on velvet pillows, paintings, and marble statues fill every wall, every surface where the eye alights. And to think that it all began with the tomb far below, that plain stone box.

No, not the box. It began with you and the people like you, who gathered there and wrote your wishes on the wall. You could not have known what would follow, what splendors and terrors would grow from the fisherman's bones.

Few places harbor quite so many secrets within their walls as the Vatican. The center of the Roman Catholic Church for two millennia, it was also a hotbed of intrigue and scandal, made all the more insalubrious because of the veil of holiness behind which it took place. Wars were fought in its name, witches burned, rebels tortured, orgies, and secrets rumored to be tucked away in its crypts and basements, enough to fill a hundred books or more. To this day, few are allowed into the truly hidden corners of the massive fortress country in the heart of the Italian capital. Tourists and pilgrims enter St. Peter's Basilica by the thousands and wander among the treasures of its vast museum, but there are entire worlds beyond the edges of these public areas. To catch a glimpse down the Vatican's private passageways, or under its floors, one must know someone, or be someone, or send a great many cajoling faxes to various Vatican authorities. (The fact that fax machines are still in use here only adds to the feeling that the Vatican is some sort of pocket reality, frozen in time, running by its own peculiar rules.)

One of the Vatican's most intriguing mysteries is an ancient necropolis hidden beneath the foundations of St. Peter's—a city of the dead, its streets and mausoleums running deep under the great domed cathedral. To enter it is to walk among the very roots of Catholicism. All the grandeur above began here growing from a single, unassuming seed—the body of Peter, chief disciple of Jesus, crucified upside down next to Nero's Circus and buried in a simple rock tomb nearby in 64 CE, about thirty-four years after the crucifixion of Jesus. The saint's name given to him by Jesus was Cephas* from the Aramaic Kepa, for "rock," and his body became the cornerstone on which the church is built. But until the 1940s the presence of Peter's bones in the marshy soil beneath the church was taken as a matter of faith. Rumors spoke of streets and ancient ruins

---

*Petros in Greek, the derivation for Peter.

▶ *View into the Clementine Chapel beneath St. Peter's Basilica during one of many excavations in search of Peter's bones.*

under the Vatican, and somewhere among them, the saint's tomb. And yet for all anyone knew, the bones had been removed for safe-keeping or disassembled to be used as relics in distant monasteries. No doubt many popes thought it best *not* to know what lay beneath their feet.

Of course, in the days of Peter, the graveyard was not under-ground. It stood on the slopes of a hill known as Mons Vaticanus, or Vatican Hill, just outside the walls of Rome. According to law, the dead were not allowed to be buried within city limits. Thus, on all the many roads leading to Rome, mausoleums and tombs sprouted like clumps of mushrooms, veritable villages of the dead butting up against the city of the living.

Roman tombs were nothing like the Gothic and macabre burial sites of later centuries (see The Bone Chamber, page 239). They were built to be places of delight. Often beautifully painted, two-story affairs, their upper floors were used for family gatherings and feasts. In some ways they were the equivalent of the European Schrebergartenhäuser, miniature houses where families, even less well-off ones, could escape the heat and bustle of the city for a quieter, greener respite outside its walls.

According to lore, the old St. Peter's Basilica was built in the direction that Peter's body was buried, its floor plan a magnified version of his corpse.

After Peter was executed, he was brought to the necropolis on the hillside and buried in the tomb of an early Christian. According to Roman tradition, once a body was interred, no one was allowed to move it. A place used for burial was a locus religiosus and to disturb a body was thought to cause pain and discomfort to the deceased. Peter's body, how-ever, quickly became a danger to powers both religious and political. Almost instantly, a cult sprang up around his grave and believers began arriving in droves, praying and scratching messages into the wall of the tomb.

When Emperor Constantine was in need of a basilica to keep his Christian population happy, he decided to bury the necropolis to make space for his new church's foundations. He ordered the old tombs be filled in with dirt, while also chopping off the upper levels and garden terraces of the mausoleums to make way for the church's floor. Constantine ordered the tomb of St. Peter to be wrapped in a box of red-veined pavonazzetto marble to represent the blood of the martyrs.

According to lore, the old St. Peter's Basilica was built in the direction that Peter's body was buried, its floor plan a magnified version of his corpse. (A basilica is, by definition, a church of exceptional antiquity or historical importance; many basilicas gained this designation by being built over the graves of martyred saints.) Peter was buried with his head toward the sun, a pagan tradition that later referred to Jesus's rising from the dead.

Around 1505, the old Constantinian church was demolished to make way for the stunning domed structure we see today. Peter's tomb and the surrounding necropolis were buried yet farther. Briefly, in 1626, the necropolis was unearthed during the excavation to build the four massive, twisted bronze columns of Bernini's grand tented altar. Workmen broke through the ceiling of one of the tombs, causing much damage. After the foundations of the altar were built, the tombs were covered up again. Whether Peter was actually buried there was not a matter anyone cared to look into too closely. It was only in 1940 that Pope Pius XII ordered the necropolis be looked into again, and not out of any particular passion for archaeology or historical facts. Rather, the excavations began because the previous pope, Pius XI, wanted to be buried as close to the grave of St. Peter as possible. To do so, the Vatican first had to make sure the saint was actually there. Alas, the new pope's decision to allow the excavation of the necropolis coincided almost exactly with the start of World War II and the arrival of the Nazis in Rome.

For the first several years, no one but a select few knew of the undertaking happening beneath the floor of the basilica. A team of ten men called the sampietrini, "the little ones of St. Peter's," hereditary caretakers of the Vatican and its buildings, set to work, but not before they were made to swear, personally to the pope, to keep their findings secret.

A German priest, Monsignor Ludwig Kaas, oversaw the excavations. He and his team were forced to work only at night and cart out the rubble of the excavation as quietly as possible. They contended with the threat of bombings, flooding, as well as the very real danger of collapse of the massive church above, at whose foundations they were now chipping. But, as they tunneled their way through the tangle of ancient structures beneath the magnificent high altar of St. Peter's, they slowly unraveled the secrets surrounding the burial of St. Peter.

One by one, they unearthed the tombs lining the necropolis's two streets. One mausoleum featured collections of red-and-white stucco roses and an epitaph trumpeting the family's success in selling linen. Another tomb's floor was inlaid with a rare black-on-white silhouette mosaic, its ceiling painted with birds. In another, they found two Christian graves, one of them belonging to a man named Flavius Statilius Olympius. "He had a joke for everyone," read his family's fond inscription, "and he never quarreled."

The Christian graves offered the first bit of hope that the searchers were moving in the right direction. The next clue came when they found a broken statue under which someone had scratched, thousands of years ago, "Peter, pray Christ Jesus for the holy. . . ." The rest was unreadable, but a mention of the long-sought-after saint was heartening.

Finally, directly beneath the great altar above, they uncovered a red-painted wall. Next to it, they found another wall of white marble

▶ *This exceptionally well-preserved Roman sculpture belonged to the sarcophagus of one Q. Marcius Hermes and his wife. It was unearthed during the twentieth-century excavations beneath St. Peter's.*

covered in what looked like graffiti. Most of the writing was in Greek or early Christian code,* overlapping and terribly difficult to read. The messages contained prayers for the dead, one to an exorcist and his companion, another to Renatus, the beloved husband. There was a small carving of a dove. And a tantalizing line in Greek read, "Peter is within."

The pope was summoned from his apartments. A chair was brought and he sat enthralled, waiting for the sampietrini to complete the excavation. One of the men reached into a recess below

*In order to express their beliefs during periods of persecution, early Christians developed a series of secret signs and symbols that they would use to mark places of worship: fish, doves, anchors, shepherds, and palm fronds. Only the cross, the most recognized symbol today, was rarely used, as it was seen as a mark of oppression, a reminder of the grisly practice of crucifixion used by the Romans.

the marble wall and pulled out a fistful of old Roman coins. Next his fingers touched bone.

In a recess in the wall, a skeleton was found, wrapped in gold and purple cloth. The skeleton's feet had been viciously cut off, a common practice in bodies that had been crucified, as it was too difficult to pull the nails out. After 2,000 years, the grave of St. Peter had finally been found.

The Vatican managed the discovery with the aplomb and eye for pacing of a thriller novelist. When Monsignor Kaas was contacted by *LIFE* magazine in 1950 to write a report on his findings, his response was sly: "For the time being, the discoveries made in the central area below the main altar of St. Peter's must remain undisclosed. The Vatican's reserve in the matter has caused some impatience among those anxious to confirm, by physical evidence, the burial of St. Peter. . . . But the last word belongs to science and cannot be anticipated."

It would take another eighteen years for the pope to publicly confirm that the bones were indeed Peter's. Italian archaeologist Margherita Guarducci succeeded Ludwig Kaas as the overseer of the necropolis project and dedicated the rest of her life to her research. Guarducci, a professor, devout Catholic, and code breaker who had deciphered countless ancient markings, was the first female archaeologist to be given such an authoritative post in the Vatican. Reportedly shocked at the way the excavation had been handled, she took matters into her own hands, decoding the graffiti around the graves and examining the bones herself. After extensive testing, it was concluded that the skeleton belonged to a man between sixty and seventy years of age from the region of Greece or Mesopotamia. By the end of her research, Guarducci firmly believed the bones belonged to the fisherman saint.

What became of Peter's bones? They have been returned to the recess in what is now called the Graffiti Wall, where they rest inside transparent plexiglass boxes. In 2019, Pope Francis gave nine of the saint's bones to the ecumenical patriarch of the Orthodox Catholic Church, Bartholomew I. The other 150 fragments remain in the Vatican.

As for the necropolis, it has been painstakingly restored. Today it is a dim, heavy place, its narrow alleys and ruined mausoleums rendered surreal by the electric lighting overhead. Dozens of tombs line its main street, called the Via Cornelia, their brick walls and frescoes still intact. One tomb contains what is thought to be the first depiction of the Christian God, his look based on the Roman deity Apollo. Another is filled with the urns of dead slaves, who in a case of postmortem justice have been allowed to slumber undisturbed while their wealthier counterparts have long since been disassembled, tested, and carted about by modern researchers.

In a recess in the wall, a skeleton was found, wrapped in gold and purple cloth. The skeleton's feet had been viciously cut off, a common practice in bodies that had been crucified, as it was too difficult to pull the nails out.

Not far above the buried necropolis, you can step through a panel, back into the sleek, air-conditioned vaults below the nave of the basilica. Pilgrims and tourists mill about, kneeling before gilded icons and elaborately carved tombs, and shushing anyone who disturbs their devotion. Here, in a small chamber called the Clementine Chapel, is a tiny golden door, which the pope may reach through to touch the place where Peter was buried. Only he has permission to do this. No more do supplicants scratch their wishes into walls or whisper hurried prayers against the saint's grave. The worshippers must contend with the veil of gold and marble and find their truth there. ◊

THE SCANDALOUS ART
IN THE CARDINAL'S BATHROOM

It is easy to forget, when walking the piously muted halls of the Vatican, that the church of yore was a rather corrupt and puerile entity. More political than religious, its popes were known for fathering countless children and having dalliances with anything that moved. Take the story of Pope Julius III, who had his brother adopt a young man from the streets (either to be the keeper of Julius's pet monkey or his lover, accounts vary) and shortly thereafter raised the barely literate seventeen-year-old to the position of cardinal. The fellow, whose name was, ironically, Innocenzo, would later be put on trial for rape and double murder. Suffice it to say, the church was a scandalous beast in those days, and its architecture reflected this.

In the pope's personal apartments, far from the areas open to the public, is a small, locked room. This chamber, called the Stufetta della Bibbiena (which translates to "small heated room of Bibbiena"), is adorned with gleefully naked gods, satyrs, and a Venus rising from a shell, all painted by the Renaissance master Raphael. Cardinal Bibbiena, for whom the room was built, was the author of several ribald plays, as well as a heavy drinker and womanizer. His bathroom was whitewashed and sanitized many times over the centuries in the hopes of erasing its sordid past. At one point it was turned into a kitchen, then a chapel. Now it is kept under lock and key, with visitors rarely granted access except through the serpentine channels of the Vatican secretariat.

So, the next time you find yourself staring in reverent awe at the pure white columns and domes of the Holy City, know that buried within its walls is a naughty bathroom, commissioned by a randy cardinal.

▶ *This decidedly unholy 1516 sketch of Venus and Adonis was made in preparation for the painting of a secret bathroom in the depths of the Vatican, now kept under lock and key.*

THE NOT-SO-SECRET ARCHIVES

Much has been made of the so-called Vatican secret archives, its fifty-three miles of shelves, ancient codices, and sealed documents rumored to hold everything from prophecies of the apocalypse to cover-ups of the church's past crimes. In his novels, Dan Brown imagines the archives as a titanium-lined bunker with soundproof walls, bursting with earth-shattering secrets.

The truth is that the archive looks like a not particularly modern university basement—shelves upon shelves of cardboard filing boxes and manuscripts, and only a few sections of sensitive material locked away behind metal gates. And just like a university basement, thousands of researchers are granted access every year. The main reason it is known as a "secret" archive is a mistranslation of the Latin, "secretum," which means "private." The archive is the private library of the pope, established in the seventeenth century by Paul V to store his personal correspondence and collection of books. (In 2019 it was renamed the Vatican Apostolic Archive, perhaps because the Vatican was tired of fielding requests by overeager tourists and fiction writers. Its reputation as a place of mystery stuck, however.)

That said, while the archive is not secret in the traditional sense, it does contain secrets, some of which are slowly finding their way to the public. In 2020, incendiary papers detailing Pius XII's role in World War II were unsealed, including proof of the church's refusal to "give back" rescued Jewish children who had been baptized as Catholic to escape the Holocaust, as well as letters displaying a general unwillingness to speak up against Nazi atrocities. In 2012, the Vatican also revealed a 184-foot-long parchment scroll detailing the scandalous accusations and confessions from the fourteenth-century trial of the Knights Templar, the brotherhood of knights that was persecuted and tortured by the church before going underground (see The Initiation Well, the Knights Templar, and the Freemasons, page 127).

The archive also featured the prophecies of a Portuguese shepherdess who claimed in 1917 to have had visions of the end of the world. The prophecies were called the "Three Secrets of Fatima." The Vatican doled out bits and pieces of the visions over an eighty-three-year period, keeping folks on the edge of their seats as to what was seen. In the end, the final secret proved disappointing, vague talk of penance and flaming swords. Of course, plenty of people immediately jumped on the announcement, saying the prophecy was false and the third secret is still being kept under wraps by the Vatican.

17

The Sleeping Beauty Apartment

PARIS • FRANCE

2 SQUARE LA BRUYÈRE • NINTH ARRONDISSEMENT • PARIS • 1940

You hear sirens in the distance.

Father is scavenging the city, desperately trying to secure transportation to take you both far south, away from Paris.

You will be leaving everything behind. You've already filled your two suitcases with clothes and books, just the necessities. Everything else, all of Marthe's precious things—as familiar to you as the soft, whispery sound of her voice—will be abandoned, to the bombs and violence and bloodshed.

◄ Marthe de Florian's cherished possessions, forgotten in a Parisian apartment for more than seventy years.

You wander through the chaotic jumble of your grand-mère's world one last time: tapestries, paintings, an ivory parasol, a gramophone.

You gaze at yourself in the full-length mirror and wonder if you look like her, your grand-mère, the famous Belle Époque beauty Marthe de Florian. Her portrait hangs nearby, an explosion of white and pink: pale skin, flushed cheeks, elegant features, a gossamer dress. It was painted by her lover Giovanni Boldini long before you were born.

You pick up a pile of letters. Your grand-mère bound her love letters in colored ribbons, a different color for each lover, and you slowly reread the yellowed card from Boldini, savoring the passion and yearning. When you finish, you tuck the letters into a drawer in the dressing table.

You run your fingers across the top of the delicate vanity. You sniff the bottles of perfume—the verdant, woodsy gush of Fougère Royale Houbigant evokes a memory of your grand-mère returning late one night, bursting into the flat with a much younger man, lingering with him in the doorway, laughing so hard her long, diamond earrings tapped her cheekbones.

You hear a honk from the street and race to the window just in time to see a family with six young children pile out of

◀ *Paintings and sheet music are placed haphazardly around the room, highlighting the intensity of those final moments before Solange Beaugiron fled Paris.*

a nearby building and squeeze into a black Citroën. Another family fleeing Paris. Soon there will be no one left on the entire block. You scan the street below, then return to the perfumes.

You pick up a clear bottle, lift the crystal stopper, and breathe in deeply. The powdery amber floral of Après l'Ondée reminds you of the time Marthe took you to drink le chocolat chaud in a warm Parisian tea shop during a hard spring rain.

The sirens wail again, but they are farther away this time.

The hint of cake and violet in Guerlain's L'Heure Bleue brings to mind the night Marthe read *Alice's Adventures in Wonderland* out loud to you on your unbirthday, while the two of you nibbled petit fours by the fire.

Happy, fairy-tale memories.

You are glad Marthe didn't live to see the Germans enter Paris.

A vehicle honks loudly in the street below. This time it is your father. He has found a car, an old Peugeot. He leans out the window, waving, and you nod down at him.

You close the shutters and the apartment dims. You clutch both suitcases and gaze around your grand-mère's apartment for the last time.

You don't know when you will return. Never, perhaps. Everything is always changing, the world grows bright and dark by turns . . . but your young heart wants this soft, luxurious, aromatic place to always be the same, preserved like an ancient pharaoh through the passing of years.

This magical apartment would serve as your grand-mère's tomb.

"Goodbye," you whisper as you close the door behind you and turn the lock. "May you rest in peace."

In May 2010, 91-year-old Solange Beaugiron died alone in rural France. Soon after her lawyers began the daunting process of organizing her affairs, they discovered something rather astonishing—Solange owned a flat in Paris and had, in fact, since she was eighteen, though she hadn't set foot inside it in over seventy years.

An auctioneer named Olivier Choppin Janvry was mandated by a provincial notary to open the rusty lock on the door of this forgotten flat in the Pigalle district. Inside he discovered an enchanted apartment trapped in time: rooms that sunlight had not stroked in decades, a sea of nineteenth-century furniture languishing under a thick bloom of dust, velvet wallpaper peeling off in long strips, paintings, jewelry boxes, elegant vases alongside a fragile porcelain tea service, bottles of perfume (long since evaporated), a stuffed ostrich, mirrors (gone milky and cloudy with age), an open songbook, and a single pink glove on a dressing table.

The most glittering of all the treasures? A large portrait of the flat's original owner, Marthe de Florian, by the Italian painter Giovanni Boldini. Boldini was one of the most famous artists of the time. Known as the "Master of Swish," for his ethereal style of painting, Boldini painted Marthe during their love affair in 1888, when she was twenty-four years old—though journalists would only discover this later, after a love note from Boldini to Marthe was found (as well as a reference to this painting in a memoir by Boldini's wife).

Janvry was flabbergasted by the discovery of this time capsule apartment, and the story of its existence caused a worldwide sensation as photographs of its interior hit the internet. The apartment's original owner, Marthe de Florian, was a Belle Époque beauty and socialite. Sources claim she was a demimondaine.

In 1848 Alexandre Dumas published *La Dame aux Camélias*, which featured the precarious, extravagant world of upper-class French men and the smart, beautiful women who entertained them. It was soon adapted into a play entitled *Le Demi-monde* ("demimonde" literally means "half-world"). This led to the term "demimondaine," which was used to describe a woman who moved through this half-world. Demimondaines were women supported by wealthy lovers. They were often sex workers, but not always.

The half-world was a place of extravagance, alcohol, drugs, theater, gambling, high fashion, and sex. Many demimondaines were actresses, some of them successful, such as Sarah Bernhardt. Another famous demimondaine was Virginia Oldoini Verasis, Countess di Castiglione, an impoverished aristocrat who eventually became the mistress of Napoleon III. (After this affair ended, she moved on to other politicians and members of royalty. Rumor has it she once charged a British noble one million francs to spend twelve hours in her company.)

For a handful of years, these demimondaines ruled Paris, dominating the gossip columns and fashion magazines.

The gilt-edged Parisian half-world ended with the start of World War I. Fashion changed, as did social conventions, and the term grew increasingly obsolete.

Marthe was born Mathilde Héloïse Beaugiron on September 9, 1864. Initially she joined the workforce as an embroiderer in the dressmaking district, but her beauty and charm quickly took her down a more interesting path.

Along with the artist Boldini, Marthe had love affairs with two future presidents of France, several aristocrats (including a young Romanian noble), and Georges Clemenceau,

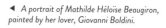

◀ *A portrait of Mathilde Héloïse Beaugiron, painted by her lover, Giovanni Boldini.*

the French prime minister. Marthe gave birth to two sons, only one of whom survived infancy, Henri, who was the son of Auguste Albert Gaston Florian Mollard, a married banker. Marthe took part of Mollard's name as her own.

A leading literary magazine of the time, *Gil Blas*, interviewed Marthe de Florian in 1894. The reporter praised her "pretty eyes, blonde hair and chubby face the color of cherry blossoms." He reported that her "aristocratic beauty recall(ed) the chatelaines of yore, when men broke lances in the name of chivalry." She was asked softball questions, such as:

What is your favorite jewelry? Pearls.

Your favorite perfume? Fougère Royale Houbigant.

The novelist you most admire? Prévost.

The musician you enjoy best? Massenet.

Your motto? "Rien ou Bien!" (Which can be roughly translated, "Do it well or not at all.")

Your chief character trait? Unwavering loyalty.

Marthe often had two or three lovers at a time, and they showered her with gifts. She lived a luxurious life—jewels, furs, a carriage. She even owned a yacht. Her apartment featured a private courtyard, a Louis XV salon, an elegant dining room, and a grand bedroom complete with four-poster bed. It was located in the old theater district, near the Moulin Rouge, which was, at the time, the heart of Belle Époque culture.

When Marthe died in 1939 at the age of seventy-four, her home passed to her teenage granddaughter, Solange Beaugiron. Within months, German tanks overran the Maginot Line. The Nazi occupation of Paris began. Solange fled with her father to the south of France.

As a teenager, Solange wrote plays under the name Solange Beldo and some believe that she was in fact the novelist Solange Bellegarde. But very little is known of her life. Her father, Henri, returned to the Parisian apartment in 1966 and lived in a small wing of it until his death, but otherwise it remained untouched, an architectural Sleeping Beauty for the next four decades.

Why did Solange never return to her famous grandmother's home? One theory is that she simply forgot it existed. One is reminded of the Frenchman Fabrice and the story he tells Linda in Nancy Mitford's novel *The Pursuit of Love*. While drifting along the canals of Venice, his mother and grandmother came upon a "little palazzo of pink marble, very exquisite." The pair stopped the gondola to look at it and rang the bell. An old servant came to the door. He told them that no one had lived in the palazzo for many years and he would show it to them if they liked. They eventually came to a salon overlooking the canal. Fabrice's grandmother was surprisingly moved by the room and remained quite still for some time. Finally, she turned to her daughter and said, "If, in the third drawer of that bureau there is a filigree box containing a small gold key on a black velvet ribbon, this house belongs to me." The key was in the bureau, just as she'd said. It turned out that one of the grandmother's lovers had given the palazzo to her years ago and she'd forgotten about it.

But one hopes Solange's avoidance came from a deeper place, a wish to let the apartment slumber undisturbed. We will never know. The secret died with Solange.

The contents of the famous apartment were auctioned off on September 8, 2010. The painting by Boldini sold for between two and three million euros. It is lamentable that a museum or nonprofit organization didn't step in, purchase the apartment, and preserve it in its untouched state. But then, maybe its allure lay in its being forgotten and lost, in its being dusty and cluttered and locked. Perhaps it is best that it is gone forever now, truly untouchable and immortal. ◈

A REAL-LIFE GRAND BUDAPEST HOTEL

If Wes Anderson's *The Grand Budapest Hotel* left you aching for a real-life version of a shabby, past-its-prime mountaintop hotel, the slowly decaying Grand Hotel Campo dei Fiori in Varese, Italy, should fit the bill.

Opened in 1910, this 200-room alpine resort crowns the top of the Monte Tre Croci. It was designed by the art nouveau architect Giuseppe Sommaruga and for more than four decades it reigned as a luxurious getaway for the European elite.

In a distinctly cinematic fashion, guests ascended the mountain to the hotel via a steep funicular. Glancing through old postcards of the hotel's interior, it's easy to picture the opulent ballroom filled with aristocrats: a sea of swishing silks, pearl necklaces, starched collars, lavish mustaches. One imagines grand love affairs in plush bedrooms, whispered secrets in dark corners, and heartbreaking drama playing out on this swank stage with all the glamour of the 1932 film *Grand Hotel*.

In the Agatha Christie short story "The Erymanthian Boar" (part of the collection published as *The Labours of Hercules* in 1947), Hercule Poirot becomes trapped in a mountaintop hotel in the Alps during a snowstorm. Was the Grand Hotel Campo dei Fiori the inspiration for this story? Perhaps. Christie may have visited the hotel during its glory years.

Sadly, World War II slowed tourism to the hotel and a fire in 1947 pushed it farther into decline. It closed for good in 1968. In the following years the owners—the Castiglioni family—lived alone in the crumbling grandeur.

The hotel sold in 2016 to a private company and was used as a film location for the 2018 movie *Suspiria*, but mostly it sits abandoned, a melancholy giant perched high above the town of Varese. Perhaps one day it will be renovated and reopened to guests, but one hopes it will always keep a hint of its faded glamour: a whiff of dust, threadbare velvet curtains, a patch or two of peeling wallpaper.

THE SCRATCHED MIRRORS
AND SECRET PASSAGEWAYS OF LAPÉROUSE

The mazelike Parisian restaurant Lapérouse, with its rabbit warren of secretive private dining rooms and corridors kept in a perpetual, luxurious twilight, was once the obvious choice for those desiring to keep a low profile. In the nineteenth century it was known as the place where politicians took their mistresses and, occasionally, gave them diamonds. Legend has it that one can still see scratches on Lapérouse's Venetian mirrors where these women tested the authenticity of their

▼ *The Venetian mirrors at Lapérouse, where you can still trace the scratches made by women testing the authenticity of their gifted diamonds.*

jewelry on their surface. And in the intimate Les Sénateurs salon, a concealed door (now boarded up) leads to the restaurant's cellar, which connects to a secret tunnel that once wound half a mile underground to the French Senate, allowing politicians to join their lovers for dinner and other delights without being detected.

Lapérouse is located in the 6th arrondissement of Paris, across the street from the Seine, on the historic Left Bank. Originally a high-end wine shop, it was opened by the king's beverage maker Monsieur Lefevre in 1766. In the mid-nineteenth century it was bought by Jules Lapérouse, whose culinary skills quickly turned its sumptuous, muraled, wooden-paneled rooms into a literary salon frequented by Honoré de Balzac, Victor Hugo, Émile Zola, Colette, George Sand, Alexandre Dumas, and Ernest Hemingway. (One can see glimpses of Lapérouse in *Midnight in Paris*, Woody Allen's love letter to Hemingway.)

Marcel Proust wrote of the restaurant in his 1913 novel *In Search of Lost Time*, better known as *Remembrance of Things Past*:

> On some days, instead of staying at home, he would have lunch in a nearby restaurant whose good food he had once enjoyed and where he now only went for one of those reasons both mystical and bizarre, which we call "romantic"; it is because this restaurant (which, by the way, still exists) had the same name as the street on which Odette lived: Lapérouse.

With a history like this, food is only one of Lapérouse's attractions (it was awarded three Michelin stars in 1933, one of the first in Paris to receive that designation). In 2019 it was restored to its original glory by interior designer Laura Gonzalez, who supervised mural renovations and and covered walls in mischievous Pierre Frey silk. The *New York Times* described the renovation as "resembling a Venetian palazzo compressed into The Orient Express."

The Lapérouse is an institution in Paris, and Antoine Arnault, a minority owner in the restaurant, fully understands this. During its reopening he mused to the press that "Lapérouse is a myth and as such immediately brings to my mind both the heritage and storytelling of a beautiful Parisian sleeping beauty."

18

King Tut's Tomb, Treasure Hunts, and Our Need to Dig

VALLEY OF THE KINGS • EGYPT

From Howard Carter's diary, written during his hunt for King Tutankhamun tombs, on November 26, 1922:

With trembling hands, I made a tiny breach in the upper left hand corner . . . widening the hole a little, I inserted the candle and peered in . . . at first I could see nothing, the hot air escaping from the chamber causing the candle to flicker. Presently, details of the room emerged slowly from the mist, strange animals, statues and gold—everywhere the glint of gold. For the moment—an eternity it must have seemed to the others standing by—I was struck dumb with amazement, and when Lord Carnarvon, unable to stand in suspense any longer, inquired anxiously Can you see anything? *it was all I could do to get out the words,* Yes, wonderful things.

◀ *A replica of King Tutankhamun's antechamber—these dazzling, golden funerary objects (over 600 of them) were the first items Howard Carter encountered after entering the tomb.*

What child can resist the thought of buried treasure? And what adult can resist the lure of adventure, greatness, the unknown? We all yearn to go on quests, like a knight of the Round Table. We all want to hunt, scavenge, dig, feel our blood beat with the spark of discovery, the hope of finding something buried, something untouched for 500 years, something long thought lost.

Fiction is littered with references. Tom goes digging for buried treasure with Huck Finn in Mark Twain's *The Adventures of Tom Sawyer*, Jim Hawkins finds a map and takes to the sea to look for gold in Robert Louis Stevenson's *Treasure Island*, Wade tries to solve a 1980s-inspired virtual reality treasure hunt in Ernest Cline's *Ready Player One*. Some have even argued that all murder mysteries count as treasure hunts, because the detective must follow clues to find the ultimate reward, the identity of the murderer.

Most children first experience this type of thrill in a scavenger hunt: Get a list, find as many items on it as you can, win a prize! Some believe that the scavenger hunt finds its origins in ancient folk games. It surged in popularity during the 1930s when author, professional hostess, and gossip columnist Elsa Maxwell began featuring them in her lavish parties, held in places like New York City and Paris.* The items included in her notorious scavenger lists were wild and varied: pick a fight with a policeman, acquire a black swan from the Bois de Boulogne, pluck mustache hairs from Kermit Roosevelt (son of President Teddy), steal a red pom-pom from a French seaman's hat, procure a goat and/or a monkey.

The University of Chicago holds arguably the largest annual scavenger hunt in the world. Known locally as SCAV, a 2012 article in the *New Yorker* described this college quest as, "a mash-up of the Intel Science Talent Search, a fraternity hazing, a pep rally, installation art, reality TV and a 4-H fair." SCAV begins at midnight on a Wednesday in May and ends four days later, on Mother's

---

*The scavenger hunt mania was a main plot point in the 1936 film *My Man Godfrey*.

Day. The first hunt, held in 1987, listed such things as a training bra (25 points), a painting on velvet (20 points), and a Hula-Hoop (10 points).

According to this same *New Yorker* article, future SCAV hunters have been asked to: "unboil an egg; induce a potato to break the sound barrier; eat their own umbilical cord (one student, having persuaded his mother to express-mail the membranous keepsake she'd saved from his birth, stuck it into a Twinkie and swallowed it); get circumcised (someone did); and bring a lion, a tiger, or a bear to campus." But you don't need to attend the University of Chicago to experience some adult scavenging. Letterboxing is both a scavenger hunt and a treasure hunt of sorts. It involves a list of clues (usually posted online) that, when solved, leads to a hidden waterproof box filled with prizes. The boxes always contain a logbook, plus a signature stamp and ink pad that players can add to their own journals. This author used to play it extensively, once locating a delightful letterbox in a tiny Scottish graveyard near the fifteenth-century Dan Brown–famous Rosslyn Chapel outside Edinburgh.

Letterboxing began in Dartmoor, England, in 1854 when James Perrott placed a bottle in the most remote place he could find, next to Cranmere Pool, a spot that required a nine-mile hike through difficult terrain. He inserted a calling card in the bottle and encouraged whoever found it to contact him and to leave their own calling card for future intrepid visitors to find. Eventually a tin box replaced the bottle and hikers began leaving self-addressed postcards, which the discoverers would then mail back to them. In 1905 a logbook was added and in 1907 a rubber stamp. The hobby grew slowly; by the 1970s, there were only fifteen of these letterboxes in existence, all located in Dartmoor.

But when Tom Gant drew a map to all fifteen letterboxes, the activity suddenly surged in popularity. In 1998 *Smithsonian* magazine featured the hobby in an article entitled "They Live and Breathe Letterboxing" and by the early 2000s there were approximately a thousand letterboxes in the United States. They now can be found across the globe.

Letterboxing's popularity eventually led to geocaching, a pastime where players use GPS coordinates (usually with the help of a geocaching app on their phones) to locate "caches," often boxes containing a logbook and small collectable items. The *New York Times* featured the hide-and-seek nature of geocaching in a 2021 article, noting that it was an excellent family activity during lockdowns, and a delightful way to discover a hidden world operating just out of view.

🗝 The Pyramids of Giza, on the west bank of the Nile in northern Egypt, could be called 4,000-year-old gravestones.

And it's true, once you find a geocache in a tree along a popular hiking trail, or hidden in a loose stone down a shadowy, cobblestone alley . . . these places will never feel the same again. They have shared a secret with you.

Treasure, and the finding and selling of historically significant antiquities, is much more controversial than scavenger hunts or letterboxing and its allure far stronger, the rewards more lucrative, and its practitioners plentiful, for better or for worse.

Recently China has cracked down on grave robbers. A 2021 article in the *Economist* reported on a restaurant owner named Mr. Wei and his team of grave robbers, who served food during the day and tunneled underground at night, eventually connecting the restaurant with nearby temples and shrines. They stole gold Buddha statues and monk bones, eventually netting close to $2 million. Mr. Wei is currently serving a fifteen-year prison sentence for theft.

In 2020, China arrested approximately 2,400 similar tomb raiders, and the government said they intend to dish out more severe punishments for such crimes. (Though they have never been exactly lenient: In 2017, a grave robber was given a death sentence.) But the success of films and video games such as *Raiders of the Lost Ark*, *The Mummy*, *National Treasure*, *Uncharted*, and *Tomb Raider* suggests that, beyond a simple desire for gold, there exists in all of us a deeper reason to find something hidden, bring it to light, and maybe even change the world with its discovery.

What is, hands down, the most glorious example of this? The discovery of King Tutankhamun's tomb.

Egypt, with its gold-soaked burial chambers, has lured countless treasure hunters into its barren sands for millennia. The pyramids, Egyptians' most impressive architecture, were meant to be stepping-stones to immortality. The Pyramids of Giza, on the west bank of the Nile in northern Egypt, could be called 4,000-year-old gravestones.

Each of the three Giza pyramids was dedicated to an Egyptian king and initially chock full of treasure—until they were broken into and robbed repeatedly. The pyramid dedicated to King Khufu, known as the Great Pyramid, is thought to be the largest building ever erected. The entrance is located fifty-nine feet above the ground and leads, via a sloping granite tunnel, to branching corridors, the 151-foot-long Grand Gallery, two empty chambers dubbed the King's Chamber and the Queen's Chamber, and a third unfinished chamber far underground. In 2017 the existence of a previously unknown chamber in the Great Pyramid was confirmed using infrared thermography and muon tomography (a method that uses cosmic ray muons to create 3D images). It is an empty void approximately forty-three yards long, located above the Grand Gallery. No one has, as of yet, been allowed to excavate the space, but the prospect is electrifying. Could this be an untouched royal tomb?

Around 3,000 years ago the pharaohs, tired of all the grave robberies, stopped erecting pyramids and started building hidden tombs.

The Valley of the Kings, situated about 300 miles south of Cairo, is the resting place of the pharaohs from the Eighteenth through Twentieth Dynasties. The tombs were largely built along the same lines: a descending passageway cut through with shafts (see The Secret Doors of the Great Pyramid of Giza, page 291) and finally

▲ *A fragment from the Book of the Dead, depicting the weighing of the heart, Thebes, Egypt, dated 1275 BCE.*

ending in treasure chambers and a room with a stone sarcophagus containing the mummified remains of the pharaoh. The walls of the tombs were usually decorated with scenes depicting the pharaoh nobly hanging with the gods of the underworld.

The most magnificent tomb art possibly belonged to Queen Nefertari, the wife of Ramses II. (This author had the pleasure of seeing the dazzling traveling exhibition *Queen Nefertari's Egypt* at the Portland Art Museum in Oregon in 2021.) It includes scenes from the famous *Book of the Dead* (a collection of spells and formulas—such as the Coffin Texts and the Pyramid Texts—that were placed in tombs to aid the dead) and gave scholars a better understanding of the Egyptians' belief in the afterlife and the role of women in ancient society, as well as insight into the more everyday aspects of life, such as current fashions.

In 1817 Giovanni Battista Belzoni discovered the empty tomb of Pharaoh Seti I of the Nineteenth Dynasty, the father of Ramses II. No treasure remained, but the tomb was beautifully painted and decorated. Belzoni was stunned by the level of preservation—the bright shining colors of the paintings, the artist's brushes still on the floor, as if they'd left only moments before.

Of the sixty-plus tombs in the Valley of the Kings, only King Tutankhamun's 3,300-year-old burial chamber remained intact, with all of its ancient artifacts still sealed inside. Tut's tomb had only two rooms, yet they contained more than 5,000 artifacts, many of them coated in hammered gold. This precious metal was tied to immortality and the afterlife. Egyptians considered it the flesh of the gods. It was the color of the sun, of Ra, the god of creation and life itself, and so naturally the pharaohs wanted their tombs to contain as much of the stuff as possible. Tut's burial chamber was bursting with gold-plated jewelry, amulets, weapons, furniture, and miniature chariots. His coffin contained more than 242 pounds of the metal, including the most famous Tut artifact—his golden funerary mask.

If King Tutankhamun's small tomb contained this many riches, imagine what might have lurked inside the larger tombs of the more powerful kings? Tut, often called the Boy King, was a relatively minor pharaoh. He ascended the throne when he was eight or nine years old and was about eighteen when he died. He ruled Egypt from 1333 to approximately 1323 BCE, a tiny ripple in the vast flow of the Egyptian empire, and yet relics from his burial chamber have now circled the globe and enthralled millions of visitors.

How did his tomb manage to evade grave robbers for three millennia? It was twenty-six feet underground and protected by piles of rubble and boulders from earthquakes and flash flooding. It took dozens of diggers to unearth its door. You have probably seen the famous black-and-white photos from 1922, depicting Howard Carter and his patron Lord Carnarvon proudly standing in the desert outside Thebes, Egypt, next to the entrance to the Boy Pharaoh's tomb. This had been the hunt of a lifetime.

The discovery of the tomb in 1922 made Howard Carter an instant celebrity and kindled the imaginations of countless future archaeologists, directors, and writers.[*]

*Look no further than Agatha Christie, who was a young woman when the tomb was unearthed, and later wrote several Egyptian- and archaeological–themed mysteries, including *Death on the Nile*, *Death Comes as the End*, *Murder in Mesopotamia*, and *Appointment with Death*.

THE SECRET LIFE OF HIDDEN PLACES

However, it was not long before rumors of a "King Tut Curse" began to spread. Carter's patron, Lord Carnarvon, died from a mosquito bite that gave him blood poisoning. Carnarvon's half brother also died of blood poisoning, as well as various other people who visited the tomb or had ties to its discovery.

Was the curse simply a way for papers to sell copies? Or were the ancient Egyptian gods angry at the desecration of a pharaoh's tomb? In fact, fifty-eight people were present when King Tut's sarcophagus was opened and only eight of these died in the next twelve years. Not a sensational number for what is meant to be a powerful pharaoh's curse.

Carter dismissed the curse as nonsense and carried out his excavations with little thought to superstitions. As it turned out, King Tut's tomb didn't just contain golden items of luxury. Wicker baskets of food were found in the chamber as well, and a 1944 edition of the *Detroit Evening Times* lauds three "withered little peas from the 3,300-year-old tomb, so hardy that they put our modern pampered peas to shame and so old they have outlived the insect varieties that used to prey on them." The article reports that one of the archaeologists who worked on the dig sent three peas to an American who planted them in his garden . . . and they subsequently sprouted as if they were fresh from the seed store and not thirty-three centuries old. The article then goes on to discuss whether or not the peas could possibly be cursed.

Modern scientists have failed to germinate any ancient grain or vegetable, but rumors of the Boy King's peas still exist, and "King Tut Purple Peas" are currently available to order online. So even current-day agriculture was affected by Carter's Egyptian treasure hunt.

Ancient Egypt's reach is long. There are claims that the high-protein grain kamut, also known as khorasan wheat, was first discovered in a pharaoh's tomb by a World War II US airman who mailed the thirty-six grains of wheat to his father, a Montana wheat farmer.

This author just read the ingredients of her Nature's Path heritage flakes cereal—kamut is the first ingredient listed. So, in a sense, it's now possible to get a taste of ancient Egypt by merely eating breakfast.

That said, if 3,000-year-old "mummy seeds" can really germinate in the modern day, then perhaps pharaoh curses are also real, and we should all steer clear of such things.

Always an incorrigible loner, Howard Carter died in London in 1939 and only nine people attended his funeral. His gravestone reads: "May your spirit live, may you spend millions of years, you who love Thebes, sitting with your face to the north wind, your eyes beholding happiness," a quote taken from the inscription on one of the first items Carter found upon entering the tomb, what he called a "wishing cup." Carved from a single piece of alabaster in the shape of a lotus blossom, it must have held a deep place in Carter's heart.

Egypt and its ancient treasures still have us under their spell. "Egypt" is the number one searched-for topic on the British Museum's website. A 2022 article in the *New Yorker* entitled "Why King Tut Is Still Fascinating" ponders the timeless allure of the Boy King:

> *I met a second grader who seemed well on his way to a doctoral degree in Egyptology. After describing the mummification process in recondite detail—not only why the brain was removed through the nose but how exactly natron dried out the rest of the body—the child drew an elaborate cartouche with the hieroglyphs used to spell my name. He then proceeded to tell me more about the pharaoh Tutankhamun than most of the other students could tell me about their own grandfathers.*

The article goes on to discuss the controversy behind Egyptology, from the selling of artifacts to the right of non-Egyptian museums to retain Egyptian finds, but added that scholarly debate doesn't dampen children's love of all that shiny, shiny treasure. And what a treasure it was: bright blue lapis lazuli scarab beetle jewelry, an elaborate falcon necklace, solid gold sandals, a fainting couch, board games, the alabaster wishing cup, Tut rendered as a gilded figure throwing a harpoon, musical instruments, a cheetah skin shield.

Is it any wonder that this minor pharaoh is far more famous in the modern day than he was in his own century? By the vagaries of chance, his tomb survived intact to the present, allowing us a glimpse into the past. His treasures for the afterlife remained untouched, bestowing him a second immortality. The Boy King now reigns over a kingdom of curious young minds, and this, at least, is a lovely thought.

Howard Carter, like the mummy he discovered, also achieved a form of immortality, one that will perhaps prove as timeless as that sought by the pharaohs. And maybe this is what all treasure hunters truly seek—not a chest of sparkling jewels and gold coins, but to

▼ *Howard Carter in the tomb that would make him famous. Lord Carnarvon is shown on the right—he would die less than two months after this photograph was taken, supposedly from the "King Tut Curse."*

survive death, to matter more than our frail bodies, to contribute something to the world that will shift scientific thought or change a historian's view of a civilization . . . to do something that will endure. Who could ask for more from life?

So go forth, all you lovers of the buried, the hidden, the clandestine. Grab your shovel, your metal detector, your flashlight (or torch) and start digging. Explore that haunted castle built above a pit to hell, knock on wooden panels, search bookcases, find the trigger that opens a hidden door and takes you to the dim, dusty stone staircase, stumble into an apartment that hasn't been opened in decades, follow a trail of amber shards back to a Russian palace, investigate an underground alchemy lab, uncover monastery floor plans that highlight a forgotten room. Who knows what wondrous knowledge you are about to unmask, what ancient secrets you will expose, what life-changing finds your explorations will bring to light. Reach out toward immortality with an intrepid heart and a curious mind.

Go boldly into the dark. ◆

AN EGYPTIAN MOVIE SET
BURIED BENEATH A SANDY SEA

Cecil B. DeMille depicted the story of Moses on screen twice; the silent 1923 version of *The Ten Commandments* required the largest set that had yet been built in Hollywood. When the turbulent director finished shooting, he took dynamite and blew up most of the plaster Egyptian scenery, either to prevent a rival director from using it or simply because he couldn't be bothered to break it down and transport it back to the city. What was left—plaster sphinxes, a temple, giant lions, and four gargantuan Ramses II statues—were buried in a 22,000-acre stretch of dunes along the California coast, north of Los Angeles.

DeMille, in his posthumously published autobiography, quipped, "If a thousand years from now archaeologists happen to dig beneath the sands of Guadalupe, I hope they will not rush into print with the amazing news that Egyptian civilization, far from being confined to the Valley of the Nile, extended all the way to the Pacific Coast."

Some of the colossal set has been excavated but a lack of funding means that most of it still remains buried in the California sands. So, if you happen to be hiking along the beach near the small town of Guadalupe, don't be surprised if you trip over the upturned nose of a century-old giant plaster sphinx entombed in sand, just like its Egyptian forebearers.

▼ *A scene from DeMille's 1923 film,* The Ten Commandments, *including one of the famous plaster sphinxes—there were twenty-one in all, each weighing five tons.*

THE DROWNED PALACE
OF CLEOPATRA

Franck Goddio is an underwater archaeologist and pioneer of marine archaeology. He founded the Institut Européen d'Archéologie Sous-Marine and has excavated nearly a dozen shipwrecks from the eleventh to sixteenth centuries, including Spanish galleons, trading vessels of the British East India Company, and the *Orient*, the ship Napoleon Bonaparte used in his invasion of Egypt.

Some thirty years ago Goddio read an account from Strabo—an ancient Greek historian—describing the city of Alexandria and Antirhodos Island, which was located in its eastern harbor. Strabo mentioned that Queen Cleopatra's palace was on Antirhodos, and Goddio was determined to find it.

Alexander the Great founded the city of Alexandria in 332 BCE. It was said to have been grander and more beautiful than Rome. It boasted a famous library. Its Pharos Lighthouse was one of the Seven Wonders of the Ancient World. Julius Caesar, Mark Antony, and Cleopatra strolled its royal quarter, and Cleopatra maintained a marble seafront palace in its harbor.

But 200 years after Cleopatra's death by suicide, several parts of the city's coastline sank into the sea as the result of unstable sediment and possibly an earthquake, taking Cleopatra's palace and all its treasures with it.

Goddio began to search for the sunken island in 1992, and eventually he discovered a collapsed palace, its rubble lying in the blue waters sixteen feet below the surface of the harbor.

Photographs of this excavation reveal haunting images of well-preserved statues, sphinxes, halls, colonnades, and crypts, where it is proposed the queen might have been interred. Her resting place has still not been found, but many other wonders have been discovered among the ruins of the palace, including a sunken ship containing all its cargo.

Feeling inspired? No need to scuba dive in distant lands. Simply buy yourself an underwater metal detector and take it to your nearest stream, pond, or beach. Who knows what you will discover.

THE SECRETS DOORS
OF THE GREAT PYRAMID OF GIZA

Two shafts run diagonally upward and outward from the King's Chamber in the Great Pyramid of Giza. Lower down in the structure, two more extend from the Queen's Chamber. For many years, the theory was that these were ventilation shafts, but recent research has suggested otherwise. It is now believed that they held a religious purpose, that they were "star shafts," allowing the souls of the regent and his wife to find their way to the heavens.

In 2010, the University of Leeds sent a lightweight wheeled robot into the shaft in the Queen's Chamber and made an astounding discovery. Two hundred feet up the tight, sloping passageway, the robot encountered a handleless stone door with traces of two copper hieroglyphics symbolizing that a soul might open the door, if not a body. (Quarry marks can still be seen in the door, including the symbol of the work gang that cut the stone, "wadi"—the green ones—and a sign that may be the hieroglyph "prjj"—"to come out" of the tomb.)

The robot, having neither body nor soul, drilled a small hole in the stone, through which it extended an endoscopic camera. Beyond the door was a chamber, its floor painted with intricate symbols in red ochre. At the far end of the chamber was another door, presumably leading onward up the shaft. Due to the country's political instability at the time, the university had to cut its research short. The final door has still not been opened.

Photo Credits